RUSH
TO JUDGMENT
The Simeon Rice Story

SIMEON RICE

WITH

MARK STEWART

THE LYONS PRESS
Guilford, Connecticut
An imprint of The Globe Pequot Press

Dedication

To my parents, Evelyn and Henry Rice,
and to the memory of my grandmother, Adelia "Big Mom" Ross.

The Lyons Press is an imprint of The Globe Pequot Press.

10 9 8 7 6 5 4 3 2 1

Printed in the United States of America

ISBN 1-59228-546-5

Library of Congress Cataloging-in-Publication Data is available on file.

Acknowledgments

I would like to acknowledge the extended Rice and Ross families for the love and support they showered on a runny-nosed little kid who only wanted to live his dreams. I wouldn't have made it without each and every one of you. And to all the friends and loved ones who remained by my side since I began living this *vida loca,* you know I am indebted to you forever.

To Brother Charles Davis and Brother Ben Furman, I thank you for the indispensable roles you played in my evolution from young boy to young man. To the people of the Roseland neighborhood (*aka* The Wild Hundreds) of Chicago, be proud that you raised one of the toughest SOBs that ever set foot on a football field. To the faculty of Washington Elementary, you taught me how to learn, for which I am eternally grateful—and by the way, I didn't break half the stuff you thought I did. To the Mt. Carmel community, thanks for keeping your promise that "you come to Carmel as a boy, and leave as a man." That phrase could not be truer. To the University of Illinois—where I discovered quality people, great times, an outlet for my physical talents, and an environment where I could stretch the limits of my intellect—Champaign is where I literally found a voice, thanks to the professors in the Speech Communications department in the School of Liberal Arts. You taught me the power of language and started me on the path that led to this book.

To the Arizona Cardinals organization (*aka* The Armpit) and their fans, you have my sincerest appreciation for putting up with an off-beat guy who liked to do things his own way. You drafted a player who wanted to fulfill his destiny and get his team to the Super Bowl, and allowed me to flourish. I established the foundation of a cherished career and put down roots in your city; my only regret is that we never went all the way. No hard feelings and God bless you all. I would also like to acknowledge the New York Giants, Minnesota Vikings, and Chicago Bears, who gave me something to prove and motivated me to be the best defensive end they ever saw—and to win a Super Bowl for the Tampa Bay Buccaneers, the team that actually had faith in me as a person and a player.

To the Tampa Bay players, coaching staff, management, and fans, I say thank you for a unique and enlightening experience. Winning the Super Bowl was one of the best moments of my life. We have to do it again sometime! To all of my teammates, thank you for your hearts. To Tony Dungy, special thanks for bringing me to the Bucs. And to Rich McKay, I told you our deal would make you look like a genius, so I just want to say "What up, Einstein?"

I would also like to extend my profound appreciation and deepest respect to the talented, courageous athletes who challenged the racial and economic status quo of sports down through the years. You made it possible for the people of my generation to get an education, control our own destiny, and accomplish great things at the highest level of sports. Much love to the old school! And finally, here's some special love for "Sweetness," the great Walter Payton, a man whose style of play, work habits, and dedication to the game I have emulated since I first discovered football.

Lastly, I thank God for truly blessing me with the myriad experiences that have helped me become the person I am today. Life is a journey for all of mankind, but it is the individual who must grow through obstacles, learn through lessons, and ultimately acquire the understanding to find his or her own truth.

—Sackmasta (*aka* Simeon Rice)

Additional thanks, appreciation, and recognition to:

Kevin Wilson	Dave McGinnis	Jonathan Miller
Lamon Caldwell	Denny Marcin	Julie Nathanson
Benjamin Morrow	Lou Tepper	John Idzik
Ty Douthard	Frank Lenti	Pete Larios
Sean Green	Dave Lenti	Sonya Rice
Aji Anderson	John Ptocki	Tonica Rice
John Anderson	Malcolm Glazer	Nianna Rice
Joe Greene	Linda Glazer	Yahshia Rice
Rob Marinelli	Joel Glazer	Diallo Rice
Rich McKay	Bryan Glazer	Mike Kennedy
Jon Gruden	Edward Glazer	
Monte Kiffin	William Bidwill	

Big ups to anyone I miss in this book. Don't charge it to the heart, charge it to the mind. Or blame my editor!

Introduction

I can pinpoint the day I decided to become a professional football player. In fact, I can tell you the exact moment. It was January 24, 1982. I was one month short of my eighth birthday. The San Francisco 49ers were playing the Cincinnati Bengals in Super Bowl XVI. The 49ers had a 20–0 halftime lead, but the Bengals were coming back. Cincinnati's quarterback, Ken Anderson, dropped back and could not find a receiver. He was in trouble, and he began to run. The field looked like a hornet's nest, but Anderson, who was not the fastest guy around, spotted an opening and took off. He slid under two tacklers just as he made a first down.

That really made me want to play football. I don't know how to explain it, but Anderson's run made me appreciate that there was an art to football, and that the players who possessed creativity could succeed even when they were seemingly surrounded by chaos and mayhem. At that moment, I saw that football was a game that required aggressiveness—but also rewarded a certain type of talent. It was a team game, but it also allowed individuals to shine.

I was at that age when I was still trying to understand what it meant to be a man. My father was a great role model, but it seemed to me that these players were celebrating manhood on an entirely different level. That day I sensed that football would lead me to celebrate and explore my own manhood, to find out what I could do physically and mentally, to discover my own artistry and creativity, and to do so within the realm of physical play.

I loved games, you see. I loved to compete. I loved to keep score. I loved being part of a team and I loved to accomplish things individually. I loved the fact that you could test your limits within the framework of a set of rules. I had played football prior to that January afternoon back in 1982, but I had never viewed it as a means of self-expression. From then on, however, I viewed football as the ultimate game. That one play in that one game was literally a life-altering event.

Fast-forward twenty-one years to Super Bowl XXXVII. Now I'm on the field banging and little boys are watching *me* on TV. I'm playing the best game of my life in the biggest game of my life, fulfilling the ultimate goal of any professional football player. My appetite for playing football is undiminished, my drive to dominate and win stronger than ever. I am at the apex of my profession, and a championship is within my grasp.

And I owe everything to football.

It's a different game than the one I played growing up in Chicago, a different game than most fans understand. Like any white light, the halo surrounding the culture of football is made up of many different colors. Through the prism of my experiences, I believe you will absorb its full spectrum for the very first time.

In other words, this is not your father's football book.

This is a book that explores the dominant forces in my world—faith and illusion—and that most curious of quirks in human nature: the rush to judgment. I am by no means a simple man, yet I am someone who likes to keep things simple. Perhaps that is why, for most of my life, I treated these three elements as separate and distinct from one another. Only when I recognized how profoundly intertwined these forces are did I achieve a level of clarity about the world in which I exist. Up to that point, life just kind of punched me in the face, and I kind of punched back. I guess you call that living and learning.

I fell in love with football when I was eight years old, and basically every important decision I have made in my life since then has taken into consideration how it might affect my dream of playing professionally. Ask anyone who knows me going back to my childhood, and they will tell you: It has always been about football for Sim.

The game has bestowed order on my life, it has enabled me to set goals, it has given me a greater appreciation of friends and family, it has let me explore my own physical and intellectual limits, it has given me fame, and it has created a financial base from which I can map out the rest of my life. Football has taught me lessons about love and trust and betrayal that most people don't learn, or at least appreciate, until they're twice my age. Football is a sport that looks to its future, but always respects and honors its past, so it has also given me a sense of where I fit into the human story, in the time line of history.

I am considered a star in my chosen profession. *Simeon Rice* is a name that has already been etched into the record books as a member of a championship team and as an individual All-Pro player. I have set team records and league records, a couple of which have already been broken. (That's football for you!) As a star in a major sport, I am a commodity. On this point the people who run football are crystal clear. I don't necessarily like it, but I understand and accept this fact. To a point. Grudgingly.

When I first set my sights on a career in football, my goal was to become a player who could bring a unique combination of qualities to my job. I was always bigger, faster, more coordinated, and more aggressive than almost everyone I played with, from grade school right through college. But that's true of most players in the National Football League. What I added to my physical gifts was the ability to accurately analyze on-field situations in real time, as they happened. I also have an off-the-field dedication to my craft that I feel is unparalleled.

You would think that a guy with that type of résumé would rank among the most coveted men in football. You would think that a guy with that type of skill set and that type of work ethic would be the last man a coach would fret about. You would think that a guy who takes care of business on the field, in practice, and in his personal life would be held up to fans as a paragon of athletic integrity. You would think that fans and coaches and the media would say, *Damn, I'd do anything to have twenty-two guys like Sim on my team.*

You would think all those things. And you would be wrong. Don't feel bad. For most of my life I thought this way, too. To my utter amazement and constant dismay, I am regarded as a very dangerous person by the football establishment.

Welcome to the upside-down world of Simeon Rice, where all things are possible but nothing is ever what it seems. Where integrity is for sale but obedience is non-negotiable. Where your best intentions beget your worst nightmares. Where risk is high and reward is maddeningly elusive. Where good is bad, black is white, right is wrong, and the only thing you know for sure is whether you've won or lost when you walk off the field.

How do I fit into this world? At times, not very well. This was once a source of anxiety for me, but now it's almost like a badge of honor. It is not every man who gets fed into the meat grinder of elite-level football and emerges with his brain unscrambled and his dignity intact. Not only does that qualify me to comment on America's favorite spectator sport, but I feel it gives me a rather unique perspective on what it means to be a football player, too. And this is what I intend to share with you in the pages that follow.

I've had to look back at my life in great detail in order to do this book, which is not an easy thing for anyone to do. Basically, I'm the type of cat who prefers to look forward. I like to examine things from a lot of different angles, to step back and analyze a situation. Doing this book forced me to explore my thoughts and feeling and actions. Truth be told, that was the easy part. The hard part was explaining my thoughts and feeling and actions. My motto was always, *If you know me, no explanation necessary. If you don't know me, no explanation will do.*

I began that process by looking at myself and my life as objectively as possible. While I've never cared that much what people think about me, I am acutely aware that many people find me somewhat, shall we say, enigmatic. If you take Simeon Rice at face value, you have someone who has unquestionably devoted his life to football, but who also did the following: (1) jeopardized his chances of playing college football by demanding to be a six-foot, five-inch high school running back; (2) passed up a chance to play in the NFL so he could goof off one more year in college; (3) risked everything in the prime of his football career to play pro basketball; (4) dared a team owned by a billionaire to sign him for minimum wage (after recording the best five-year start of any defensive end in history); and (5) achieved his dream by winning a Super Bowl—the ultimate expression of team-sport success—then celebrated alone in a hotel room.

Everything you just read is true. That's me in a nutshell, and I will be the first to admit that I can be a tough nut to crack.

Let me also forewarn you that my life story is not typical of most professional athletes. I came from a stable family, my parents both had good jobs, and I went to excellent schools. I don't do drugs, I don't drink, I don't have a posse, and while I've probably made less than half the dumb-ass mistakes most players my age have made, I've made some beauties, too. My life would be damn boring were it not for the fact that, somehow, I always seem to find myself cast as the villain. I'm not sure what that says about me, but I think it says a lot about the game I play and the people who run my sport. And ultimately I think you'll agree.

Just do me one favor: Don't rush to judgment . . . take your time before you make up your mind.

1

I am truly a product of my parents.

My father drilled into me that you can do anything if you put your mind to it. You set a goal, you understand what it will take to achieve it, and you never waver from that path. We both like breaking things down, trying to find that point where logic meets philosophy so we can wrap our minds around something. As a young man, he was an athlete with explosive ability—fast, powerful, and coordinated. He wasn't a big guy, six feet five like me. He stands about five feet seven. But he never gave up, and he never backed down from a challenge. That's the Simeon Rice you see on the football field.

The Simeon Rice you see off the field—from the way I move, to my mannerisms, to the way I express myself—has a lot to do with my mother. She is a long, lean, elegant woman with a relaxed manner. She was also very athletic as a young woman, a basketball player and a runner. I'll bet she could fly.

My mother taught me about the importance of faith. She is a religious woman, but that's not what I'm talking about. It's more like having faith in yourself and in the people you are close to. In my case, by extension, that came to mean my teammates, my coaches, my teachers, and eventually the teams I played for and the professional league I joined. This aspect of my personality is what defines me. I have faith that people will do the right thing; that their intentions are what they say they are. The benefit of this approach to life is that it enables you to be steady, to be consistent. It also helps you pull back and see the big picture.

In sports—and particularly in football—almost everything you do is an act of faith. Why else would you kill yourself doing drills in practice? Why else would you run plays you know aren't going to work? Why else does a guy like me work out eight hours a day in April when my next game is more than four months away?

The more I think about it, the more I realize just how much my faith has defined me. Everything good that has come to me in my life has in one way or another stemmed from the faith I have in myself, in my family, in my friends, in my teammates and coaches, and in the basic goodness and fairness of others. And not surprisingly, every time I get screwed, it's a product of my faith as well. It's an uneasy trade-off, but so far it's one I've been able to live with. I honestly believe if I'd had the kind of personality that enabled me to see the bad stuff coming, I'd never experience the good stuff, and I'd have closed off the avenues that have helped me explore my world with the depth and humor and intelligence that make life truly worth living.

My mother, Evelyn Ross, was born in Castleberry, Alabama, to Adelia and Jesse Ross. She had two sisters and three brothers. My grandfather worked for International Harvester, and my grandmother worked as a nurse's aide. The family moved to Chicago's South Side in 1956, when she was eight. I don't think my mom liked the city at first—it was nothing like the friendly environment in Castleberry—and to this day she has a lot of love for the country. Still, she's lived in and around Chicago ever since. My mother got her degree and worked in special education for twenty years. She retired the same year my father did, 1997, but still works with some after-school programs.

My father, Henry, was born in Youngstown, Ohio, and came from a very large family: He was the thirteenth of fifteen kids. His father worked as an engineer in the coal mines of western Pennsylvania. Education was the top priority in my dad's household, and he graduated from Youngstown High, an integrated school, at the age of fourteen, in 1956. Pops decided there were better opportunities for a smart young black man in Chicago, so he moved there hoping to acquire some advanced training or, ideally, get into college. Three of his brothers lived in Chicago already, so he had family there.

Unfortunately, the state of Illinois wasn't interested in his Ohio diploma, and made him return to high school—Dunbar High—where he was basically on hold for three years until he graduated again. He went to college to become a chemist but didn't like the field, so he took a job at Boeing in California. He returned to Chicago to earn a degree as a machinist. He worked at Portic for a while, then in 1969 took a job at Ford with more responsibility, better pay, and more benefits. He worked there for almost thirty years.

My father taught a little tennis on the side in Palmer Park to pick up some extra cash. He never took a lesson himself, but picked it up from watching other players in the park. He was always adept at breaking things down for people to understand, and he turned out to be a good instructor. That's how he met my mother, in 1971. They got to talking and discovered they were on the same level—professionally, intellectually, and spiritually. Both had very high standards, and I think they were a little amazed to find such a good match on a tennis court, no pun intended. Within two months they were married. As my dad says, "She filled my prescription."

My father was raised by a Baptist mother and a Methodist father, so he got a heavy dose of the Bible growing up. He was resistant to religion at first, but after moving to Chicago, he met a woman named Lilly Green, who became his surrogate mother. She was an Adventist who kept an eye on a lot of the kids in the neighborhood, and eventually he came around to her way of thinking. My mother began going to the Adventist church, and that's how we were raised. Today I would describe them as nondenominational Christians.

My older brother, Diallo, was born in 1972. I came two years later. My mother says she knew I was going to be an athlete when I was five. We were walking together and reached State Street, one of the busiest streets in Chicago. As we stood on the curb waiting for the light, I looked down the street and saw a car coming toward the intersection. I wanted to see how fast I was. I waited . . . waited . . . waited . . . and then I darted across, just in front of it. My mother nearly had a heart attack.

That wasn't the first time I had tempted fate. A year earlier, on a trip to the Lincoln Park Zoo, I wriggled into the lion enclosure when no one was looking. Before anyone knew what had happened, I was balanced on the edge of the moat that separated me from the lions, roaring at them. Some guy reached in and grabbed me, and they got me out. No trips to the zoo for a while after that.

After Diallo and me came four girls: Sonya, Tonica, Nianna, Yahshia. We moved to the Roseland section of Chicago when I was four. My parents bought a big house on 117th and State Streets. It was a fourteen-room Victorian that had been updated, so it was very strong and sturdy. All the kids had individual bedrooms, and we had a rec room and a TV room. We watched a lot of *Sesame Street* in that room. My parents approved of *Sesame Street* not because of the letters and numbers (we were all pretty sharp where that was concerned) but because of the values it taught.

This was the late 1970s and early '80s, and my parents would talk about how society's values were eroding. Our neighborhood wasn't disintegrating the way others in Chicago were, but it was getting wilder and more dangerous, and that was a concern for two parents raising so many kids. If things had gotten really bad, Diallo and I were ready to protect our homestead—we made sure to watch *Kung Fu* reruns and plenty of professional wrestling.

All of the Rice kids had interesting names. My parents wanted us to have strong, individual names. They preferred that we create our own identities instead of taking on names of relatives. They also believed names like this would inspire us to greatness.

For me, greatness equated to football. I was completely focused on the sport growing up. And by that I mean I made a lot of decisions based on whether something would enable me to play or prevent me from playing. I thought a lot about what I had to do on and off the field to get to be a man like Walter Payton, to achieve greatness. Payton was my hero. I had his football cards and his posters on my wall. I knew all the minute details of his life, and I'd talk to my father about him constantly, the way kids do when they become infatuated with a particular subject. Pops was always amazed how much I knew about him, and how I emulated him.

I wanted to play in the NFL like Payton. I knew the odds are against someone fulfilling this kind of dream, but that only made me work harder. My parents supported me in my dream because they could see I was going about it in such a way that—even if something prevented me from being an NFL player—the path I was on would lead me to success in some other way.

My father was like that when he was a kid. He was full of energy, very athletic and strong-willed. Pops always saw a lot of himself in me. My father has told me that I fulfilled all the dreams he had as a young man, and I can't even begin to explain how proud that makes me. Even when I was creating problems and he was getting called in to school from work, I think he could draw parallels to the way he was during his own childhood. That's the only way I can explain why he didn't drown me.

Not that he didn't try. More on that in a moment.

I was a handful as a kid. I misbehaved, I tested the limits, I had some physical encounters—

I was a little whirlwind, a high-energy kid. Teachers found me extremely annoying. I was tough, very physical, and, whether I meant it or not, I could be very intimidating. I also questioned everything. If something didn't make immediate sense, I expected an explanation or an answer.

I respected adults, but I did not feel they were infallible. When I went from pre-k at the Miss Rufus School, which was run out of a neighborhood woman's home, to kindergarten at Scanlon, the public school around the corner, I was convinced that I had already *been* to kindergarten. I knew my colors and numbers and letters already, and I thought someone had made a mistake.

When I went from kindergarten to first grade, my parents moved me out of Scanlon and sent me to Washington Elementary, which was on the East Side, in the more upscale Hegewisch section of Chicago. They weren't happy with the quality of the teaching at the school near us, so we rode the bus every morning and afternoon. Well, I was convinced that someone had screwed up again, and that I was actually repeating first grade. When the teacher offered to ease me into my new classroom, to help me get acclimated, I pulled away and demanded to be placed in second grade. I spent the entire school year looking around wondering why they had me with these other kids. My mind was always racing ahead, and other children just seemed to be operating at a different speed.

My parents and teachers may have a different story to tell, but looking back I think I was just trying to figure out who I was. I don't mean this to sound like a cliché. I literally was trying to figure this out. I would wake up each morning in an all-black home in an all-black neighborhood and get on a bus with all-black people each morning. As this bus headed across town, the black faces would begin to melt away, replaced by white ones. Then I'd get off the bus, walk into Washington Elementary School, and almost all the faces were white. I never did anything really bad. I was just doing things black kids do, and they didn't understand.

The way I talked and the way I walked, the way I laughed, my body language—these were things that were frowned upon, and I could feel it. Imagine going from your home environment, where acting one way is totally accepted, to a place where everyone interacts with you like you're from another planet. Now imagine experiencing that as a kid. A big, strong, smart, fearless, physical kid. I did something to get in trouble every day. That's not an exaggeration. And I'm not exaggerating when I say that there were weeks where my parents got calls from the school every single day.

It took me a while to figure out what was going on.

One of the things that clued me in was that anytime something went missing, either me or Jeffrey Jordan, the other black kid in my class, would be asked whether we'd seen it or whether we had it. When I got older I understood what was happening, but at that age—what was I, seven, eight?—it was really puzzling. If someone said, "I can't find my pencil," someone else would invariably say, "Look in Simeon's drawer."

I grew up in an incredibly honest and honorable household. I didn't know about stealing. It never occurred to me to take something that belonged to someone else. And I certainly didn't understand that white people thought everyone who lived in black neighborhoods stole. Try to put yourself in my shoes and imagine what you would make of this situation, which, seriously, went on for years. That's a bad thing to put a little boy through, and I think it affected my relationship with white people for a long, long time.

Naturally, I started rebelling. I remember thinking, *If I'm going to get in trouble every time something goes missing, or something's broken, or for something else I didn't do, then I'm going to get my money's worth and do whatever the hell I want to.* I was big and strong and I had a short fuse, and I was angry a lot when I was in school.

My father was always looking for creative ways to channel my frustration in more positive directions. He thought it might be a good idea to enroll me in a martial arts class. He hoped it would teach me discipline and give me an outlet for my energy. It took me a couple of months to catch on, but once I did I became very good. And very dangerous. I already had the strength and the explosiveness and the balance and the body control. Now I knew how to pack all of that into one punch. Dad pulled me out of that class fast. He told me to stick with football.

I'm lucky I had my football. It was a way to work out some of the aggressive feelings I had, and a way to cut loose after a frustrating day in school. It also helped me stay out of really major trouble, because if I fucked up in school I wouldn't be allowed to play. By the time I was eleven or twelve, I started to get really focused on the game, and my father got called in to Washington Elementary less and less.

I still got in hot water, though. The most frustrating thing for me was when I would get in trouble for doing what everyone else was doing. In the boy's bathroom next to the gym, they had one of those heavy tile drop ceilings. It had to be ten or twelve feet up. The kids at Washington played this game where they would run up to the wall, jump against it, and take a few steps vertically to see how close they could get to the ceiling. When I tried it, I put my foot through the wall and also pushed it over an inch, so that one of the enormous tiles dislodged and came crashing to the floor. It looked like a demolition team had been in there—you could actually see through to the gym! It was a bunch of kids playing, but the wall gave way on me. So the school made it out like I had been vandalizing the bathroom. You'd better believe Henry got called in for that one.

Looking back, I'd have to say Pops handled the discipline aspect very intelligently. Another man would have killed me, I'm sure of it. As I mentioned earlier, my father came close once himself. I had been sent to the office because of an incident that would probably be categorized as sexual harassment today. These girls were messing around, pinching my

butt in the hallway. I pinched one back and she turned me in. So my father was called into school—for the third or fourth time that week. He
didn't want to come in because he was working nights and needed to
get some sleep. But the principal said they'd put me on a city bus home,
so he dragged his ass out of bed and came to get me. That must have dri-
ven him over the edge, because when he came to the office, he saw me
sitting in the hallway (I wore out a spot in that hallway) and he didn't
even want to talk to me. I guess they showed him the file on me, which
filled almost a whole drawer, and he lost his mind.

We got in the car and he practically refused to acknowledge my existence. I tried to get him to say something, but all he'd say was, "Simmy,
I don't want to talk."

When we got home I asked him what he wanted me to do. He was
acting all somber. He said, "Just go sit in the TV room and I'll be there in
a moment." Then he came in and said, "Let's go upstairs."

"What're we going to do?" I asked.

"You'll see." We went up and he turned the water on in the bathtub.

"Simmy," he told me calmly, "this is the end. If you keep going on
like this I'm going to have a heart attack. You won't have no dad. Diallo
won't have no dad. And your sisters won't have no dad. To keep that
from happening, I've decided to go ahead and take you out."

Take me out? I didn't know what he was talking about. Then he
told me to take my clothes off, and I got confused. "Why do I have to
take my clothes off?" I asked.

"You'll see," he said again.

I took my clothes off like he said, and he came into the bedroom,
took me by the back of my neck, and marched me into the bathroom. I
saw the water in the bathtub and asked him what that was for. He told
me to put my hand in the water.

"That water's cold!" I said.

"That's where you're going!" he shouted, and he shoved my head
down to the waterline. "This is going to hurt me worse than it hurts you.
Let's just get it over with and drown you. Then I can sleep every day."

"Please Dad! You love me! You can't kill me! I swear I'll do better!
Just try it and see! I won't get in no more trouble!"

He let me go and I was good after that. For about two weeks. Years later, he admitted that it was all he could do to keep from cracking up. I must have looked terrified.

I was never terrified of anything in school. School was terrified of me, maybe. In terms of where I stood compared to the other kids athletically, it was like night and day. At Washington Elementary there was me, and then there was everybody else. I've talked to a lot of people who are considered stars in their sports, and this is a common story. Athletically, we were in a different place than our schoolmates.

I didn't lose a race in my school, to anyone, after third grade. I was doing backflips off garages. I was slam-dunking basketballs in eighth grade. There wasn't anything physical that I couldn't do. My balance and body control were ridiculous. I don't care what you're talking about—basketball, football, gymnastics, track—I was the best athlete any of my friends had ever seen. When I wrestled in high school as a freshman, I won All-Catholic League.

Of course, the big test if you're a young athlete doesn't come against kids your age. You need to find someone who's already up there in the stratosphere, and determine out how much of a gap you need to close before reaching that level yourself. I played basketball against older guys, and football against older guys, but that's not what I'm talking about. I'm talking about pure, raw speed and power—pitting yourself against the best.

My uncle had a farm south of the city, and I used to go down there with Pops. My uncle knew a kid who lived around there who was supposedly planning to qualify for the Olympics, and he got the idea of racing us to see how fast I really was. I was only eight or nine at the time, and this kid was graduating from high school. We got up one Saturday morning and drove to the farm, and this kid was waiting for me. My father and my uncle wanted to see how close I could stay to him in a footrace. Well, he beat me, but I kept it close. That's when I knew without a doubt that there would be some exciting times ahead for me in sports.

That was the last footrace of any kind I lost until eighth Grade. I went fifteen or twenty track meets without losing once, and I have almost 150 track medals to prove it. My specialty was the 100 and 200, as well as the long jump. Even when I was a member of a relay team, and we were behind, I'd run the anchor leg and just burn it up. My string ended in a city meet, when I finished second in the 200.

Being a football player on Chicago's South Side was interesting. Basketball was the city game, and it was embedded in the culture of the community. I played hoops then, and I still do today. But as a kid, I saw the game as something everybody did, and it wasn't in my nature to follow the crowd. Even after I became good at basketball—I was dunking in pickup games at age fourteen—secretly I thought it was a bullshit game compared to football.

You play basketball with all these tough dudes and the second you touch someone—*Foul!* To me, that was girl stuff. Also, compared to football, basketball was a slower-paced game, especially at the organized level. Between all the whistles and the time-outs, I never felt like I was going all out. Football was a game you could play with total abandon. It had more stoppages than basketball, but out of necessity. You needed those moments to regroup and get ready for the next play.

The world between the white lines of a football field held for me limitless possibilities. It was 100 yards of total bliss. To be able to play the game and play it well made me feel special in ways no other sport could.

As I've already mentioned, the player who amplified these feelings for me was Walter Payton. Sweetness. Man, I loved how he played. He never stopped until the whistle blew. He was relentless, dragging tacklers an extra few yards at the end of a play or giving them a shot before he veered out of bounds. He was an extremely physical player, yet he also had the ability to make people miss. When he needed a yard near the goal line, he dove over everyone and seemed to float right into the end zone. I read everything about Payton I could lay my hands on. I watched videos of him. I saw how he carried himself, how he always tried to be a role model. Whenever he was interviewed, he always seemed to say the right thing. I saw how hard he trained and how committed he was to the sport, and it turned me on to football even more. Payton played with his heart, and by doing so he showed me how much he enjoyed the game at that level. This affected me very deeply. More than a decade before I played a down in the NFL, I already loved the game like a pro, like Sweetness.

I met Walter briefly in the San Diego airport when the Broncos and Packers were playing in the Super Bowl after the 1997 season. The second time I met him, I was flying out of New Orleans with my friend, Marquisa, and our seats weren't together, so she sat down next to me hoping the person would switch when he showed up. Well, who should show up but Walter Payton! He was cool with it, and we made the switch. I spent the entire flight explaining to Marquisa who Walter Payton was, what he meant to me, and how incredible it was that we would meet this way. After a while I started regretting that she had taken his seat. I had just blown the chance to spend four hours with my hero.

Luckily, I got a third chance. During my third year in the league we had a conversation before one of my games and I was able to tell him how much he meant to me. Obviously, it's a rare thing when you get to talk to your childhood hero, man to man, and articulate for him the important role he had in your life. I could see he appreciated what I said. Then he said, "Sim, if I had your ability I'd still be playing."

I was blown away. Really, really blown away. I was stunned. I called home and told my mother the whole story. He was the best. It was an unreal moment.

I also remember my first football helmet. I had been asking my parents to get me one for a while, but after that 1982 Super Bowl I turned up the heat. The next Christmas, there it was, under the tree. A brand new white Sears, Roebuck helmet. I'm not sure who made the purchase, but they must have told the sales clerk my age, not my head size. It was like three or four sizes too small. I squeezed the helmet on anyway, though, and wore it around the house all day with my Walter Payton T-shirt. It took two of my sisters pulling as hard as they could to get in on me, and my head was busting out of it, but I felt like a football player, and that was all that mattered.

I played football whenever I could find a game—in the street, in front yards—it was a good time for me. I usually played with kids who were older and bigger than me, but I loved the contact and the challenge. Early on I was able to catch the ball and put moves on people that made them miss. The older guys would say, "Yo, this kid's got talent." That felt great.

Once I went to the park and got into a tackle game with a bunch of grown men. I was ten years old at the time, and this was without pads and helmets. I caught a kickoff and was running it back when I was hit really hard. That's the day I learned you keep your mouth shut when you're tackled. I had it open, and it raked across the grass. My mouth was full of dirt, and I couldn't breathe. My eyes got wide and I started to panic. I thought I was dying, but it was just the first time I'd had the wind knocked out of me. I think everyone was a little scared when they heard me making that gasping noise you make. They asked the cat who tackled me, "Yo, why you hit Shorty so hard?"

"If he's going to play with grown men," the guy said, "then he's going to get treated like a grown man."

I could tell from the way he said this that he didn't want me on the field anymore. One of the other men asked me, "Are you going to quit?"

I was still gulping for air, wondering whether I was dying or not. I was terrified. But there was no way in hell I was leaving that field. "Nah, I'm okay," I said. Then I got my breath back and kept playing. Those guys had a lot of respect for me after that.

My friend Bennie Morrow used to introduce me as the best athlete in the world, and this goes back to like third grade. To a large degree, I think many of my friends in the early days were my friends because of what I could do. That's a very physical age, and it was entertaining to them to see me dominate games and try crazy shit. I was physically gifted. I knew it and they knew it, and it was cool. There was an innocence to it at that time in my life. I didn't know where my gift would take me; I didn't know there was a process. All I knew was that no one could beat me at anything. I felt that anything I put my mind to, I could make my body do.

My physical abilities came to me at a crucial point in my life. In the second grade I was labeled LD: Learning Disabled. I had a minor speech impediment at the time—I slurred certain words—but I was in a speech therapy class for that. So I'm in the Learning Disabled section, but at the same time, when I took the Illinois state reading test, I placed three grades ahead.

The situation confused me. When I asked my mother about it, she said there was a certain quota of black kids they needed in the LD class. I don't know if that was true, but that's how I remember it. And I remember how angry this explanation made me, so there must have been something to it. I was pissed. I mean, I was in there with kids who were eating paste and playing with fucking crayons. I'll never forget, they brought me in there and had me sounding out letters—kindergarten stuff—and I was already reading chapter books. I've never understood it and I never will.

I know the administration knew I didn't belong in the Learning Disabled class. Why did they keep me there all those years? I think they saw that I just went off by myself and drew, and felt that was an outlet for me. That's my secret talent—I could just look at something and draw it really well. Maybe they figured here was an hour a day where I wasn't running or shouting or breaking something.

My social life at Washington Elementary wasn't very exciting. Mostly, I hung with the dudes on my block. I met Bennie in church when we were in the third grade. He never asked me how old I was, and since we didn't go to the same school he didn't know what grade I was in. I was a lot bigger than Bennie, so he naturally assumed I was much older, and he kind of looked up to me as a big brother. That was kind of cool, so I led him to believe that I was three years older for years and years. It wasn't until 1988 that Bennie finally figured it out. He came over to my house and saw my eighth-grade graduation picture, and then noticed the date was the same as his eighth-grade graduation picture.

"You're in eighth grade?" he said.

I was busted, but I tried to keep up the facade. "Nah," I lied.

Bennie went and asked my mother, and she told him to come back and ask me again. Eventually he squeezed it out of me and discovered he was actually four days older than me, and I swear it broke his heart. He was in shock for days. Finally he said, "Sim, I don't care, you're still my big brother."

Bennie was a straight arrow, an A student in elementary school. There wasn't much I could teach him about academics. But I did teach him how to fight. He was getting bullied and I showed him how to defend himself. One day this kid pushed him around and Bennie popped him. Bennie's grandmother got a call from his school, and my father got a call from his grandmother. She complained that I was changing his attitude. Pops took me aside and said, "Simmy, don't go messing up that boy!"

Bennie is the funniest person I've ever met. He enriched my soul, made me smile on the inside—and continues to do so. He was the product of a good family but a broken home. His father left and his mother had some health issues, so his grandparents raised him. He spent a lot of time at our place, and called my father Pops. Dad would speak to Bennie like he spoke to his own children, so we considered him a member of the family.

Actually, Bennie saw something in me that others, including my parents, have pointed out. In terms of how I processed information, I always felt that I was older—chronologically—than other kids my age. That was probably one of the things that got me into trouble so often. My teachers would look at me and see a nine-year-old trying to do and say things a teenager would. So what might have been natural for an older child became a "behavior issue" for me.

Two other key figures in my Chicago days were Charles Davis and Benjamin Furman, who were deacons in the Morgan Park Seventh Day Adventist Church my family attended for a time. They were monumental people in my early life, and my relationships with these men molded much of who I am today.

Brother Davis was a Pathfinder leader who gave of himself without limit or reservation. He took this boy off the block, from the heart of Chicago, and taught me how to survive in the wilderness. By the age of thirteen, you could have dropped me in the middle of nowhere without food, water, or supplies, and I would have found my way home. He also taught me life skills, how to deal with certain situations, not to mention everything from photography to sewing.

When I was eleven, Brother Davis took a group of us on a big trip out to Colorado. We were white-water rafting down the Colorado River, when I decided to stand up for a better view. Just then we hit a patch of rapids and I was catapulted out of the boat. I had a life vest on but no helmet, so I was in trouble. By some miracle, I popped up within reach of Bennie, and he grabbed me and hauled me back into the boat. He saved my life.

The adventures Brother Davis invited me on, along with the summer trips my family took, really opened my eyes to the fact that there is a big, wonderful world out there. To this day, I explore some part of the planet every off-season. I love to learn about different people and places. I'm fascinated by the way people think, and there is no better way to understand a new culture than by immersing yourself in it. The cool thing is that, ultimately, what you learn about most is yourself.

You know, people think all football players are big, dumb jocks, but I can tell you that's definitely not the case. There's a lot more depth and variety than people think. When Jon Gruden says "Simeon's from another planet," he means it as a compliment, and I take it that way. It's the press that misses the point. They're thinking I'm some weird, self-indulgent prima donna football player, when what Jon means is that I have a unique perspective borne of unique experiences. Part of the problem is that I don't think black athletes are perceived that way. And maybe an athlete actively broadening his horizons is just a threat to the status quo. Who knows? The point is, I am very satisfied with the path I'm on, and that path is one I can trace back to those early years with Brother Davis.

Brother Furman was more influential in my teen years. His door was always open to me and my friends. Practically every Saturday after church, Diallo, Bennie, and I would go over to his house for lunch. We would have these long conversations about where we were in life, what was important in life, and where we hoped our lives would go.

There is nothing this man wouldn't do for us. When I wanted to get my drivers license, he let me practice with his car, then helped me prepare for the test. He was a big brother, a father figure, a friend—whatever we needed him to be. He was never controlling, never judgmental. He was pretty cool for an older man, especially one who was a school principal!

Brother Davis and Brother Furman expected nothing in return except my promise that I would extend myself to others in my life the way they had extended themselves to me—basically, the old "Each one teach one" philosophy. If you come away from this book understanding only one thing about Simeon Rice, it should be that I have always taken this promise very seriously. I have devoted a lot of time to the people who matter to me because time is the most precious thing there is. Giving money to someone is a nice gesture, but you can always get more money. Giving time is something different, because you can never get it back.

Offering someone an open hand may have come from the deacons, but offering an open heart is something I learned from my Aunt Francis. She was my mother's older sister, and she never had kids, so the six of us had the luxury of a "second mom." When my grandmother passed, Aunt

Francis filled her role as family matriarch. She was always a pillar of strength, yet at the same time sweet and kind, and she never turned us away, regardless of what we needed.

Francis had big shoes to fill. Adelia Ross—we called her "Big Mom"—was not your typical grandmother. She was healthy and vibrant right to the end. She was a very wise woman who could zero in on an issue and get right to its heart, or pull back and see the big picture. Everyone in the family could lean on her, myself included, so when she passed suddenly and unexpectedly after suffering a stroke during my senior year of college, we were all totally unprepared.

You knew Big Mom was a unique person, because everyone in the family eventually took something from their relationship with her and carried it on in themselves. In my case, I saw how much courage and dignity she had, right to the very end, which made me more determined than ever to become a success in football, and a success in life. The thing I missed the most about my grandmother was knowing she was out there somewhere watching me play. She saw every one of my games in college—she was either in the stands or watching on TV. Just before my first NFL game, as we prepared to take the field, I started to get very emotional. My teammates thought I was just nervous, but the truth was I realized that, for the first time, Big Mom wasn't going to see me play.

With Brothers Davis and Furman, Aunt Francis, and Big Mom providing a watchful eye and a safety net above and beyond what my family and friends offered, there was only so much trouble a kid could get into. Of course, I still perpetrated my share of mischief.

What's the worst thing I ever did? I never did anything that embarrassed the family, nothing that jeopardized our standing in the community. The police never called home and said *We've got your son* or anything like that. Once we were exploring an abandoned building and ran into this dude with a gun, but that was as close as I ever got to anything really serious. Some of the guys I knew as a kid slipped into crime and drugs, and over the years they moved or died or just disappeared. But they weren't anyone I spent much time with. I more or less kept my nose clean. I think when I was little someone pissed me off so bad I ran into our house to find a butcher knife, but my mother stopped me before I got back out. That was probably the most extreme thing I almost did.

The thing my parents talk about is the time our neighbor, Mr. Roosevelt, was having a yard party. My father had a collection of classic 45s and LPs, and Diallo got this great idea that they would fly like Frisbees. I was only eight, so this sounded reasonable to me. Diallo and I started throwing the records out the window, and they made a cracking sound when they hit. Everyone in the yard thought someone was shooting, so they were running and diving for cover. My parents found out and they were furious. They made us go over and apologize, pick up the records, which were ruined, and offer to clean up the entire yard after the party. What's interesting about this story is that they were less mad that we had taken something that belonged to our father than they were that we had intruded on a private celebration. My mother was so angry that she actually told Mr. Roosevelt he could whup us, but he didn't. I think he was impressed that Diallo and I came over and took responsibility for our actions, because he was very friendly to us after that.

What gave my parents the most pride? Incredible as this may sound, I think they appreciated how early I developed self-restraint. The incident my mother recalls was when she heard my friend, Chris, using a lot of foul language in front of our house. She came to the door and called me in. I asked her why she had done that, and she told me she was afraid I was going to put some damage on the boy. I said, "Ma, Dad said as long as he doesn't hit me, it's cool. Words can't hurt me." That was a big moment, because it showed my parents that I was processing all the advice they had been giving me. I was only eight at the time, so I guess that was a pretty mature thing to say. The funny thing is, Chris wasn't cursing *me* out, he was going after some other kid! Chris was a trip. He had no back-up (all of his siblings were grown up) but he would still get in your face because he had this dog, Smokey—a big Doberman—that he would run home and get if he got beat up. So no one messed with Chris.

Meanwhile, I developed a delay mechanism that kept me from instigating physical contact. As I got older, I got to where I could turn it on and off. In football there are times when you have to read what's in front of you instantly and then react an instant later. If it's you against another guy, the one who reacts first usually wins the battle. In this case, having a delay mechanism is not an advantage. So in most football situations, I switch into a read-and-react mode. In some cases, though, you want to take a half beat to consider your options. In those situations I would hesitate for an instant, process the information, make my decision, then make my move. I've always had the kind of body where I could buy that little bit of extra time, so learning how to control my thinking was a major step in my football development.

What were my options outside of football? I never considered anything else. My father had a woodworking shop where he would build beautiful furniture. Diallo loved to work with Pops in that shop, but I didn't. He tried to pass along his love for woodworking by making me help him, but I couldn't stand it. I just wanted to get out of there. So when he would ask me for a chisel, I'd give him a screwdriver. If he asked for a pair of pliers I'd hand him some clippers. Finally my father said, "Simmy, you're not using common sense. Skills like these give you a second option in life. If you don't achieve your dreams, you have this valuable skill to fall back on. We could open a father–son shop and make a nice living."

I was fourteen years old and starting to see that I had a future in football. "Dad," I said, "this is not going to be my profession. I am going to be a football player. I'm going to the NFL and I'll be a millionaire. You've got me wasting my time here—why don't you just let me go do what I want to do?"

He sighed and said, "Simmy, a man should know how to build a home."

Let me tell you, at that point I probably *could* have built a home. Diallo and I were always helping Pops fix our house. We could lay a foundation, put on siding, level a porch—we were the young, black Bob Vilas of our neighborhood! I hated doing that stuff. It was so time-consuming. The summer I was thirteen, we leveled our entire house. Sometimes, my father would stare at that level of his for a half-hour. I was like, *Damn, Pops, the bubble is in the middle. Can we please move on?*

I understood and respected what he was trying to teach me: You don't half-do anything. And today, I totally embrace that philosophy. Also, you have to add dimension to your life, use different parts of your brain. I just couldn't stand carpentry! It didn't feel natural to me. But my father's words took hold. Since then I have always embraced new opportunities and tried to expand my horizons.

I have a son of my own, something not many people know about me. I'll delve into the details later on. But I see now how difficult it must have been for my dad to guide me. On the one hand, he recognized in me all the earmarks of a potential star athlete. I had the quickness, the power, the balance, the focus, the intelligence, and the skills. But my father also knew that the odds were against me. Life is full of unpleasant surprises, things that can trip you up on the way to your destiny. I know he thought about these things all the time, which is why he was always trying to get me interested in a fallback skill.

My mother was just afraid I'd kill myself. She was sure I'd be seriously injured doing the daring things I did . . . and she didn't even hear about the worst stuff. I think she was relieved when Diallo quit football. He was a great running back, but he didn't love the game the way I did.

The dilemma, of course, is that if a parent is too insistent on playing it safe—whether that means keeping options open or just not taking physical risks—it might actually be the thing that trips the athlete up. Somewhere, deep down, he may be getting the message that his parents don't think he can make it. Finding the correct balance between unbridled parental support and a dose of common sense here and there is a daunting task. My parents did a great job. I hope I do half as well.

Sports may have been the focus of my childhood, but the good times were not limited to playing fields. My parents were very involved in the church, so the church community was almost like a second family for us. There was a program within our church called Pathfinders that Diallo and I loved. It was similar to the Boy Scouts and operated summers and on weekends during the school year. It was great. There always seemed to be some activity to keep us occupied and interested, and I believe that it was what first got Diallo interested in the military.

We also attended Christian camps when we were kids. Mostly they focused on building self-confidence, self-reliance, and camaraderie. It was at one of these camps, the Circle Wild Camp in Michigan, that I encountered the only thing in my life that truly scared me.

I was only five years old and we were there for a two-week session. We all piled into a yellow bus at 111th Street and drove around to Michigan. As we pulled into Camp Wild, I noticed that it was next to a graveyard. I didn't understand much about death at five, but I knew there were dead people buried there, and it stuck in my mind as we un-loaded our stuff, ate lunch, and went through orientation.

The only time I had experienced death was when I lost my pet tur-tle. It was just a tiny thing, and I used to take it in the yard in one of those styrofoam meat trays and let him wander around. Every time my father came home from work and saw that turtle outside, he would say, "Simmy, bring that thing in."

One day, I brought the turtle out to play and got distracted by something. I forgot about it and left it outside, and sure enough my fa-ther ran it over in the driveway. When I found that turtle it was as flat as a pancake and I starting bawling. My father was so annoyed that I'd left my turtle outside after all his warnings, all he could think to say was, "Stop crying and clean that thing up."

So at this stage of my life, my lone experience with death involved a squashed turtle and my dad telling me to stop crying and shut up. I had already seen a cemetery next to the camp, and after lunch we went out-side and the cooks had a great big snapping turtle they'd caught in a trash can. I looked inside and thought *Whoa, that's not like any turtle I've ever seen.* I asked what they were going to do with it and someone joked they were going to make soup and feed it to us. I hadn't even gotten to my cabin and already my brain was on overload.

I stayed in a cabin with a bunch of kids and three counselors. It had bunk beds and wire screens on the windows. Diallo was in a different cabin, with older kids, so I would be sleeping alone and out of my house—for two weeks—for the first time in my life. Camp Wild was right smack in the middle of a forest. I'm sure I'd find it beautiful today, but at that age it seemed dark and mysterious to me. It was extremely scary at night. There were some big-ass trees, and they would cast strange shad-ows everywhere.

That first day the counselors told us we had to memorize a certain number of Bible verses. That was cool. But then, as if I weren't rattled enough, they said if we didn't memorize our verses—or if we were disobedient—Red Moses would come get us. *Red Moses?* This was just a device used to keep us in line, of course, but it was a bit much for little kids with fertile imaginations.

Naturally, everyone wanted to know about Red Moses, and these guys just made stuff up as they went along. The more we asked, the more apocalyptic their description became. The thing that really scared me was when they said that Red Moses doesn't go after girls, only little boys. I looked around and saw nothing but little boys. Oh, man, I thought, this cabin is going to be a Red Moses magnet!

The Camp Wild experience grew more terrifying by the day for me. We would swim in this river every day, and on one of the first days this dude with a megaphone started sounding an alarm and screaming for us to get out of the water. "Water moccasin! Water moccasin!" I'm like, *What's a water moccasin?* It sounded like a shoe to me. When I finally saw it and realized it was a snake, it didn't seem that dangerous to me. But everyone was so hysterical that I knew it had to be bad. That made a huge impression on me.

One night, I woke up and looked out the window of our cabin. I saw a man in a top hat and tails with a cane. He was standing less than 50 yards away and we just stared at each other until he drifted back into the woods. Now my mind was playing tricks on me. And it was only going to get worse.

The thing that really sent me over the edge at Camp Wild was when they made us watch a film about the Rapture. This movie was totally inappropriate for little children. It was made in the '60s or '70s for an adult audience and was indescribably violent. There was one part where all these people were being beheaded and it really freaked me out. It would be considered NC-17 by today's ratings system. They showed this movie to us after dinner, and when it ended they said, "Okay, everyone back to your cabins and go to bed."

What? I couldn't believe this. Not only did I just see the scariest shit of my life, but now I had to find my way back in the dark? We all traipsed through the woods with our little flashlights, not saying anything, all frightened out of our minds, when the camp's watchdog, an enormous Bull Mastiff, started barking like crazy. We called him the Lion Dog because he was so big and we were so small. He had a chain attached to his collar with a padlock, which we found especially intriguing.

Anyway, when the Lion Dog started going crazy, some kid shouted "Red Moses is in the woods!" and all hell broke loose. There were kids running all over the place, smashing into trees, crashing into each other, weeping uncontrollably, dropping their flashlights—it's a miracle someone wasn't seriously injured. I remember running faster than I ever had, flying through the woods, trying to outrun the beam from my flashlight. My heart pounding so hard I could hear the blood pumping though my head.

Man, this was too much stress for a five-year-old. What was next? The Tooth Fairy would show up with fangs? The Easter Bunny would eat people? I was in little kid hell.

Diallo, meanwhile, is in heaven. He was having the time of his life. All the stuff that was freaking me out he was totally into. All I could think about was making it to that first weekend, when parents were allowed to visit. I was going home.

That was if I lived that long.

A couple of nights after the Red Moses incident, everyone in the cabin was startled out of their sleep by a loud clanking sound. We laid back down in our bunks, but only a few kids fell asleep again. You know how darkness can cast its own light, create its own shadows? Well, I started seeing these weird shadowy figures move across the ceiling of the cabin. I was on the top bunk, so they all seemed to be moving toward me. First, there was a muscle-bound man. Then an elderly lady. Next came a baby.

Do you know how afraid I was? I was horrified. To this day, I don't know what it is. But I can tell you this much: I wasn't the only kid to see these shadows because we discussed it the next day.

Ah, the next day. After breakfast, the counselors told us we had a choice of activities. We could go horseback riding or spend the day in the House of the Red Moses (this is what they called the Arts & Crafts center). Where do you think I went?

Well, I had the time of my life that day. We got to ride these beautiful animals, and then Diallo and I snuck into the barn and played on these ropes, pretending we were Batman. All the bad memories from the past couple of days melted away. That's the beauty of a child's mind.

When we gathered together for dinner, however, the terror returned. The kids who went to the House of Red Moses were full of stories. They claimed that the front door slammed behind them after they entered, that the lights went out, and that all this other supernatural stuff happened.

Okay, now I really had to go home. I started packing my stuff, getting ready for my parents' visit. I had it all planned out. I was going to tell them that I was being mistreated, that I had refused to go to bed so the counselors made me sleep outside the cabin, in the woods. When I told Diallo what I planned to do, he said, "Simeon, Ma and Pops aren't coming."

First I was crestfallen. Then I began to panic. *How am I going to make it through another week of this craziness?*

That night, after midnight, things got totally out of control. I woke up and looked out the window, and right there, a few feet away, was a figure who looked like he was made out of fire. It was Red Moses.

I was so scared I couldn't even scream. I look around and everyone else was awake and seeing it too, including the counselors. Everyone jumped out of their beds and huddled behind the counselors. One counselor ran over and locked the door. Another one went to the window and was yelling at this thing and praying at the same time. This was the most tumultuous moment I have ever experienced in my life, and I can still remember exactly how I felt. It was total, unadulterated fear.

And just like that, Red Moses disappeared.

The counselors told everyone to double up, and they burrowed underneath the kids, almost like they were using them as shields. That freaked me out. Even worse, no one wanted to double up with me, because I had soiled myself. So I ended up sleeping alone—not just that night, but every night, while everyone else continued to double up for the rest of the time we were at Camp Wild.

Finally, the day came when it was time to go home. And check this out: As we left Camp Wild, one of the counselors said, "Everyone check your luggage. You don't want to take the Red Moses spirit home with you!"

I was so scared, I had to sleep next to my mom for a year. Every time I saw a shadow in my room I would scream and claim there was a man in my room. This was when Pops was working the late shift, and he would get annoyed when he came home and found me taking up space in his bed. One night, Mom told me to go sleep with Diallo, who had a big bed.

Diallo never believed my camp stories and he would laugh when I talked about Red Moses. But that night, I swear, his mattress rose up and dumped us both on the floor at the foot of the bed. My mother came up because she thought we were fighting, and we tried to explain what happened. Needless to say, when my father came home that night he found all *three* of us huddled in his bed!

"What's going on here?" he demanded.

"I don't know, Henry," Mom said, "but something weird is happening."

Would you believe, after all of this craziness, that my mother still wanted to send me back to Camp Wild? My father finally intervened and said I didn't have to go. I am not exaggerating when I say that was the happiest day of my life.

When we weren't at camp, the family would drive all over the country in our motor home, which my parents purchased when I was four. Every summer we took a trip—to places like Washington, DC, California, New York, Virginia—which gave me a real sense of the size and history and geography of the country.

Our neighborhood had a lot to offer, too. We had a good group of friends there. We didn't go to the local school anyway, so we weren't part of that crowd. Besides, there was always something to do after school. Our parents both worked, so we spent a lot of time at the YMCA.

My parents always knew what we were doing. We had a family meeting once a week. We would talk about what we were involved with, where we were going, and my parents would outline the expectations they had for us. They weren't about to let anyone slip through the cracks. We would also do Bible study at home every week. Mom's father was a church deacon, so she appreciated the importance of setting aside regular time for religious discussion. This type of interaction not only kept us from straying toward the temptations offered to young people in a city like Chicago, but also gave us a sense of purpose, taught us about love and respect, and, in the end, gave us a spiritual foundation that enabled us to go out and explore the world on our own.

My sisters? They're my babies. I got along with them very well. In fact I was, and am, extraordinarily close with all my siblings. We have very similar personalities; we are all extremely determined people in our own way, very goal-oriented. We also are similar in the way we think and the way we approach life. Being older, I think I was kind of an idol for the girls. When they were at odds with my parents, I sometimes served as an intermediary, giving them perspective on what was going on with Mom and Pop. I know they enjoyed having me for an older brother, especially after people in the neighborhood started recognizing me as a football player. Being Sim's sisters wasn't such a bad deal.

They were great athletes who had terrible coaches. They had elite-level skills but lacked elite-level training in their formative years. That was frustrating for me to watch, but unfortunately that's the reality of girls' sports. Most of the time, schools don't take it seriously enough to hire a talented and committed coach who can develop the really gifted athletes who come along.

That's a shame, because—I'm not bullshitting—my sisters all could have been on Olympic teams. All four ran track and played basketball. I always tried to help them out in sports. On the weekends, I would put them through their paces. By junior high they had a really strong base—they had great form and they were in the habit of practicing. Let me tell you, they were the fastest girls in the neighborhood. I worked them out, ran them up hills and whatnot. I trained so hard that they would start crying. I'd yell at them, "C'mon, you can make it!" One time I ran Sonya up a hill backward and sideways until she was screaming "I hate you!"

We communicated as well as any brothers and sisters I've ever seen, and still do. When I come home we fall right into our old ways. They want to know all about what's happening in my life, and they tell me everything that's happening in theirs. We all view the ups and downs of life the same way, so we can be very honest and get right to the heart of things. We can talk to one another about absolutely anything.

Unfortunately, I'm afraid they've ruined me for marriage, because I don't think I could spend my life with a woman if I didn't have that same kind of connection. I'm not sure what effect I've had on them in that respect, but given the level of honesty I have, I've definitely enlightened them about the male psyche. They know what to expect from their boyfriends, what they shouldn't put up with, and what they're going to have to tolerate if they want to move a relationship along. I started having these talks with them around the time each went off to college.

What qualified me to give this advice? My father once told me, "If you know yourself, you know all men." He cautioned me that you have to know yourself completely, from the most mundane and basic, to the most innocent, to the wildest and most extreme. I am a reasonably introspective person. I think a lot about what I do, and why I do it, and I can be brutally honest with myself. So I think I'm a good resource for my sisters in the men department, and they seem to agree.

The most important nugget of wisdom I imparted to them is to appreciate that—depending on a man's age and maturity level—they are getting an entirely different person than he was at a previous stage. A man of eighteen is different than he'll be at twenty-five, and at twenty-five he's different than he'll be at thirty. Understand that if you hook up with a dude at one age, you have to be prepared to go through all the twists and turns and potholes on the road to who this person will ultimately be. And recognize the biggest irony: Once you get that man to where he's stable and has a fully developed personality, he may no longer be the man you wanted.

I remember a conversation I had with one of my sisters about love. I told her that the reason she'll fall in love with a man is because he'll say he loves her and really mean it. She'll feel that honesty and that passion and believe it's forever. But with men, I warned her, it's not always forever. The farther you get from the moment, the more likely it is that a young man's mind will change. It might get to the point that he doesn't even remember the moment. It's like when a dude borrows money from you. He really needs it and he swears he'll pay you back, and you lend it to him because you believe that truth and that passion. Then you see him a few days later and he can barely remember borrowing the money!

I know that's a cold way of looking at love, but I'm the big brother. I need to open their eyes so they can recognize the bullshit, but also recognize the real thing when it does come along. Sorry, boys, the Rice women know all our sweet little secrets now.

Diallo and I were best friends. We loved each other and agreed on almost everything. Diallo looked out for me all the time, because he knew I had this energy in me and I might try anything that popped into my head—shit that might get me hurt and him in trouble for not stopping me. Diallo seemed to feel that if someone wasn't keeping an eye on me, I was going to injure myself or someone else. He could read me, too. He'd say, "Watch out, Dad, Simmy's about to do something!"

As we got older, Diallo and I remained very close, but developed different personalities. I became more outgoing, more public. Diallo became more serious. He had a small, tight group of friends. Everyone else he kind of kept at arm's length. He looked out for me until I was about thirteen or fourteen, when I got to be as big as he was. After that I continued to look up to him and respect the hell out of him, but that quasi-parental part of our relationship was over.

The thing we had in common was that we both wanted to be great at what we did. We were both determined to be successful. It took Diallo a while to get a grip on what that was, whereas for me it was always football. So for a time, I had surpassed him in a way. Looking back, the fact that our parents had us attend different high schools was a good thing, because we were each able to develop our own identity.

Still, the one year we went to the same school and played on the same team was fantastic. I was in seventh grade at Washington Middle School, playing serious organized football for the first time. Naturally, I wanted to be a running back, like Walter Payton. I also played nose tackle. Diallo was an eighth grader and an All-Star. He was the *man*. I was still living in his shadow back then.

Diallo and another eighth grader, Willie Condrado, were the stars of the Minute Men. But I got my props, too. I'll never forget when the coach pulled my father aside and said, "You make sure your sons get to practice, because they're going to make you a lot of money someday. They're that good. They're special."

My father had just gotten off work and he had come by to pick us up. I happened to overhear this conversation and I was like, *Wow. I'm just a kid and he's already saying that about me.* I didn't even think about how it reflected on my potential. I was just impressed that someone could look that far ahead.

I was one of the biggest kids on the field at that point, which gave me a nice advantage when I ran the ball. It usually took more than one man to bring me down. I didn't envy some of those kids who tried to tackle me, because I played hard and I was extremely aggressive when it came to contact. Sometimes when I was carrying the ball, I felt like it was me hitting them, not the other way around.

Some kids are good football players because they are angry or frustrated or just mean, and they channel it into their play. I was different. It was just my personality to play football at that high level of intensity. The more fun I was having, the more aggressively I played. It was a joyous thing, and I think that's what the coaches saw when they projected that I might be a "special" player.

This is an aspect of football, I might add, that fans just don't get. When you're down on the field, the personality of the players is very obvious. Their faces may be hidden inside a helmet, and their body language may be masked by pads and the uniform, but one football player can tell a lot about other football players by the way they play. I've always loved this about the game. It's like a hidden language that enables you to express yourself in a very pure and honest way. There's a lot of freedom in that, a lot of joy.

As tremendous an athlete as my brother was, he never really liked football. He was just as big, just as fast, and just as hard a hitter as me, but I loved the game and he didn't. He was good at football, but as I said earlier he didn't have any passion for it. Diallo's passion in eighth grade was girls. He basically gave up sports because of his interest in girls. There were many times he would go to cheerleader practice instead of football practice.

I was just the opposite. My head was in the playbook. Girls were a distraction that was going to keep me from achieving my dream, so I wasn't really interested. At that age, given the choice between hanging out with girls and looking at my football cards, I would have chosen the cards. I had a nice collection, too—thousands of cards. I gave them to a friend before I went to college. I felt like I was going to be a star and didn't need them anymore. Now they're probably worth something!

Anyway, Diallo was a superior athlete who simply didn't like sports. I understand now, as a professional athlete, that this is part of a weeding-out process that leads to the ultimate talent pool of pro sports. You lose the guys who aren't big enough, strong enough, fast enough, quick enough, smart enough—the list goes on and on until you are left with a very select group. Well, part of that process is taking out the athletes who have all the physical and mental attributes but lack the passion. It makes sense to me now, but back then I didn't understand it. Diallo excelled in every sport from track to wrestling, but would drift away from each game just as he began to master it. Seriously, he would score 30 points in a basketball game and come home and not even mention it. Then he'd quit the team because he didn't like basketball practice. He'd beat the fastest guy in a race, and feel like there was nothing left to prove. So he stopped competing in track. There was nothing exciting to him about athletic achievement. In a weird way, I'm not even sure he understood that what he was doing constituted an achievement.

That year we played football on the same team. I thought having a brother as the team's star would be great, but it kind of backfired on me. He was good enough as an eighth grader that he could blow off practice once in a while and still start. In order for me to start, I had to make every practice. Fridays were half-days, and Diallo and I often went home to eat lunch before returning for practice. One Friday, it was very cold and Diallo said, "C'mon, we don't have to go."

I told him I *had* to go, but he insisted I didn't and I let him talk me into staying home. At that time my mother said I couldn't go on the bus by myself, so what choice did I have? On game day, the coach announced the starting lineup. Diallo was in and I was out. I had waited all week for my first start at fullback, attended all the other practices, played my heart out, and now I was on the bench. I was pissed off. I was in tears.

In defense of my brother, you have to understand how kids think at that age. We all believed great players didn't have to practice, and Diallo was a great player, so he didn't like to practice. He thought of himself as a superstar—*we* thought of him as a superstar—so there didn't seem much point to him practicing. We didn't understand the team concept of football yet. We still thought of it as an individual game, played by a handful of our favorite players, and everyone else just seemed like props on a movie set. Diallo was to our Washington team what Walter Payton was to the

Bears, and we didn't grasp how Walter fit into Chicago's team concept. It was just too abstract for a bunch of kids in junior high. In Diallo's case, he was thinking, *Why should I become part of the team? Hell, I am the team!*

I always thought my brother could have been a great college athlete, but by the time he was finishing high school he decided he wanted to join the military. That didn't surprise me. Diallo always struck me as being military-minded, and he was always talking about it. He loved the Pathfinders and the Boy Scouts, with the uniform and all the equipment. We used to watch a lot of war movies together, and he was really into them. They didn't really excite me, but I understood what appealed to him about it and I've always had a lot of respect for people who make the decision he did. Diallo wanted to go to West Point, but he didn't have the grades, so he enlisted in the navy.

Even so, when he announced his decision I was angry. I really wanted him to go to college so I could go visit him and find out what that life was all about. I had this fantasy that he would invite me to his dorm and we would hang out, and now that wasn't going to happen. I had spent my whole life looking up to him, letting him open doors for me, letting him hack his way through life so I would have a clear path. Basically, I didn't want to stop being his little brother. Anyway, the day Diallo left was crazy. I was still hot at him, and thought he was making a bad move. I was convinced he could walk on to any team in the country and play football at a high level. He was still a special athlete, and I still didn't fully comprehend that he just didn't like sports. The family didn't make a big deal about Diallo's impending departure, but as brothers we were really tight. I wasn't sure how to act. I stayed downstairs with a friend while he was upstairs packing, and my mother had to tell me to go up and see him.

My father took Diallo's enlistment very hard. He had gotten used to the rhythm of life with two sons, and he would come back from work and half expect to see Diallo there doing his homework. They used to have long talks about life and school, and now they hardly communicated anymore. Weekends were the most difficult, because the three of us used to do things together all the time. Now there was just me and Dad.

By contrast, I don't think my leaving had as big an effect. My parents were already used to one son being away, so it was easier on them. I was going to college, too, not joining the military, and regardless of what parents say they are always apprehensive when they know a child might find himself in harm's way. In general, they didn't worry about me. I think my parents viewed me as a man wrapped in a boy's body—I was focused, I had a plan, and my path was clear. Diallo was still finding himself to a degree.

Although football was everything to me, it wasn't the only game that interested me. I loved track and field, too. I loved to watch and I loved to compete. Jesse Owens was the single biggest inspirational figure in my childhood. I used to read everything I could find on him. I knew the story of the 1936 Olympics by heart—how he'd gone to Berlin and beaten everyone in front of Adolf Hitler. He seemed like a mythical figure to me. I was especially captivated by the stories of Jesse racing against horses, and only later did I find out he did this because it was one of the few ways he was able to earn money. The most surprising thing I learned about Owens—and this was just recently—was that he was my father's childhood hero, too.

The one sport I never got to explore was baseball. I wanted to play very badly when I was a kid, but our family went to church on Saturday, and that's when the games were scheduled. My cousins Aji and John Anderson played, and their father coached their Little League team, so naturally I wanted to play on it. If I had started playing as a kid I might have kept playing, and maybe you'd be seeing me in a different uniform. John, by the way, is my oldest friend. There were times when we were together 24/7, and to this day we can still talk about anything, any time of the night or day. He was a fine athlete, too, and a huge influence in my life.

I did watch a lot of baseball as a kid, especially the Cubs. My grandmother was a huge fan, and we used to watch the games together. She would make me hot dogs and we'd sit in front of the TV and root for Andre Dawson, the "Hawk." Dawson joined the Cubs in 1987, and even though Chicago finished with a losing record that year, he still won the MVP. That was impressive to a boy of thirteen. That told me you could get your props—your credit, your respect—as an individual even if your team sucked.

At the time I didn't fully understand the events that led to the Cubs signing Dawson, who was a free agent. But as I came to understand the circumstances, I gained a new appreciation for how he handled that negotiation. The year Dawson left the Expos and put himself on the market, he was one of the best all-around players in the game. Yet every time he knocked on a door, he was told teams either weren't interested in him or couldn't afford him. Dawson's reaction was, *How could you not be interested in me? I'm a premier performer. And how do you know you can't afford me if you don't know what salary I want?*

Baseball fans will remember this as the year of collusion, when the owners secretly agreed not to sign one another's star free agents. The players had a collective bargaining agreement forbidding this, but no one could prove it was going on. Dawson knew that the players needed proof, so he contacted the Cubs and told them he wanted to play for them badly enough that he'd take whatever they were willing to pay. I think he even sent them a signed blank contract and literally dared them to fill in a number. When the Cubs sent it back untouched, the players knew they had baseball's nuts in a vise.

The Cubs realized their mistake and made Dawson an offer—for a fraction of what he was worth. Andre took the money, had a great year, and sacrificed potentially millions of dollars to make the case for the players. There were guys who were screwed during the collusion era who were seeing paychecks years later thanks to the lawsuit that Andre's actions helped create. No, it wasn't exactly Jackie Robinson or Curt Flood, but it was a big moment in the history of sports labor. I know the story because, when I became a free agent, I found a lot of doors slammed in my face. I basically had to sign a blank contract, too. Although the circumstances were totally different, I had an eerie feeling of déjà vu.

My parents liked to think that I told them everything growing up. If something bothered me or puzzled me or hurt me, we had the kind of relationship where I could go to them and talk it out. That didn't mean I went to them with everything, though. Like most boys, I held a lot inside. There are some things you just keep private—it's part of the process of building your own unique personality.

But in the end you are unquestionably a product of your parents. As soon as I accepted this, I took comfort in the notion that I could look at them and get a glimpse of how I would turn out. The weird thing was that, as they got older, my parents actually started to reverse roles. I'm still trying to figure this one out!

My mother, whose empathy and compassion make up a big part of my personality, has become less tolerant. She was always the parent who would never come down on someone, who would always strain to understand the motivating factors or extenuating circumstances in a situation. Now it's like, *Damn, she's stricter than Pops!* My father was always cut-and-dried about stuff, kind of intolerant. Now he's a creampuff. Dad still gets mad, but like most guys he gets over it. Mom? She can hold a grudge. And if she gets really pissed about something she'll hold on to it for a good long time.

The more I've come to understand my parents, the easier it has been to figure out some nagging questions in my own life. For example, I recently discovered where my push-the-envelope attitude and occasional impulse-control issues came from: my dad. Slowly but surely, I've come to realize that Henry Rice—Mr. Steady, Mr. Discipline—was a wild man in his youth. He was a member of a motorcycle rodeo as a teenager, the kind of daredevil outfit that would play at state fairs. These guys were crazy. They were doing things on motorcycles that you see kids do on BMX bikes today. And since my dad was the youngest, they always asked him to try the most dangerous stunts first.

After that, he built and raced cars. He ran them on dirt tracks and drag strips. He had an accident in his early twenties, and the steering column smashed into his chest. It cracked a rib and left the jagged end so close to his heart that it hurt every time it beat. The doctors thought he was going to die, but three days later he was back on his feet. Apparently, he calmed down after that.

Okay, so I know where my wild youth came from. But what can I look forward to as an older man? Well, if Pops is any indication, I'll still be pushing the envelope. One summer when I was in Champaign, the family took a trip to Niagara Falls. There's a spot where you can walk up some stone steps and get right near the waterfall as it cascades down. Pops climbed up these steps and got it in his head to touch the water. No reason, he just wanted to.

He climbed up some rocks so he could stretch his hand out . . . and slipped. From where my mother was standing, it looked like he had

gone over the edge—she damn near had a heart attack. By some miracle, this lady grabbed his foot before he went all the way over. She
started screaming and a couple of guys came over and pulled my father
out. To this day he can offer no explanation why he did this, and he ad-
mits that, had he actually put his hand in that water, it would have pulled
him in and killed him. No explanation at all.

Like father like son? Sounds like I have nothing on Pops.

2

The happiest man in Chicago in the fall of 1988 was Henry Rice.

I had started high school at Mount Carmel Academy in Chicago, an all-boys Catholic school of eight hundred or so with a great sports tradition and a reputation for discipline and academics. Many kids in my class traveled more than forty miles each way to attend Mount Carmel. There was this one kid who came from Michigan who left his house at five o'clock in the morning and traveled three hours each way. It took me an hour each way on a city bus.

Mount Carmel provided just the atmosphere I needed, different from anyplace else I'd experienced. It had the feel of a military academy, yet there was a very paternalistic environment. I responded to the fact that everything was regimented. You always knew what you were supposed to be doing, and what you were supposed to be doing next. They told you what you had to get done, and you got it done. Period.

I had been disciplined more times than I care to remember at my old school, but at Mount Carmel the discipline had direction. They used to say we go into Mount Carmel as boys and leave as men, and there was a lot of truth to that. Everything had a reason, including rules, regulations, and punishment. I liked that.

I became a dedicated individual. I was dedicated to my school, my fellow students, my coaches, my teammates, my teachers, and my academics.

I saw where it was all leading, and how I would benefit. I still tried to bend the rules from time to time and assert my will, but I quickly learned where that line was that you couldn't cross.

At Mount Carmel they were very clear on the matter of sports: If you fell behind in your work, you could forget about playing. Athletics was the carrot at the end of the stick. If you bucked the system you paid the price. It didn't take long for me to wrap my mind around that—I was still on my way to being the next Walter Payton, remember, so I was careful not to jeopardize my situation when it came to football. They also drummed into our heads that athletics last you only a few years, but your education has to last you a lifetime. I was like, *Yeah, sure, whatever.* But over the years those lessons became ingrained in me, and by the time I got to college I appreciated this idea.

The academic demands could be intimidating, and let me tell you, the teachers knew how to intimidate you, too. They took no shit, no nonsense, and they would physically handle the students in class. You really believed that a teacher or coach might lose it and beat your ass.

I was smart enough and focused enough to do what I needed to get by. I always did my homework, though sometimes I didn't do my best. Looking back, I could have done more, but there were nights when my father came home from the late shift at the Ford plant and I was still up working. So I didn't exactly breeze through high school. I'd start each term slowly but I'd finish with damn near all A's. I never worked as hard as I could have, but by the same token I knew when it was time to work hard. When I needed the grades, I got them. Most important, my average was always good enough to keep me on the playing field.

Socially, Mount Carmel was cool. Everyone came from a different part of the city, so there wasn't a lot of hanging out off campus. But at school I felt like damn near everybody was my friend, which was a big change from grade school. I made some really close friends at Mount Carmel, like Stewart Sharpe, Bobby Sanders, Patrick Whitfield, and Charles Edwards. I also became very tight with Lamon Caldwell, and we still work together today. Lamon was probably my best friend there.

I'd actually met Lamon before Mount Carmel. He lived in my cousin John's neighborhood, and we'd crossed paths on the basketball court and the football field in our younger days. Funny thing is, we'd never talked. He was a big kid like me, and very talented, but it was like we were always in the same game but never communicated. The one time we interacted was when I came out wearing a St. Leo's shirt. Leo's was another all-boys school in Chicago, and at the time I thought I'd be going there. Levicius Johnson was recruiting me, as was Frank Lenti at Mount Carmel, although I think technically I'm not supposed to call it "recruiting." Anyway, Lamon saw the shirt and asked about it. I told him I was going to Leo to be a running back. He said he was going to Mount Carmel as a defensive lineman. Then lo and behold I end up at Mount Carmel and I see him there, and we've been inseparable ever since.

I can honestly say Lamon is a great man. Very righteous, always positive, super dependable. I've never met anyone else like him. He's a very progressive dude—into poetry, classic jazz, reads the Bible, very involved in the black community—he is utterly unique. His personality was still forming at age fourteen, but you could tell he was a good dude. I call him the Black Socrates.

There was a lot of talent at Mount Carmel when I was there. Donovan McNabb, the future NFL quarterback, and Antoine Walker, the future NBA All-Star, were sophomores when I was a senior. I was friendly with Antoine, and we were both good, strong basketball players. Donovan was the backup quarterback on our team to Mike McGrew, so I actually saw a lot of him when he ran plays against the defense in practice.

I arrived at Mount Carmel as a fourteen-year-old running back. I was big, around six feet tall, and I was fast, but I was still getting used to my body, so the explosiveness wasn't completely there yet. We had a great varsity team that lost just one game in 1988 and 1989, and won the state championship both seasons. I played on the freshman and sophomore teams those years. The freshman coach was Ron Szczesniak and the sophomore coach was Curt Ehrenstrom. We practiced across the street in Jackson Park, while the varsity used the field next to the school. After the sophomore team, you either played varsity or you stopped playing football. But I don't think they actually cut anyone at Mount Carmel. If you were willing to put in the practice, you got a uniform, and Coach Lenti would make an effort to get you into the game.

I also wrestled my freshman year. I wasn't really into it, but I was good at it. Still, I didn't see how this was helping me reach my goal to play in the NFL, so I stopped. Looking back, this was probably a mistake. So much of my game today relies on balance, body control, leverage, and feeling what my man is trying to do when we are body on body, and I realize a lot of the special things I do are a direct result of that one year of wrestling. In football you have to be reactive and proactive at the same time. The same is true in wrestling. I was quick as hell back then, but I still had to respond intellectually and physically to my opponents, even as they were reacting to me. It's an interesting sport.

Wrestling also gave me a more acute awareness of my body at a time when I was starting to sprout up. This can be an awkward stage for even the most coordinated athlete, but I never had a problem. I just kept getting wider and longer, and I knew instinctively how to use my increasing size to its fullest advantage. I have to believe that wrestling was a key part of that process, too.

After my sophomore season, I shot up several inches. Coach Lenti got me into a summer league and said my friend Bobby Sanders was going to play a lot of tailback, so he wondered if I'd be willing to play receiver. I'll never forget, I was catching everything they threw my way, making great runs, scoring touchdowns. I also played linebacker that summer. I had fun, but it never occurred to me that I would be asked to play those positions at Mount Carmel.

Come the fall, he brought me into his office at the beginning of the term and asked if I'd like to contribute like Jasper Strong. Jasper was two years ahead of me. Originally, he had been a tailback at Mount Carmel, but switched to receiver and now he was playing wideout for the University of Illinois. I wasn't impressed. I still wanted to play tailback.

Coach told me I was now too tall and gangly to play running back. He said someone was going to come in low and blow my knees out. He asked me to think about playing on the defensive line, and said I'd also make a good tight end, and we'd see how things developed from there. He thought at those positions I had a chance to earn a college scholarship.

Coach Lenti told me the story of Chris Calloway, a Mount Carmel alumnus who made it to the NFL. Calloway was a running back like me his freshman and sophomore years, but when his body type and skills translated better to receiver, Lenti moved him there. Coach said he got anonymous letters telling him what a dumb-ass he was. But he saw

Chris's future as a wideout. Long story short, Chris made All-State, started three years at Michigan, and had a long NFL career. Coach Lenti had also sent Nate Turner to Nebraska and Frank Cornish to UCLA. They both made it in the NFL, too. So he knew his stuff.

Still, no more Walter Payton? I didn't care how many guys went to the NFL. I still wanted to quit. I thought, *This is some bullshit. I came here to play tailback.* I was a very results-oriented kid, and from my perspective I was having success as a running back. I didn't understand why they would switch me, and I was unwilling to play anything else.

I fought the idea my whole junior season. I would mess up all the time in practice, but the coaches wouldn't switch me back. I would drop passes and say, "See, I can't catch it. You've got to hand me the ball." On defense, I would just stand there while everyone was running around me, like I didn't know what to do. I thought I was being very clever, but the coaching staff knew I was doing it on purpose.

That whole season was a test of wills, and I'll admit that it was a wasted year. I refused to remember my plays, and I was a disaster in practice. I kept saying, "I don't know what I'm doing at these positions—just give me the ball and let me score some touchdowns for you." Not surprisingly, I spent most games on the sidelines, playing here or there, basically doing mop-up action. And that was mostly on defense. I had played so little that I was willing to do anything to get on the field.

I was so obstinate that I could not give in. Coach Lenti was doing what he thought was best for me and best for the team, but I didn't see that. I hadn't yet learned that you can't always do what you want when you want, which of course was—and to some extent still is—my natural inclination. Recognizing these situations is something you need to do to be successful, but it can be a hard pill to swallow, especially at that age, when you think you're smarter than everyone else.

We traveled to Cincinnati to play Moeller High to open my junior season and Lenti didn't put me in for a single play. This game was played in Riverfront Stadium, so it was a big deal. I stood on the sidelines with a ball in my hands, waiting to go in, and the call never came. I looked like a real jackass. My parents drove all the way from Chicago for the game, and I felt embarrassed and angry. Afterward, I saw them and the tears came. My dad was pissed. He asked me why I hadn't played and I told him I didn't know. He said, "You wasted my time, Simmy. You embarrassed me. Forget football and get your education."

This was devastating to me. My father and I weren't close in a chit-chatty way during high school. Mostly we would have long, serious talks. But I desperately wanted to make him proud. Pops had always been supportive of my football, but now it seemed he was ready to pull the plug on my dream. When we got home, I went out to the swing set in our backyard and soon I was in tears. My sisters went running into the house and told my parents. My dad came out and I told him that I was ready to transfer. A couple of months earlier, in summer league, the coach for Chicago Vocational—where Dick Butkus had become a legend—said I could come play for him anytime. That sounded good to me, but there was no way my parents were going to let me leave Mount Carmel.

Later my father told me that he believed this was a disciplinary issue, and that the discipline might be good for me. He used to say, "Simmy, your coach is just like me. At home I expect you to follow rules and regulations. On the team, you can't just do what you want to do. You have to do what you're told."

I was incredibly stubborn as a teenager, often to my own detriment. I recognize that. People say, "Sim, you were a smart kid, you liked to analyze everything. Why did you throw away your junior season like that?" I think a big part of my problem was that I didn't like defense and I didn't understand defense. People always ask me, "Didn't you look up to Richard Dent and Lawrence Taylor?"

Well, not to slight those guys, but no, I didn't. Yes, I was aware of the Bears defense and the Giants defense, but the individual names never stuck out in my mind. Generally speaking, it takes a whole defense to stop a play—I knew that then and it still holds true. You can have the greatest linemen and linebackers, but if you have no secondary the other team can throw the ball on you all day. A guy who makes a 50-yard touchdown run can win the game by himself, and that was the guy I wanted to be.

You have to remember the way a teenager thinks. I'd been rooting for the offense my entire childhood, and to me the defense was that thing that's preventing you from making that 50-yard touchdown. I don't think I could name more than a handful of defensive players in the NFL at that time, but I could tell you the names of the running backs, quarterbacks, and receivers. There was no glamour to defense. I couldn't understand why anyone would even want to play it. I sure as hell didn't want to.

Coach Lenti liked to say, "The best friend a coach has is the bench." And in my case, it turned out he was right. I could have played all year as a junior and gained the attention of a lot of colleges, but I blew that chance. Suddenly my path to the pros wasn't so clear. That spring I realized the best way to get back on track was to do whatever the coach wanted, secure a scholarship at a college that would let me play running back, and just start making my mark in the NCAA. So at the end of the 1990–91 school year, I went to Coach Lenti and said, "Coach, I'll do whatever you want me to do. I just want to play."

Lenti explained that I could be a third-string running back, a second-string tight end, or a difference-maker on defense. I had only one season left, but he promised me, "You work hard, and I think you'll earn yourself a Division I scholarship as a defensive player."

From that point on I was the ultimate team player. I never thought *me*. I always thought *we*. It helped that we had a really close-knit team my senior year. Everyone watched everyone else's back, and we went out of our way to help one another. If I needed a ride to a game or practice, there was always somebody willing to swing by and pick me up.

It's interesting how the same coaches whom you were convinced were idiots when you were warming the bench suddenly become geniuses when you're playing every down. I now appreciate just how special a group these guys were. Frank Lenti was the head coach, and he also handled the offensive linemen. His brother, Dave, was the defensive coordinator, Pete Kammholz coached the linebackers, Don Sebestyen coached the secondary, and John Pitaki was my position coach. Tom Sulo coached the quarterbacks and runners, while Mark Carmen worked with the receivers. These guys were on the same page on everything. I won't name names, but there are plenty of people in the Big Ten and the NFL who could probably learn a thing or two hanging around the Mount Carmel sideline.

I showed my appreciation for my big chance by playing hard on every down. I didn't take one game more seriously than the other— each one for me was like the Super Bowl. My father used to give me pregame pep talks. He would say, "Simmy, when you look across the line, you should see peewees. You go out there and look down on them. Be a giant. Fear no one and play to win."

I'll give Pops credit. Ever since he put those ideas in my mind, that's how I've approached every game. I don't care who's across from me. When I picture him before a game, I picture him with his ass on the ground, watching me go past. Watch a tape of me against the Raiders in the Super Bowl and you'll see what I mean.

That senior season at Mount Carmel, my body was like a wrecking machine and my brain was like a computer. Every time the ball was snapped I would try to dominate or surprise or disrupt the other team. There were times when I was unstoppable; the only thing that kept me from tackling the ball carrier was that someone else on my team got him first. I was what college scouts call a standout performer.

I also stood out because we had an undersized team. Don Veranisi and I were the only players on defensive who were six feet tall. We called ourselves the Ninja Turtles, although I didn't make a very good turtle. We played a 50 scheme with an odd front, and I played something similar to a defensive tackle. The idea was to set me up so that opposing teams would have to put two players on me. That would give a defensive end or linebacker a clear path to the backfield. Kevin Kilroy and Matt Crimmons made a lot of plays in these situations. If opponents tried to deal with those guys and didn't double-team me, they were in for a long afternoon.

We opened up that season with an overtime loss to Joliet Catholic, and then lost 6–4 to Simeon (really!). All of a sudden our string of three straight state titles was in jeopardy. At that point we made a few changes in the lineup, the seniors stepped up, and everything came together—we just dominated. Over our next ten games we had nine shutouts. During that time, I began to realize how well my skills translated to defense. I was amazed how many different ways I could strangle an offense. I still hadn't given up my dream of being a running back, but this shit was now fascinating to me. It got so I could do anything I wanted to on the football field. In practice, the coaches asked me to ease up, or else we weren't going to be able to accomplish anything running our offense.

By the end of the year I started to get some recognition as a defensive player. I made All-Catholic and All-State. When recruiters came to the school, they couldn't find my name in the records and wondered where I'd come from. Coach Lenti had to tell them the whole story about me not wanting to switch positions, and—knowing the way football people think—I can tell that a lot of them wanted nothing to do with me after that. A school has only so many football scholarships, and can't afford to waste one on a kid who sounds like a head case.

Coach gave it his best shot, though. He would point to the guys on the walls who were major college players or pros and say that, athletically, they couldn't compare to me. He tried to make the negative into a positive, saying, "Here's a kid who's only played one year of defense, he's one of the best players in the state, and he doesn't even know what he's doing yet!" When Lou Tepper and Chris Cosh of Illinois came to Mount Carmel, they asked Lenti flat-out how good he thought I was. Coach answered, "Someday that kid is going to be playing on Sundays—that's how good I think he'll be."

He sold me as a defensive lineman with the feet of a running back. Tepper, who was putting together a great linebacking crew with Kevin Hardy of Evansville and Dana Howard of East St. Louis, liked what he was hearing. I didn't find out about this conversation until many years later.

The state championship game was against Wheaton Central. Whereas most teams we played in 1991 were running teams, Wheaton was about 50–50 pass and run. We played a bad game and made a lot of mistakes. Our quarterback, Mike McGrew, had a sore shoulder all year, and he couldn't get the offense going. In the fourth quarter we were down by a touchdown, and as I was coming off the field Lenti grabbed me and said, "Simmy, you're supposed to be the man. You have to find a way for us to turn this game around."

A couple of series later, toward the end of the game, they dropped back to pass. I broke through and stripped the quarterback of the ball, and we recovered it. I could feel the momentum shift. We scored to tie the game, then won 21–14 with forty-seven seconds left. If you're wondering whether there's a better feeling than making the game-turning play in a high school championship game, well, the answer is no.

Because I played defense for only a year at Mount Carmel, the colleges that were interested in me were recruiting me as an "athlete." That means they know you're raw, but you've got skills they think they can mold to suit the needs of their program. They size you up like a side of beef, stamp you GRADE A, and then figure out which cut you are once you get to the school. I knew this was how it would go for me, so I accepted it and was ready to say yes to the first decent offer that came my way.

People assume I was a big recruit, but the truth is no one was that interested in me. Also, I didn't really understand how the recruiting process worked. And I had no concept of what college football was like, since I'd never played anywhere near that level before.

I was not listed in the top one hundred in the state, which meant that someone would be taking a chance on me. The possibility actually crossed my mind that my football days were over. That's how it is for most of the guys you play with in high school: You have your fun, you graduate, and you move on with your life. I wasn't ready to give up football yet—I still loved it and wanted to play—so I would have enrolled at a junior college, like Marine Valley or College of DuPage, until I could make a Division I school notice me.

That was really my plan, because at this point all the major schools had handed out their scholarships, so guys like me were left to fight over the scraps. As it turned out, I did have a handful of recruiting calls, including one from Nebraska, which was a great honor. The Cornhuskers were always in contention for the national championship, and my pops really wanted me to go there. But after they came to our home and told me how much they wanted me to play for the 'Huskers, I never heard from them again. I guess they found someone they liked better.

During my final semester of high school, I narrowed my choices down to three schools—Boston College, Louisville, and Illinois—and visited each. To say I had three different experiences would be an understatement.

I went to BC first. Tom Coughlin was the coach, and I was really excited. I knew they were going to try to sell me on the school, but as far as I was concerned, the moment they called me to visit, I was going to Boston College. It was far away but not too far, a little over an hour by plane.

A week before I flew out, I put my foot through a glass door and needed stitches. My father was furious—he said they'd see me hobbling around campus and they wouldn't want me.

My trip was still on, though. I arrived in Boston on a Friday after-noon and liked it immediately. It was similar to Chicago in many ways, so I felt comfortable in the environment. In the BC dorms I also ran into a guy I'd known at Mount Carmel named Mario Mowatt. He and his twin brother, Enrico, had been honors students three years ahead of me. Mario told me I'd love the school. I couldn't believe I knew some-body at BC. At that point I was ready to sign on the dotted line.

The first evening, I saw the school's highlight film, they did a little jersey ceremony, some former players talked to us, and I met some of the other recruits. It was a cool setting. This took place at a restaurant that supposedly served the best lobster and crab in the city. They really tried to impress me, but back then I didn't eat that type of food. They looked like big bugs to me. The coaches thought there was something wrong with me. They were like, "C'mon, son, you've got to put on some weight if you're going to play here." All I ate was a little bread and some water.

The next night they took me out to a fancy steak house. Well, we never had steak at home, and although Chicago is supposed to have great steak restaurants, I never ate at one. So to me, steak just looked like a big, unappetizing slab of meat. I watched the other people tear into it and I couldn't understand it. I kept ordering more bread!

The coaches made a point of saying how I was their number one recruit, which probably wasn't true, but from their expressions at dinner I started to sense that I was slipping down the board. They probably thought I'd never put on another pound. I had a problem with that, any-way. I felt that as I grew, the weight would come. Anyway, after two meals, I don't know what they thought about me. Maybe they expected a kid from Chicago would be a little more sophisticated, but I had never been exposed to these types of situations, and I was incredibly naive.

The first night of the trip I ran into a player who had transferred from Michigan. He was selling me on BC as a party school. He told me I was going to do a lot of drinking if I came to BC. I kept telling him I wasn't into drinking, and there was no way I was going to get drunk every night. We argued back and forth, him guaranteeing I was going to become a big drinker and me telling him there was no way that would happen. I blew him off. I was actually more interested in getting to know college women. The guy who was my host threw a party that same night and it was off the hook. There were more fine women there than I'd ever seen in one place. These were college girls, not girls from the 'hood. It was a delight, like nothing I'd ever been a part of.

My foot ached too much to do anything but stand off on the side, but before I knew it I was surrounded by a group of these girls, asking me how's my foot, where am I from, wanting to know all about me. When they found out I was from Chicago they said it was too bad about my foot because I should know how to dance. All the cats from Chicago know how to dance. One of these chicks was really exotic, light-skinned with green eyes—I'd never seen anything like her. I can still remember her. And her friend, whom everyone called "Cat," was just as fine. I ended up hanging out with both of them.

Cat was twenty-three or twenty-four, a grad student. She's telling me about how she's going to be a lawyer, and I'm thinking that sounds cool. Mind you, I'm seventeen and she's a grown woman. I don't have a game, I don't know how to talk to girls. So I start lying. *Yeah, I'm the number one recruit in the nation. Yeah, I got two Chevy Blazers, one red and one white.* Meanwhile, I didn't even have a driver's license at the time!

I realize now they probably saw right through me, but eventually they asked if I wanted to go out with them on Saturday. It was crazy loud, and I thought they asked if I wanted to go out with the coaches. So I said no. Smooth, right? Well I could tell from their bewildered expressions that I must have heard them wrong. I asked Cat to repeat the question, and this time I understood it. We made a date, and I was feeling good. In my mind, the night was a success. Of course, at this point I hadn't really mixed it up with any females, so I had no idea what I was getting myself into.

The next day I got a tour of the athletic facilities and met the coaches. I spent most of the time with Steve Szabo, Coach Coughlin's right-hand man. He followed Coughlin to the pros, and I think he was with him when he took the job with the Giants after Jim Fassel got fired. Anyway, everyone with the program asked me how I liked the school, and I told them all that I did. Then I mentioned that I had a date. That made them really happy. "Man, you work fast! You came up big!"

They were honestly excited for me. So were the players I met. They gave me my props and it felt good. "Man, you've been on campus one

day and you got it going already! You a player! You got you some game!"
Hey, what better way to sell a school than to have your recruits find a
little romance? Unless you work for the University of Colorado.

Well, after the big tour and my second dinner of bread and water, I
prepared myself for my big date. It was kind of exciting. Remember, I
had hardly kissed a girl at this point in my life, and I was definitely a
virgin.

Cat rolled up in this fine Camaro and my eyes got wide. *Wow, she's
doing it!* I folded myself into the passenger seat, and looked back and saw
three more girls in the backseat. They decided we were going to go to
some clubs. I reminded them I was only seventeen—I don't know what
the legal age was in Massachusetts back then, but I know it wasn't seventeen. One of the girls in back said she was seventeen, too. She was a fine-
looking Puerto Rican girl who lived in Boston.

Cat handed me a fake ID, and that got me into the first bar. The
Puerto Rican girl didn't have an ID and couldn't talk her way past the
bouncer, so she had to take a taxi back home. I was disappointed about
that. I really wanted to talk to her because we were the same age and I
figured we would have more in common. But I was in and she wasn't, so
that was the end of that.

This bar, meanwhile, was unlike anyplace I'd ever been. It was a real
scene. Everybody's drinking, people are partying, all sorts of stuff is
going on. It's a crazy atmosphere, and I'm a wide-eyed seventeen-year-
old taking it all in.

When we went to leave, the girls stopped by the coatroom. Back at
the car they threw their coats in the trunk—but they still had coats on.
The next place we went, it was the same thing. Oh, shit! These prissy, in-
nocent-looking girls were stealing coats! This blew my mind. In
Chicago, the people I know who steal look like they steal. But not these
girls. I confronted them and they said, "Why, do you want one?" I said,
"Nah, I'm okay." I didn't know what to do. I couldn't believe this was
happening!

Toward the end of the evening we stopped at a jazz club, but knowing what was going to happen I was too nervous to enjoy the music. I
slipped away and called my host back at the dorm. I said, "I'm here with
Cat and—"

"Wow, you're out there with Cat? Man, you doin' it! She's one of the hottest girls on campus. You gonna hit it?"

I had been obsessing on the coats, but now I realized the stakes had become higher. Now I had to act cool, like *I'm with it, like I know how to close the deal.* It dawned on me that I'm away from home, everything is going my way, and from the perspective of being a sexually inexperienced person, this is definitely the situation I want. If you're out looking for the late-night come-up, this is it!

Now that I was actually faced with it, however, I started getting nervous. Cat asked me who I was calling, and I told her it was my host, but he wasn't there and I didn't know where to find him. I was trying to come up with a story so they would drop me off, but she gave me a look and said, "Don't worry, I'll take care of you, baby."

That was strong talk for me at that time. I was thinking, *Oh my goodness, I've gotten myself into something I can't get out of. I'm going to lose my virginity tonight whether I want to or not.* I was acting cool, but I was really nervous. We got back to her dorm and were walking down the hall, and I said, "Let me call my host again."

This time I got him on the phone and gave him a quick rundown of what was happening. I told him I thought I should leave. "Are you crazy?" he said. "You got to seal the deal, man." I guess there were a lot of guys who wanted to be with this girl.

Now I couldn't go back. If I did, I'd be known for the next four years as the guy who couldn't seal the deal.

Cat asked me if I'd found the guy, and I lied and said no. "Okay," she said, "you can stay here tonight."

As we got closer to her room I started to panic. I assumed she lived in a suite like the BC football players I had met, so I thought I could just sleep on the couch in the common area. When she opened the door, I realized she was in a single. There was a bed, a dresser, a television, a desk and chair, and that was it. Oh, shit!

I wanted to get out of there bad, so I tried to stall for time. Cat did some modeling, so I looked through her modeling pictures. Very slowly. Then I looked at pictures of her friends and family. Then I looked at pictures of her old boyfriend, who was a football player. Then

I turned on the TV. But it was so late that most of the stations just had test patterns.

Cat was getting tired, but instead of falling asleep, she just got more aggressive. She came over and sat on my lap. "Sim," she said, "you're wasting time. We can't do this all night."

I said, "It's cool, I like looking at your pictures."

"Listen," she said, "unless you plan on sleeping in my desk chair, we're about to go to bed. I'm going to get changed."

I was like, *Damn!* Cat walked out the door and returned a couple of minutes later wearing things I'd only seen in a Victoria's Secret catalog. She had a see-through negligee and garters. I had turned the TV to *The Andy Griffith Show* while she was out, and it was over, and I'll never forget they were whistling that tune at the end. She walked over to the TV and turned it off, and turned on some music. It was Jodeci, the first time I'd ever heard them. I stretched out in the bed—with my clothes on and facing the wall.

She turned me over and started taking my clothes off. I was so shy I didn't want to take them all off, so I just rolled my pants down. I'll spare you the details, but suffice it to say I had no idea what I was doing. There was no foreplay, no kissing, no warm-up, and the whole experience felt like sandpaper. It was not a pleasant moment for me, and it had to be horrible for her. I thought, *This is it? This is what everyone's bragging about?* Then I fell asleep.

When I woke up the next morning, there wasn't any morning left. I walked back to my host's dorm and all the guys were saying, "Man, you got us all into trouble. You've missed half the stuff already."

You see, the rule is that a recruit can't be on campus more than forty-eight hours, and during that stretch he has to spend a certain amount of time looking at the nonfootball aspects of the campus. At BC, this was what Sunday was for. If a recruit doesn't balance his visit right, I think the school is technically in violation of NCAA rules.

When Coach Szabo found me, he started screaming at me. "You're irresponsible! We're gonna redshirt you! You'll never start here!" I knew Coach Coughlin really wanted me, but now they were yelling at me like I was a little kid. The day before, I was sure I was going to BC.

Twenty-four hours later, they were treating me like trash. In their minds, I was already a bad kid. I'd been through that before. I'll never forget, while Szabo was yelling at me, I was literally thinking, *Oh well, guess I can cross Boston College off my list.*

It was disappointing the way my first recruiting trip turned out, but all I cared about was that the school didn't call my parents and tell them what happened. *I* wanted to be the one to do that. What Coughlin did was call Frank Lenti at Mount Carmel. When I got back to Chicago, Frank was pissed. He said, "Mount Carmel is all about discipline. You went there and you embarrassed Mount Carmel."

Oh, man, I thought. All I needed was for Henry Rice to find out and all hell would break loose. He'd keep me in a room for three hours lecturing me. And my mom, I didn't want her seeing me like that—as the jerk who blows a college scholarship because he overslept. She really wanted me to go to BC, because it was a Christian college, so I knew she would be very disappointed. I was so paranoid they'd find out that I eventually told them—not the lurid details, but just enough to let them know I'd screwed up.

I'm pretty sure they knew there was more to the story, because Cat kept calling the house. She even said she'd come to my senior prom. My father said, "That girl doesn't want you. They hooked you up with that girl."

I'm like, "No they didn't. C'mon Dad, give me my props!"

In light of the big scandal at Colorado, I'll go on record right now saying that my experience at BC was not a setup. It was just about me putting it down. That was Sim being the handsome, charming, irresistible seventeen-year-old kid that I was!

The next school I visited was Louisville. This trip was a bit less exciting, although they did the whole "hostess" thing. I went to some parties, but nothing jumped off. It was a totally different scene at Louisville. Wild. One party I went to, guys were getting arrested.

I met with Howard Schnellenberger. He had built programs at Miami and Duke, and was a bona fide college coaching legend. He asked me what every coach did: "Sim, what position do you see yourself playing?"

I gave him my standard answer: "What position are you recruiting me for?" He told me if I came to Louisville, I could play any position I wanted. I asked him about tailback, and he said, "Okay." It was tempting, but deep down I sensed that I was being lied to. Part of a successful college recruiting program is the ability to sell kids a pipe dream. Schnellenberger was a master at it, because I was listening to him even though I knew there was no way he'd let me play the position. When I left his office I was like, *I'm going here!* But deep down, I must not have believed him, because that feeling faded pretty quickly.

During the Louisville trip I started to get a clearer picture of what it meant to be a college football player, and I also began to be more honest with myself about my goals and expectations. The NFL was still the pot at the end of the rainbow, but I was starting to have doubts about whether I would get there as an offensive player. I also found the idea of living on a campus and furthering my education increasingly appealing.

I was excited to be part of an environment where everyone had one thing in common: learning. At Mount Carmel, they taught us how to learn. They gave us the structure and academic skills that would enable us to take the next step, but I didn't understand this until I visited a couple of colleges. Here I would be exposed to more knowledge than I could ever hope to soak up, while at the same time enjoying all the personal freedom that was denied to us at Mount Carmel. I felt this way after returning home from Louisville, even though, honestly, I met some students there whom I considered pretty marginal. Academics didn't seem as important at Louisville as at BC, and that rubbed me the wrong way. No disrespect, it's just the feeling I got during my short time there.

So I had crossed Louisville off my list, and Boston College had crossed me off theirs. We hadn't heard anything more from Nebraska, even though they'd sent a recruiter to Mount Carmel and to our house. Things were looking bleak until Illinois stepped up and invited me down to Champaign.

By the time I arrived on campus, I had already made up mind I was going there. It was a big school with a great social scene and excellent academics—perfect for me. There were also a lot of guys from Mount Carmel there already, which was a bonus. I went down with a couple of my classmates, Bobby Sanders and Charles Edwards. By the time I left for the trip, I had my whole weekend planned, including lining up a girl. The only problem was that Coach Lenti had called all the Mount

Carmel guys and told them what had happened in Boston. So about the time this girl and I were ready to go back to the hotel, Bobby said "Nah, Sim. You've got to go back to your room."

Other than my coed interruptus, the trip went well. I loved how big everything was at Illinois. From the campus to the athletic facilities to the parties, it was like a different world. And the possibilities for finding a major were limitless. Illinois was a Big Ten school—it dwarfed Louisville and BC—and it really felt like the big time. That had great appeal to me, because it meant I could do my thing on the grandest of stages. All I could think was, *I'll be playing my games on ABC!*

Greg Colby, one of the linebacker coaches, took me around and had dinner with me, and we got along great. They had one scholarship left, and they offered it to me on the spot. I gave them an oral commitment, and it was a done deal.

The players were cool, too. At least most of them were. While I was there I met a cat named Mikki Johnson, who was a redshirt heading into his first season. He asked me what position I played. I said I was a rush linebacker (I was just making it up—I had no idea where they wanted me to play). He said, "You better find you another position. That's my position."

Charles overheard the conversation and said, "Forget about him, dog. He's an asshole."

Mikki and I ended up playing four years together and had some good times.

I returned to Chicago feeling pretty good about things. The only obstacle that remained was passing the ACT. I actually scored too low the first two times I took it, and I've always suspected that's why Nebraska cooled off on me.

Here was the problem. At Mount Carmel I'd worked hard to keep my grades up. I was really good at absorbing information and spitting it back. But the minute we had finished a section or I'd passed a test, I'd put a lot of the material out of mind. Well, the ACT determines what you've accumulated and retained in high school. Oops. Also, there were some parts of the test that covered materials to which I'd never been exposed. Not to say it was racially biased, but there were some terms and references I swear I'd never seen before. I don't care how smart you are—if you're seeing something on a test for the first time in your life, you're not going to master it. The upside was that I went to a really good school, and once I reached out to the teachers they prepared me beautifully. On my third try I whipped right through the ACT and passed with flying colors.

My father was disappointed that a Nebraska offer never materialized, but he was happy I was going to Illinois. He just wanted me to go to a good school with a good football team. My mother was still sad I didn't get the Boston College offer. Me? Illinois might not have been competing for a national championship, but it was as big-time as college football got—and I knew I would walk out of there with a diploma that carried some weight in the world.

Unfortunately, accepting the Illinois scholarship meant closing the door on my dream of being the next Walter Payton. I accepted this change of course and moved on. Would my life have been different had I continued to pursue this dream? What would have happened had I found a school that was willing to recruit me at that position? I honestly don't know. Maybe I would have been a third-stringer like Coach Lenti said.

Then again, maybe not. Until I sat down to write this book, I hadn't thought about it. I had the same skills and body type as guys like Eddie George and Eric Dickerson, both of whom were at least six feet three and probably weighed 225 or 230. I was a little taller, a little heavier, but just as fast.

No regrets, though. I made the right choice.

3

My Illinois experience started in the summer of 1992. When I signed my letter of intent, Lou Tepper told me about this fantastic summer program and said he'd pull some strings and maybe I'd get in. He said it was all young people my own age, including a lot of girls. It sounded like a vacation. "Beautiful," I said.

Well, it was a bridge program. Basically, it was summer school to help people who might not be up to snuff academically prepare for their freshman year—although they told my parents that it was more to help kids make the transition from home life to college. Whatever it was, when I got down there, I was like, *Whoa, this is the military!* The dean wore fatigues, there were curfews, everyone was yelling—I'm thinking, *What the hell is this? Is that what college is like?*

This was not a program for athletes. I think there were only two other players besides me there. One was Dennis Stallings, with whom I became really tight. He played in the NFL with Tennessee for several years. The other was Ty Douthard, who became like a brother to me. So in that respect, the bridge program was a positive experience.

Ty and Dennis were like kids in a candy store that summer. While I was hitting the books, they were hitting on the females. I would go off to my room and they would go out trolling, and they ribbed me all the time about it. I was not exactly Don Juan at this stage of my life, plus there was a curfew, and I didn't want to get in trouble. Ironically, it was during the bridge program that I was first smitten by a young lady named Kiela. I don't know why, there was just something about her. Unfortunately, the relationship never jumped off, so I missed out on the first love of my life.

When football practice began, I assumed I would be redshirted, or on the bench, for my freshman year. So did Tepper and his staff. It had been five years since a true freshman had started for the Illini, so becoming an impact player didn't enter anyone's thinking. But I began to realize that I would be playing a lot once I saw how good the other players were. To my mind, I was the most athletic player on that team. I may not have understood all the schemes we played, but I was faster, quicker, and stronger than the other guys. It was a revelation. I remember thinking, *Man I'm a better football player than everyone else here. This is kind of interesting.*

What I didn't realize is how this would affect the older players. In the Big Ten, the talent level is very high, but it's more or less consistent across the board. Recruits come in and work their way into the team's system, and if everything breaks right they get a shot to start as a junior or senior, or maybe in a rare circumstance as a sophomore. In my case, I leapfrogged over the other linebackers as the season wore on, and got more and more playing time in key situations. You would think the seniors would be happy to have a young player contributing the way I was, an X factor, so to speak.

But just the opposite was true. They were resentful that I was getting upperclassman treatment. They felt I hadn't earned a spot, that the coaches had just handed it to me, and this upset the balance of the team. When we traveled, I ended up sitting by myself all the time. I had no one from my class on the traveling squad, and I felt like I wasn't part of the team. It was crazy—they acted as if I was being pampered, like I had been elevated above them in some way. I couldn't believe it. I swear, they would rather have had someone on the field who was doing less to help the team, just so they could maintain their pecking order.

They had no idea who I was, and had no interest in finding out. They treated me like an outcast. I don't mean the whole team—a lot of people didn't care—but the major guys, the key starters, seemed very jealous. I think they assumed I was some hotshot high school prima donna who had been promised all this stuff if I came to Illinois. And of course, just the opposite was true. No one had heard of me in high school; Coach Lenti had to convince Coach Tepper to take me. At Mount Carmel I was the low man on the totem pole for three years. Everything I had, I earned; I wasn't given anything.

The only people rooting for me was the group of guys who had played at Mount Carmel. There were a bunch of us: Ola Ali, Andre Collins, Charles Edwards, Pete Gabrione, Bobby Sanders, Toriano Woods, Jasper Strong, and Matt Cushing, who made it to the NFL with the Steelers. They explained there was nothing I could do about the situation, so why not use that frustration and play like I had a grudge. *Every time you make a tackle, you show these guys why you're playing and some upperclassman isn't.* And that's what I did.

In games I had the mind-set that I was going to outshine my teammates. I wanted them to know I was the best player on the field at all times. Charles Edwards and Bobby Sanders would give me pre-game pep talks to get me through that first, lonely season. They were really good—they would remind me how I played with a chip on my shoulder back at Mount Carmel and I'd get all fired up. I wouldn't do anything to jeopardize the team—in fact I did everything I could to help us win— but when the headlines were written the next day, I wanted to be in them. And often I was. Of course, this just pissed everyone off even more. A lot of these guys had pro aspirations, and they needed those clippings. Here I was the "frosh phenom" getting my picture in the paper, and it drove them crazy.

If you look back at my scrapbook freshman year, you'd think I was on the field thirty minutes a game from the stories they ran. The irony is that I played somewhat sparingly that first year. I was used in special situations, like passing downs. I asked why I wasn't in on every play and they said I wasn't strong enough. I weighed 220 and I was going up against offensive linemen who outweighed me by 100 pounds, and they thought I'd get worn out or I'd get hurt. That didn't make much sense to me, because I had the footwork of a tailback, which meant blockers rarely squared up against me where they could use their size and strength. In fact, I was taking what I had learned in wrestling and martial arts all those years ago and using it against them, jujitsu style. I was wearing *them* out using their own size and strength!

In terms of getting hurt, well, I was never a cat to get pancaked. That had as much to do with heart as with skills. I'm just not going to let you do me like that. In fact, I'm going to do *you* like that. Period. That's still my approach all these years later. Anyway, I kept my mouth shut and went with the plan. Still, the more I played, the more I became convinced that no one in the college game could stop me.

It was frustrating and fun at the same time. I would watch most of the action from the sidelines, and try to determine what kind of rhythm the other team had. I would also look around at the crowds—and we had incredible crowds in the Big Ten—and start to absorb their energy. I couldn't wait to go in and bury somebody. I so wanted to help my team win, and I knew I could only do that on the field. Hell, I wasn't helping them win on the sideline. When I finally got in it was like unleashing a hurricane.

By the same token, I wasn't greedy about my playing time. On short-yardage situations and some other running downs, they would take me out of the game, and I had no problem with that. There is definitely a learning curve for freshmen in the Big Ten, and I respected that.

Coach Tepper did a good job in 1992. It was his first year at the helm and he didn't have to take a chance with a freshman, but he did. Lou had been with the program since 1988, when John Mackovic was hired as head coach and brought him in as defensive coordinator. Later he was elevated to assistant head coach, and he took over the team when Mackovic agreed to become the coach at Texas. Lou actually coached the Illini in the 1991 John Hancock Bowl and almost beat UCLA, a Top 10 team.

The 1992 Illini played a lot of close games. We lost to Minnesota 18–17, then beat Ohio State a week later, on the road, 18–16. We lost to Northwestern 27–26 then beat Wisconsin the following week 13–12, again on the road. In our last three games we beat Purdue 20–17; tied Michigan, which was in the running for the national championship; and took care of Michigan State 14–10. I can't explain it, but for my career at Illinois we always seemed to do better against Big Ten opponents in their building than in ours.

The first time I made headlines was in the third game of the season, against the University of Houston. They killed us, but I got three sacks. In general I performed well when I was in the lineup, and made enough plays to be voted Big Ten Freshman of the Year.

At the end of the season we were invited to play Hawaii in the Holiday Bowl in San Diego. If there was one game where I felt I could have done more, that was it. They obviously had prepared for me, and they attacked me with the option, which they ran to perfection. Normally, I dominated that play. I could tell whether the quarterback was going to pitch out or hold the ball, cut inside or pass. But they executed well, and their ball carriers were especially fast. We lost 27–17.

What an experience my first year at Illinois was—not just from a football perspective but from a life perspective as well. In college you are exposed to so much, so fast, that either you are overwhelmed and retreat into your own little world, or you start expanding your view and understanding the big picture and how you fit into it. A lot of athletes stay inside the cocoon that the athletic department creates for them. In many cases, I think the coaches prefer that their players go this route. I honestly believe that's a reason why some athletes do poorly in class, or don't graduate, or don't develop their social skills. They don't mix with the general population and just stick to what they know. In the end, they realize too late they don't know shit.

In my case, I embraced the college experience on every level. Not just the social aspects, but the academic aspects as well. I was a big-picture guy, and for me the big picture included pro football. After my freshman season, when I did so well against guys who were earmarked for the pros, I saw that this was a strong possibility. So my goal was to enjoy the hell out of college while I was there, take courses that would help me the rest of my life, and get my degree. I knew that playing Division I football and going to class didn't always add up to enough credits after four years—and I had made a promise to my parents, my grandmother, and myself to graduate—so right away I began taking summer school classes. This was a great decision. I remember that first summer how I felt that everything was falling into place.

I stayed in Champaign and worked a bunch of different jobs—my first summer and the next two also. I paid for my basic expenses, and spent the rest of the money to help Bennie Morrow and my cousin John Anderson with their tuition. My parents had set aside a little money for Bennie to go to college, and I wanted to help out. Each year I brought Bennie and John down to campus for the summer, and we would work our asses off, share my apartment, and bank as much as we could for tuition. I loved these guys and wanted to do right by them any way I could.

John and I would often play basketball after work. I got him to the point where I phoned the coach at Parkman Junior College, which was nearby, and arranged a workout for him. Eventually he got a scholarship, so his tuition fees were waived. Later, when I made it to the NFL, it was like they'd made it, too. I covered their remaining tuition and expenses, I bought them rides—anything they needed, I provided. I couldn't conceive of my doing well and not taking care of them.

The best part of college for me was the freedom. Something that trips up a lot of people is being on their own for the first time. This happens to athletes, but I saw plenty of regular kids who just couldn't handle it as well. In my case, I loved it. I also abused the hell out of it. From the discipline of Mount Carmel and my home situation, it was like all the rules went out the window. That first year, I would stay up talking to my friends all night. Every night. Not partying, but talking, hanging out, laughing, joking, listening to music. Mind you, I had to go to class and practice, sometimes on only one or two hours of sleep. It's a miracle any of us graduated, but in the end most of us pulled it off. I'm convinced that this is when I permanently messed up my sleeping pattern, because to this day I can't sleep most nights.

The thing that actually threw me my first year at Illinois was that the football players didn't get the special treatment you always heard about when the recruiters came calling. They are very good about painting a picture in which you are the most important people on campus. You'll get preferential treatment, you'll get all the perks and such—but they are very meticulous about not specifically promising anything. I don't know what it's like at other schools, but at Illinois that was a fallacy. Not only did we get shorted on all the perks, I think we had it harder than most regular students.

From the moment I arrived in Champaign, I was told that anything looking even remotely like an impropriety could result in an NCAA investigation. You can't get a job during the school year, so you don't have any spending money. The only money I had in my pocket was what my mom sent me. You can't even get discounts at stores, so the money you do have doesn't go very far. That blew my mind. I mean, everyone who had a friend working at Foot Locker or some other store could get a few dollars off. In many instances, employees are encouraged to do this to keep their fellow students coming in. If I bought something at a store, though, I wasn't allowed to get one penny off because you never knew who'd be looking over your shoulder. Everywhere you turned, in fact, you encountered some type of restriction. You felt like if you sneezed it would be an NCAA violation.

I can't tell you how bad this sucks. What these rules ignore is that you're still a kid, and you're still in college. You need to have some bread in your pocket. I was fortunate that my parents both had good jobs, so they could give me an allowance. Other players came from more desperate backgrounds, and they were tempted to break the rules. Many did break the rules. It was frustrating to see, because if they got caught, they might put my future in jeopardy by bringing down NCAA sanctions on the Illinois program.

Well, it forces you to be resourceful in ways you never imagined. For instance, my freshman year, I was wondering how I would ever get a date, since I couldn't afford to take a girl out to a nice dinner and all. Thank God I finally figured out that you could get the girl to pay, because she could go and say *I had a date with Simeon Rice.* I know this sounds chauvinistic and manipulative, but it's true and it saved my life. I always wondered whether doing this was against NCAA rules. Hey, I was still profiting from my status as a football player, right?

Anyway, the whole situation got me paranoid, because they don't explain everything up front. You kind of learn it on the fly, mostly when some other guy gets in trouble for something. You say, *Oh, I guess I can't do that.* You just pray that next time, you're not that other guy. What complicates matters is that, if you're a football player, everyone is always offering you stuff. I felt like the sanctions should be on the dudes who were creating the rules violations—and so did a lot of other players.

One of the choices you have to make in college is whether or not to be in a serious relationship with someone. I had no experience in this, so I just followed my instincts. I met a girl named Nicole one day when I was out walking around campus, and we ended up in a two-year relationship. I don't regret the time I was with Nicole, but I'll admit that sometimes it made me miserable. I would watch my boys go off to parties and I'd be sitting around with her. They were kicking it. They were playaz. That's the time you should be out there mixing it up and having fun. But you can't do that when you are in a relationship.

Later, my life got a lot more complicated when I messed around with one of my good friends, a young woman named Jayna. It was a case of one thing leading to another, of a close friendship suddenly becoming sexual. Well, nine months later, my son, Jordan, arrived. Marriage wasn't in the picture, but I took care of my responsibility. Despite a couple of major bumps along the way, we've remained friends and I've been as good a father as I can be. We both recognized Jordan would never have an ideal parental situation, so my goal was to do whatever I had to keep it from becoming completely dysfunctional. I felt bad that my son might never have the stable family environment I enjoyed growing up.

It was a tough thing telling my father about Jordan. I said, "Listen, Pops. I knew better and I was taught better. I didn't do right and now I have to suffer the consequences."

I'll give Henry Rice credit. He had some sage advice. He said, "First, don't think of it as suffering the consequences. And second, remember, it's not just you that's responsible—two people made this baby. Find an equitable arrangement that gives everyone room to grow."

Back to football. Heading into my sophomore season, everyone was excited because Greg Landry was brought in to coach the offense. He was a bona fide NFL star who'd quarterbacked the Lions and made a lot of highlight plays in the 1970s. I didn't remember him well, but I'm sure he beat the Bears. Everyone did back then. Our team had trouble putting points on the board in 1992, so we had high hopes that Landry would energize us. We felt like he would give us the shot of offense we needed. Our defense was very good, so all we needed was for the other unit to stay on the field and we had a chance to be dominant.

Long story short, we finished the 1993 season 5–6. What happened that year I'm still not clear on, but it had a lot of the players scratching their heads. Landry had an excellent quarterback at his disposal named

Johnny Johnson, and he was working hard to develop him. For whatever reason, though, Tepper didn't like Johnson. Some people thought it was a "black quarterback" thing, but I didn't see that. And Tepper will say he had nothing against him, but sometimes he started him, and sometimes he didn't, and it wasn't always clear to the players why that was. If he had just left Johnson in there to grow into the quarterback position, I think we would have done better in 1993 and maybe challenged for the Big Ten championship the following season, in 1994.

My theory is that Tepper felt threatened by Greg Landry's presence on some level, and began to play mind games with the offense. Landry had a big name, and was rumored to be Tepper's successor. He was getting the job done, and even undermining Tepper's authority somewhat. That's when Lou got more involved in the offensive decision making and we lost some momentum.

Anyway, early in the 1993 season, it seemed like Landry had the offense going. We were less predictable than the previous season, and we were becoming more sound in the fundamentals. We lost our first three games—to Missouri, Arizona, and Oregon—but then we started to put some points on the board. We took five of our next six, including a 24–21 win over Michigan at Michigan. More on that in a moment.

On most Saturdays, however, it still fell to the defense to win games. That was cool with me. The coaching staff had decided I should be a full-time player, and told me they believed I was now strong enough to be on the field for every down. I was surprised that this was their reasoning. Strength was never an issue—I'd been strong enough the year before. But that's the way football people think. Just because everyone outweighed me, it didn't mean they had more strength or more stamina. I was overpowering everyone I played against as a freshman—how do you explain that? Thankfully, at this point the coaches had abandoned the idea of building up my weight and realized they should just put me out there as is. All their talk of getting me up to 290 ended, which was good, because I was never going to get that heavy.

I understand that there are formulas in football that everyone follows, where there is a direct relationship between weight and strength. But there are players, like me, who bring other things to the picture that should also figure into that formula, but often don't. I am six feet five and I come off the line like a wide receiver. That kind of quickness and explosiveness counts for a lot, but when you're a coach used to dealing with similar types over and over again, sometimes you don't think outside the box. So a player can get a tag that follows him around his whole career—like me being undersized, or not big enough to play the run.

It was exciting to think of myself as a full-time player, but I was sad, too. It meant I was going to replace a senior starter, whose name was Todd Leach. I actually felt bad about it. Some people on the team didn't take to Todd—he could be a know-it-all sometimes. But I liked the dude. He had always been very open and honest with me, and he was great to talk to because he had a lot of interesting things going on in his life. He wasn't your stereotypical jock. Now Todd was going to be my backup. During the year, there were a lot of times I took myself out of the game so he could get more playing time.

The switch from role player to starter wasn't as difficult a transition as a lot of fans think. You have to read and react to more stuff, but that's a process that started a year earlier. They don't just decide you can handle the mental aspect of the job—you've already demonstrated you can do it. Physically, it means you have to work harder, which was easy for me. From a football standpoint, I am a workaholic. I outwork everybody else because that's just the way I am. Even then, I spent more time lifting, running, and doing everything I needed to do to get myself right. From there, you just go out and let the chips fall where they may—either you get the job done or you don't.

In my case, everything went as well as it possibly could. I never really struggled as a starter. The only tough game I had that year was against Korey Stringer of Minnesota. He was around my height and outweighed me by a hundred pounds, but he had something the others didn't—he was quick and he was smart. He decided he would play me physical and get right up against me so I couldn't use my agility to its full effect. He would drive into me, grab me, shake me, smash his helmet into mine—I couldn't get him off me. Korey played mean and I played mean and it was a great battle that we won, 23–20. After the game, I thought, *Man, I guess I do need to get stronger.* But he was just a great, great player who knew what he was doing. I'll never forget him; when he passed away from heat exhaustion with the Vikings, it was a real loss.

My signature game of the 1993 season came against Michigan. Illinois hadn't beaten Michigan at Michigan in twenty or thirty years. Let me say that, as players, we don't really care about statistics like that, even though the papers write about it and the coaches and students talk about it. We're all young guys full of ourselves. That history isn't your history, so you aren't intimidated. When I heard we hadn't won in Ann Arbor in that long, my reaction, was, *Man, those older guys were bad. No way we're going to lose like that.*

I understand the importance of history in sports, and I respect the people who came before me. But the second you let history affect your thinking, you allow your mind to become conditioned that you can't beat this team. In college especially, you want young guys who think of themselves as rebels, as guys who make history and change history.

The Wolverines were ahead late in this game, but we had the ball. Our end Ken Dilger got hit by Ty Law, and Dilger fumbled the ball. Michigan recovered, and everyone on the sidelines had their heads down. As our defense started to move toward the field, I went up to Sherman Smith, our running backs coach, and said, "Don't worry, I'm going to get the ball back. *Personally.*"

We had no time-outs. All Michigan had to do was run out the clock. After making two first downs, Todd Collins could have taken a couple of knees and killed the clock. Instead, he handed off to Ricky Powers. The tackle fired out at me. I spun and he went right past me. Then I saw Powers and dove at him, going for the strip. I was good at that. I ignored the man and tackled the ball, tore it out of his grasp, and fell on top of it.

The rest is history. With just over a minute left, Johnny Johnson drove us down the field with short passes to Ty (who caught six passes in all and ran for over 100 yards) and to Jason Dulick, then threw a touchdown pass to Jim Klein to win the game 24–21. That was the most uplifting part of that whole year. It was incredibly emotional for me and everyone.

When the game ended, Todd Leach came up to me and he was crying. "Simeon, I knew you were going to do it!" That made me start crying, too. Before the game I'd wanted to do something big for the seniors, and here I had made exactly the same play I had made in the state championship game my senior year at Mount Carmel. I thought, *Wow, guess that's my trademark play.*

And it was. Tackling the ball instead of the man is the key, but finishing the play is equally important. When you make a successful strip, you're the only guy on the field who knows where the ball is going, and that gives you a huge advantage when it hits the turf. You should have two bounces to recover before anyone else can react. Still, many guys strip the ball and then watch it go loose with the rest of the players. You've got to press your advantage and grab it.

We defeated Northwestern and Minnesota after the Michigan win, then closed out the year against two top-ranked schools, Penn State and Wisconsin. They basically trounced us, and as I mentioned earlier, we finished with a disappointing 5–6 record and no bowl trip. When the year-end awards were announced, I was a unanimous All-Big-Ten pick. I thought, *Wow, All-Big-Ten as a sophomore?* It got me jazzed about my remaining two years, thinking about what we could accomplish. We had the number twelve defense in the country in 1993, and Dana Howard, Kevin Hardy, and I were just scratching the surface of our potential. What would 1994 bring?

My second spring at Illinois was a good one. I was more acclimated to the academics and just the pace of life, and I had created a good circle of friends. A lot of credit for my transition to college life I owe to a woman named Josie Rahn. Josie was a retired teacher who was friends with the wife of the president of the Quarterback Club, an Illinois booster organization. She was approached with an idea the athletic department wanted to try. They had found that, despite the summer bridge program, many players still had problems adjusting to life in college, especially the way the football season gets started right at the beginning of freshman year.

I didn't realize it, but I was going to be the guinea pig for a kind of mentoring project.

Normally, freshmen like me get redshirted. But when Coach Tepper and his staff saw I could play right away, they worried I might be overwhelmed, my grades would drop, and I'd have eligibility problems. You know me well enough by now to guess what my reaction was: *No way!* But I agreed to meet Josie and check it out.

We sat on opposite ends of this long couch, like neither of us wanted to be there. She said she was not a tutor, but more like a guide dog. She suggested we try meeting once a week, and if it didn't work, we could stop. I agreed, and we began getting together in the football office. After a couple of months we knew each other well enough so we could communicate comfortably.

The day-to-day homework and studying I could handle. And I was a goal-oriented kid, so we were usually on the same page in terms of what I hoped to accomplish long-term. The medium-term stuff, like papers, was where Josie really helped. She refined the writing and composition skills I had acquired at Mount Carmel. She explained how to create a thesis and organize my thoughts so that I could be successful on the college level. During exams, she would quiz me and help me prepare. Josie also helped me with things like opening a bank account, and some of the other basics, like rules about doing laundry, because for a while there everything I owned was slowly turning the same shade of pink.

In some respects, Josie was almost like a substitute grandma. She would scold me and treat me like a big overgrown baby sometimes. But all in a loving, caring way, never condescending. We spent most of our time discussing general things, like organizing my time and keeping a schedule. I can't say she had a huge impact on me my first year, but eventually the lessons began to sink in. The one area where Josie tried and failed was getting me to arrive places on time. I was constantly late for everything. It's still hard for me to keep a precise schedule, but I was *really* bad back then.

One of the things I liked about Josie was that she had no interest in football. I called her my "football idiot." She told me if I became a scholar, she'd become a fan. By the time I left Champaign, I had a diploma and she had season tickets.

Josie was a big reason I stayed in school through graduation. She was among the chorus of voices that told me to play my last year and get my degree before moving on to the NFL. She said, "Look, buddy, you could go out and fall down a flight of stairs and your career would be over. But no one can take your degree away from you. It's a lifelong thing."

Based on our four-year relationship, the University of Illinois widened this program so that now there are more than two dozen Josies. She never took a dime for it, and she was the one person I knew at Illinois whom I could be sure had my best interests at heart 100 percent of the time.

What Josie did for me made me want to help others. It was an op-portunity to keep my promise to Charles Davis and Benjamin Furman, and to use the influence I'd acquired at Illinois. Lou Tepper once said that he had never coached a kid who exerted so much influence on other players, and I believe it. Within the football context, I would do the little things, like making sure Robert Holcombe woke up and got to meetings on time. I tried to do big-picture stuff, too, like rounding up the skill-position freshman and pushing them past even what our strength trainer expected. It got to the point where these dudes would run and hide when they saw me coming! I tried to explain to them that developing this kind of attitude would pay dividends long after they played their last down of football.

Sometimes, my desire to help others blew up in my face. I remem-ber one instance during my sophomore year, when a friend of mine was struggling in a class and didn't know what he could do about it. He didn't realize you could sit down with one of the Teaching Assistants and they would help you work things out. So I thought it would be a good idea to go in there with him to talk to his TA.

Bad idea. Her eyes got as wide as saucers when I entered the room. I explained that I had been in a similar situation as a freshman, and asked what needed to be done to fix the situation. She wasn't even listening to what I was saying. She kept accusing me of threatening her. I sensed she was intimidated by my size and my color, but the irony is that I wasn't being the least bit confrontational or disrespectful. See—you never know when someone will rush to judgment!

My first year at school I lived in a dorm. I got along with the guys, but I basically marched to my own beat. My closest friend freshman year was Ty Douthard, but as soon as I was allowed to I moved into an apart-ment and began to enlarge my circle of friends. Besides Ty, there were two other individuals I met at Illinois who became major parts of my life: Sean Green and Kevin Wilson.

I met Sean in the university's bridge program the summer before freshman year. He was from the suburbs of Chicago. Sean was a low-key guy like me, but he was very outgoing and very resourceful, too. He also had a knack for seeing past the veneer of a person or a situation to what was real. We didn't hang out that much at first, but we became tighter as the years passed. I could see how smart he was and how much potential he had. So when it came time to build a circle of trusted friends who would accompany me on my road to success, Sean was a no-brainer. He and I shared the same dedication to being the best, and he put maximum effort into everything he did. Not surprisingly, Sean turned out to be a fantastic business ally.

I met Kevin after I got to know Ty. They were best friends going back to Cincinnati, where they'd grown up together. Kevin lived in the football house on campus, and things could get kind of wild over there. It would get so bad sometimes he couldn't take it, so he'd come over to my apartment, which was stress-free. Kevin was a big believer in a stress-free existence, just like me. He would practically sermonize on the importance of living this way. I liked Kevin right away because he was comfortable being himself. He and my old friend Bennie Morrow were a lot alike. Both were good guys who had a big appetite for life. In fact, Kevin and Bennie eventually became real tight, and then Kevin and I became tight.

Kevin was a source of endless fascination for me. This dude was the chillest cat on the planet, but he was fucking brilliant, too. He was taking the same course load I was, and yet I never saw him work. I didn't kill myself academically, but I hit the books pretty hard when I had to. Kevin? I never saw him crack a book. Did he miss a party? Not any party I went to. Then I'd see his grades: straight As! He was so placid, he savored life so completely, that I couldn't picture him excelling in an academic environment. By the time I graduated, though, he was going after his master's!

After college Kevin worked for the government and saw some wild stuff go down. I can just picture him, totally calm and collected while everything's going crazy around him. Today Kevin and Sean both work with me. I trust them with my reputation and my finances, and I'd trust them with my life.

My junior year at Illinois was my breakout season—both as a person and as a player. Everyone has a point in their lives they can look to and say, "That's when I became an adult." As much as I may have resisted this transition, I really felt like a grown-up that year. On the football field, I matured, too. The process started that summer, when I increased my workout routine to four hours a day, five days a week. I was incredibly strong when practice began, and I could feel the difference every time I made contact with someone.

Our opening game was against Washington State, a team that throws the ball a lot. I sensed I was going to have a big impact on this game, but never imagined I would do what I did. These guys were ranked in the Top 25, but we were playing them in Soldier Field in Chicago, so we had the home crowd behind us, and I had more family and friends at that game than I could count.

The defense was great in this game, and I was in the zone from the opening kickoff. I set a school record with five sacks, I caused and recovered a fumble, I knocked down a pass, and I blocked a field goal. I was splitting double teams so easily they had to put three guys on me, which opened things up for my teammates. The only touchdown Washington State scored was on a fumble by our quarterback, Johnny Johnson. They scooped up the ball and ran it 71 yards, and we ended up losing 10–9. Ty Douthard missed this game because he was being benched for coming late to a team meeting. He had been our best runner and receiver the previous year, and I'll bet we would have won if he'd been in the backfield. It seemed stupid to us that he would be benched for such a minor infraction. There had to be a better way to send him a message.

Our second game was as satisfying as our opener was frustrating. We dominated Missouri 42–0, allowing just one first down all game. One! The last time the Illini had a game like that was in 1935! I was named Big Ten Defensive Player of the Week for the second time in a row, but that was crazy—how can you pick out one player on a day like that? Our offense was in high gear, too, with 540 yards. Ty was back in the lineup, along with Robert Holcombe, a sophomore. Both guys would go on to play in the NFL—not bad for one backfield.

We crushed Northern Illinois in our next game, 27–10. I broke the school's career sack record, and we allowed just 22 yards in the second half. Three weeks into the season and we were the top-ranked defense in the nation.

This is when talk about my possibly going to the pros began to pick up. I was playing at an entirely different level than the year before, and our defense was making me look good even when I wasn't making big tackles. The seniors projected for the NFL draft didn't include a lot of standouts, and it was conceivable that I might go in the top ten if I passed up my senior year. Mel Kiper, the draft expert, said that I might even be the top overall pick. That got the people at Illinois upset—they knew that if that were the case, I would probably leave the school. It's always nice to hear that type of praise, but l knew this was a little far-fetched.

I did give the possibility of heading to the NFL a tremendous amount of thought that fall. When I wasn't thinking about it, someone usually came up and asked me about it, so there was no sidestepping the decision. Whether it was my friends, or teammates, or the media asking, my answer was an honest one: I wasn't sure what to do. The response to this answer was either: *You stay in school and get your diploma—football will always be there,* or, *Are you crazy? Passing up all that money to stay in school?*

The funny thing was that my head was in a completely different place. Those may have been the choices articulated on my behalf by the press, but they were not the choices I was weighing. To me, the decision came down to testing myself against the best competition in the world versus getting to be a kid one more year. Put in those terms, you can see what a complicated decision this was for me. I could always go back and get a diploma, and I could always make money playing football. The choice was more about my desires and feelings than about some bottom line, and that's what made it so difficult.

As an underclassman, I had until early January to inform the NFL that I wished to be considered for the draft. I was allowed to contact the league prior to that to informally ask where their scouts thought I might be selected. This was actually a program instituted to keep college coaches happy. They had a panel that gave young guys a realistic evaluation of how high they might go, so they could make an informed decision and not throw away their final college season. My teammate Dana Howard had thought about going early after the 1993 campaign, but when he found out he would not be a first- or second-round pick, he stayed for the 1994 season.

After our first three games in 1994, I was probably leaning toward the NFL. We were so good, and I was playing so well, that I thought I would have nothing left to prove on the college level. But as the season wore on, the thought of staying another year became more appealing.

We lost four more games that year to finish our regular season 6–5. And each loss was excruciatingly close.

Purdue, led by my future teammate Mike Alstott—a guy I also played against at Mount Carmel—came to Champaign and edged us 22–16. After upsetting Ohio State in their building and blowing Iowa out of ours, we lost to Michigan 19–14. We scored road wins over Northwestern and Minnesota before losing to second-ranked Penn State 35–31, then Wisconsin 19–13. Despite our so-so record, we were good enough to receive a bid to the Liberty Bowl, where we shut out East Carolina 30–0.

We played some monster teams in 1994 and either beat them or played them right down to the wire. We were maybe ten great plays away from an unbeaten season. How could I leave a situation like that? I had to stay.

The deadline came and went and I was still in school. It was like a 51–49 decision, and I'm not saying that for effect. It was a really close call. A lot of people were pulling me in a lot of directions, and they were all making very good arguments for going one way or the other. I thought I was at peace with my decision come the spring, but the night before the 1995 draft, I was driving around Chicago and all of a sudden I was overwhelmed by the feeling I should be in the draft, that it was happening without me, that I was missing a big opportunity. It was too late, but I swear, if I had known who to call I probably would have tried to get in.

Once I decided to stay at Illinois for my fourth year, I started to think almost like a coach. I worked with sophomores and freshmen between seasons to make sure they were ready physically and mentally for 1995. I tried to impart to them the wisdom I had acquired, and told them what I wished I had done differently. I felt I had the credibility to do this, because at various times our coaches had used me as an intermediary between themselves and certain players. Sometimes a comment or criticism does not have the desired impact when it comes from a coach. Either a player will take it too personally, or he won't take it seriously enough. At these times I was asked to intercede, and in most cases it seemed to work out.

Heading into senior year, Mike Pearson in the sports information department started putting together a media campaign designed to get me attention for some of the big awards, like the Lombardi Trophy and maybe, just maybe, the Heisman. This is not an unusual strategy for a school with an impact player—in fact it goes on much more than fans even know. The university benefits from the publicity and so does the player, especially if he performs up to expectations.

It's a little different when the player does not play a so-called glamour position, like quarterback. In my case the school came out with a brochure that said, "In a typical football season, quarterbacks get all of the glory, leaving the best defensive player more than a little crushed."

Then you'd open it and it said, "But this is 1995. And the eyes of the nation are riveted on a defensive legend who's shattered almost every record for doing what he does best . . ."

And then the flyer opened again and there was a picture of me about to bury Scott Dreisbach of Michigan. The final piece of copy said, ". . . leaving the best quarterbacks more than a little crushed."

This is pretty mellow compared to the way some guys are hyped in Division I—especially when they aren't elite-level players at all. I was rated by a lot of scouting services as the best returning senior in the country, so I was already on the radar screen. The University of Illinois knew how to work the national media, and I received a lot of attention. They put me on a time line with their other great linebackers, Ray Nitschke and Dick Butkus, which was an incredible honor. The big score was when *Sports Illustrated* did a big feature on me in its college football preview issue.

Illinois was also smart enough to know how not to use the media. If they needed to make a point with me, I didn't like to read about it in the papers. My father and Coach Lou Tepper had an understanding. If the coaching staff sensed anything was wrong, or felt I needed a pep talk, they could call my father and he would contact me. They were smart to recognize the closeness of our relationship, and realize that certain things could best be conveyed to me in this manner. I was not someone who responded to public embarrassment or histrionics, so if a coach had something to say, he would either take me aside and discuss it man to man, or channel it through my father. I wouldn't say they coddled me, but they were interested in protecting their investment.

With the way the school got behind me heading into 1995, I was half expecting to be named a team captain. When I wasn't named, it was a big letdown. I didn't let on to anyone at school how I felt, except maybe Josie Rahn, but that was a big, big disappointment with all the work I had put in with the younger guys, and the leadership I felt I had shown. No matter. We had a season to play and some major teams on our schedule, including Michigan, Oregon, and Arizona within a fifteen-day period that September. Everyone was going to have to show leadership to get us off to a good start.

The opener against the Wolverines was going to be a war. We had tied them, beaten them, and then played them very close in my three years. Michigan had already played a game in 1995, beating Virginia in the final seconds a week earlier. Now the Wolverines were looking to send a message to us.

The setting was perfect. The game was played at Illinois, in Memorial Stadium, and we had a sellout. This was the first time in more than a decade that the Illini had opened the year against a Big Ten opponent, so the crowd was in midseason form. This Michigan team was very good. Running back Tim Biakabutuka was hurt but still very dangerous. They also had Amani Toomer and Charles Woodson, who were game-breaking-type players.

We played tentatively in the first half, but we stayed close, and the score was 10–0 Michigan at halftime. Then the dam burst. The Wolverines completed two long passes at the beginning of the third quarter, and Biakabutuka scored from the 5-yard line. We fumbled on our next possession and Woodson recovered. Moments later, Biakabutuka ran for 17 and then 11 yards for another score. We fumbled again a few minutes later, and Biakabutuka ran one right down our throat for a 35-yard TD to make it 31–0. They blocked a punt in the end zone to make it 38–0, then we made a couple of trash scores late to make the final 38–10. A bad loss.

We had another second-half meltdown on the road against the Oregon Ducks a week later. Our defense was making big plays, forcing turnovers in Oregon territory, and Johnny Johnson was turning them into points. We missed some extra points and 2-point conversions, however, which came back to haunt us. Still, we were up 19–7 at the half and 31–20 early in the fourth quarter. I forced a couple of fumbles and got my thirty-sixth career sack to tie the Big Ten career record, so everything was going smoothly.

Then, with about six minutes left, we were pinned back in our own territory and they blitzed Johnson, who fumbled; they recovered for a touchdown. That got the crowd into the game and took us out. Our offense couldn't move, and they continued to blitz with great effectiveness. Our offensive line had some inexperienced guys on it, and we paid the price, because they just kept coming and coming. They sacked Johnny half a dozen times, and forced him to make four bad passes on our final possession. At that point we were trailing 34–31. The game just got away from us, and we were 0–2 with another test against a top-ranked Pac 10 team one week away.

The defense had to step up against Arizona the following week, and fortunately we did. Kevin Hardy and I rained hell on their quarterback, Dan White, and I nailed anyone with the ball who came near me. Our defensive backs played their best game of the year, and that gave me time to create a lot of havoc in the backfield. I got 3.5 sacks, Kevin got 2, and we combined for like thirty tackles between us. The game was tight all the way—no one was moving the ball, and the defense scored our only touchdown—but we prevailed 9–7. It was the first time in more than twenty years the Illini won a game in which they scored in the single digits.

The second time came a week later, against East Carolina. They defended us well, and Ty Douthard was out with a sprained ankle, so we basically gave the ball to Robert Holcombe. He gained 130 yards and set a school record for carries, but he was booed on his record-breaking carry because he lost 3 yards. Kevin and I kept the pressure up all game and got a sack apiece, again thanks to a great job by the secondary. Duane Lyle, a guy who'd been on the team for four years but was starting for the first time, picked off three passes—including one on the goal line with twenty-six seconds left—to preserve a 7–0 win. Now, this was the defense I'd dreamed about when I'd decided to stay for my senior year!

Indiana was up next, and the defense played a third great game. We set up two touchdowns on turnovers, which helped Scott Weaver, our new quarterback. Johnny Johnson wasn't moving the ball, so Lou Tepper had made the switch. Scott played all right. Another new face in the lineup was a running back named Steve Havard, who threw a great block on the game-winning play. The key moment in this game came in the third quarter, when Dennis Stallings, a member of our linebacking crew, picked off a pass and ran it back to the Indiana 17. Three plays later, Havard neutralized a blitzing linebacker and gave Weaver time to find Ty in the end zone, and we won 17–10.

We were now 3–2 after being left for dead. Michigan State was next, and we could smell blood. Their QB, Tony Banks, was hurt and wouldn't play. Their backup, Todd Schultz, was injured, too. It's not that we were expecting a win or looking past the Spartans, but we definitely had the best D in the Big Ten and still believed we could contend for the conference championship. Unfortunately, the game was a turning point in a bad way. Their O-line out-executed us, and they ran us out of the building. Marc Renaud gained more than 100 yards, and Scott Greene scored four touchdowns. Schultz made the passes he had to, and they won 27–21. They played me very smart in this game. Someone made a point of chipping me on every play, and I only got in on a handful of tackles.

Our season continued to go downhill against Northwestern. As long as I could remember, they were like the Big Ten punching bag, but they had really turned it around in 1995 and came to Champaign on a five-game winning streak. We blew this one, no doubt about it. We had a 14–0 lead in the first half and let them back in. They played mistake-free football and we didn't, and that turned out to be the deciding factor. We had some bad holding penalties that killed drives in the third quarter, and then botched a chance to either tie the game with a field goal or score the winning touchdown in the final seconds. The Wildcats won 27–24.

We evened our record against Iowa a week later, 26–7, but took our fifth loss against Ohio State, 41–3. The Buckeyes had a great team, and for my money Eddie George was the best offensive player in the country in 1995. He certainly did a number on us. Eddie ran for 314 yards despite playing only three minutes of the fourth quarter. As Tyrone Washington, our strong safety, put it, "They had a hot knife, and we were the butter."

This was one of those games that was actually worse than the score. Ohio State missed a couple of field goals in the game, and had a touchdown nullified by a penalty. Also, their passing attack was not at full strength, because Terry Glenn was sitting out. We had the tenth-ranked defense in the country before the game, and I don't even want to know where we were when the final gun sounded.

Coach Tepper chewed us out after the Ohio State game—the most emotional I'd ever seen him—and some of the younger players were like, *Fuck this.* I got together with Johnny Johnson and Mikki Johnson, our big nose tackle, and we called a players-only meeting. We explained that the seniors were about to play our final home game, and we didn't want to hear any negativity.

Robert Holcombe was one of the young guys who needed to get more focused, and he really came through against Minnesota. He ran for more than 200 yards and we won 48–14, to continue our Jekyll-and-Hyde season. Mikki got into a goal-line play as a fullback à la Refrigerator Perry and scored the one and only touchdown of his career. I scored my only college touchdown in this game, too. Kevin Hardy forced a fumble, and I picked it up and ran it in 27 yards. Kevin actually had a dream about this play before the game, only there I'd forced the fumble and he'd scored the TD.

The last game of my college career came at Wisconsin, and in many ways it typified my experience as an Illini football player. We needed to play a great defensive game against the Badgers to get a bowl bid, and we did play a great game. But the offense couldn't manage more than a field goal, and the game ended in a 3–3 tie. Holcombe went over 1,000 yards for the season in this game, but it was a run that got called back I remember most vividly. There were two minutes left and he took the ball down to the 20. That would have meant a 37-yard field goal to win, which was well within the range of our kicker, Bret Scheuplein: He had already kicked one 51 yards. Well, we were whistled for holding, which put the ball back on the 41, then Johnny Johnson was called for intentional grounding, which pushed us back past midfield. Those two penalties eliminated any chance of my playing another college game. Our AD, Ron Guenther, had us lined up for a possible shot at the Independence Bowl, but we didn't hold up our end, so that was that.

4

The spring after my final season was spent mopping up my final credits, enjoying my last semester as a college student, and attending awards ceremonies and football banquets. I graduated on time with a degree in speech communications. It felt strange knowing I was moving on with my life, yet not knowing where I would be the following fall.

As the NFL draft approached, I knew there were a lot of people evaluating me, trying to project what kind of impact I would have both short- and long-term. It's only natural in this situation to take a step back and try to view yourself through the eyes of your potential employers. It didn't take long to see that I was coming to the NFL with more baggage than I'd thought.

I sat down with Marvin Lewis, the defensive coordinator of the Baltimore Ravens, who had the fourth pick. He laid it out for me. He said, "Simeon, they're saying a lot of bad things about you. I just want to put them out there so you can address them."

"Okay," I said.

"Word is that you work hard, but you do it your own way. What does that mean?"

"It means I go all out," I answered, "but that I ask questions."

I told him I was a gamer, but also a cerebral player. Lewis knew I liked to put my own personal twist on things, but I was trying to convey the idea that this was my creativity coming out, and not me being rebellious. I could excel within a game plan, I added, but you're not going to sell me a pipe dream. Here I was hoping to illustrate that I could follow logic, and that I had a sense of honor and purpose and ethics. In my mind, I was out to impress the NFL with my honesty and intelligence. Little did I know this made me the kind of player that makes NFL coaches wake up at two in the morning in a cold sweat.

Lewis didn't really react to my answer, but I think he saw a spark of what I was trying to show. At least he had enough respect for my honesty to tell me who was bad-mouthing me. It was Lou Tepper.

Given this intriguing piece of information, it was hard to predict where I would be selected. I was prepared to go between six and fifteen, but still secretly expecting to be a top-five pick. I really wanted to play for the New York Giants, who owned the fifth selection and badly needed a defensive end. I liked the fact that they had visited me in Chicago that spring. They not only showed interest in me, but understood my game, too. They even said my skills and playing style were kind of similar to Lawrence Taylor's. LT had just retired two seasons earlier, and they needed somebody to put pressure on the quarterback. Thinking back on it, I'm not even sure where they planned to use me, at linebacker or the D-line.

The Giants had a good team, but they'd lost a lot of close games in 1995, so they were higher in the draft than they should have been. This is the kind of situation a high pick loves to find. I definitely could see myself playing for Dan Reeves, the coach, and on draft day I really felt it would go down that way. In fact, when I woke up that morning I was sure it was going to happen.

On draft day all the top players gathered at Madison Square Garden. In the audience were my family, my friends Bennie Morrow and Lamon Caldwell, my brother, and my cousin John Anderson. The Jets had the first pick, and they took Keyshawn Johnson, which caused a big commotion. Jacksonville had the next pick. Some people predicted the Jaguars would take me, but the coach of that team was Tom Coughlin, who remembered me from my visit to Boston College. They had contacted my agent, Roosevelt Barnes, and asked if I was interested in playing for them. I won't lie. I wasn't too excited about the prospect of hooking up with Coughlin's crew again. So the Jags took my teammate Kevin Hardy. I was extremely happy for him. It also looked like I would be around when the Giants selected.

The Arizona Cardinals had the third pick. When they announced my name it came out of nowhere. They hadn't even talked to me! They called me on my cell phone and asked me how it felt to be a Cardinal and I did the honorable thing and said I was excited, but it was in as unenthusiastic a voice as I could muster. The truth was that I was kind of in shock. I did not want to be in Arizona.

In fact, Arizona was one of the two places I specifically did not want to go. I had been there once while I was in college, after I was chosen as a *Playboy* All-American. I didn't like Phoenix. I felt uncomfortable there on a number of levels—it was too white, it didn't have the culture I was looking for, and it was so different from what I was accustomed to. It was weird being in a place where I didn't see any black people. Nothing bad happened to me there, I just didn't like it.

The other place I didn't want to go was Green Bay. It had nothing to do with the weather—I'm from Chicago, so don't talk to me about weather. As was the case with Arizona, Green Bay seemed like an alien environment to me. I definitely wouldn't have been comfortable up there.

P.S.: When the Giants picked fifth, they took Cedric Jones, a defensive end out of Oklahoma.

After the draft I headed back to my apartment at the University of Illinois. This was the beginning of a long summer of contract negotiations with the Cardinals. Arizona was known for being cheap, but I knew they needed me badly so it wouldn't be hard to make the money right. The trick was not to get locked up for a lot of years in a place I thought I wouldn't enjoy living. The irony was that this turned out to be a flash point in the negotiation . . . and years later I still live in Arizona!

The negotiation process for rookies is strange in the NFL. A team and its draft choice are essentially contractually bound already. You just have to come up with an arrangement that is acceptable to both sides. So while my agent was working with the Arizona front office, I was working out and training back in Illinois, harder than when I was in college.

For some reason—I'm not sure I'll ever know why—everything got bogged down. We reached a point that summer where it looked as if no one would budge. That's when I started talking to Michael Jordan's trainer, Tim Grover. I figured if my rookie year wasn't going to happen in the NFL, I could make it known to NBA teams that I'd be available for ten-day contracts as a bench player. Someone might have taken a chance on me. I had skills—I could have been a contributor. Playing in the NBA was always a fantasy of mine, and I was curious to push the edge of the envelope. Meanwhile, rookie camp had opened for the Cardinals, and then training camp for the rest of the team. And I still was not close to signing. The coaching staff was anxious to have me in camp, the fans were worried that I wouldn't be in shape for the season, and the press was heralding me like the Second Coming. I knew when we got the deal done, there was going to be a ton of pressure on me.

I was anxious to play. I wanted to see just how good these guys in the NFL were. When I first went to college, remember, I thought I'd be sitting on the bench for a year or two, just as I had in high school. But then I saw that I could bang with experienced Big Ten players. Would the same be true in the NFL?

The only clue I had as to what I would be facing had actually come at a banquet that spring. I had been quoted in the press as saying I could be better than Lawrence Taylor—which, by the way, I didn't say. At this event I sat with an old Pro Bowl tackle for the Washington Redskins named Jim Lachey. He was a cool guy. He asked me if I'd really said I was better than LT, and I explained that I hadn't. But then I told him that for all I knew I could be. The way I saw it, when you hit the NFL, you pay homage to the great players and show them respect, but you never tell yourself you can't achieve what they did. You have to be your own player and set your own standards.

Lachey had the most interesting response. He said, "I can watch ten minutes of film on you and know every move you make." And he said it so matter-of-factly that it threw me.

I was like, *Wow, this is some league I'm coming into.* I was wondering what I'd gotten myself into. For a tackle to be able to break me down and figure out my game in ten minutes—well, think of how much experience he has and how many hours of film he's watched. He approached his job like a heavyweight champion. All summer, this conversation went through my head. Whenever I needed to do extra reps or run extra miles or train just a little harder, I thought about facing guys like Lachey, who already knew every move I had. I devoted myself to getting faster and stronger and developing new moves no one had ever seen on film.

Toward the end of August I was in my apartment playing a video game when my agent called me. He was really excited. "Simeon," he said. "Good news—we got that deal done."

All of a sudden the reality of my situation began to sink in. I was insulated in my safe little world of college. The summer school students were finishing up, and some of the fall students were trickling in. Football camp would start shortly, and some of the guys were already on campus. I was happy and sad at the same time. I was a multimillionaire, but I couldn't think of what to say and I didn't want to talk about it until I came to grips with my emotions.

"Let me call you back," I said. "I'm taking a dump."

I got off the phone and thought, *Wow, my life's about to start.* The clock had started ticking on my professional career, and I spent that whole day realizing that I wanted to delay it some more. Of course, at this point I had missed all of training camp and all but one exhibition game—and the Cardinals were going insane.

I flew to Phoenix a day before our final exhibition game, against the Atlanta Falcons. During the flight I had a lot of time to think. I thought about everything in my past that had led me to this moment. I thought about what this moment represented in the scheme of my life. And of course, I thought about my future. Then it all hit me when I got off the plane. There was a media frenzy (at least by Phoenix standards) at the airport. People were calling me the franchise savior, and I realized that everyone in town was expecting me to take this team to the next level. Adding to the pressure was the fact that the Cardinals had to release some guys in order to get their salary-cap number right. I was making $9.5 million over four years, and back in 1996 that made me the highest-paid player on the team.

When I met my teammates I could tell that there was some resentment about all the publicity surrounding me. They'd been working their asses off all summer, they had lost some key guys like Clyde Simmons so I could join the team, and for all they knew I'd been kicking back all summer while my agent squeezed a few extra dollars out of the team. Instead of being the guy who comes in to help them win, I could tell they were wondering now if I'd be the guy who ended up holding them back.

I answered that question the next day when I suited up for the game against the Falcons. I was matched up with Bob Whitfield, an All-American tackle out of Stanford who'd left school as a junior and was the eighth man taken in the 1992 draft. Hell, it was just like college. Here was this Pro Bowl lineman and here I was literally walking off the street, and he couldn't handle me. I played a few series, showed I was in shape, and got two sacks. In football, that's the equivalent of a rookie hitting two homers or scoring 40 points in his first game.

After the game, I was pumped up. The reporters asked me what my goals for the year were and I predicted I'd be Defensive Rookie of the Year and get the rookie sack record. They asked if I'd expected to have this kind of immediate impact, and I said, "Yeah, I definitely expected it." I reminded them that some people thought I would have been the number one pick in the draft the year before, and I was a year older and wiser. I was young, full of confidence, high off an amazing game, and just tooting my horn.

Football was the easy part that first year in the NFL. The life changes I faced were far more challenging. The hardest thing for a young man to do when he's making the transition from college star to professional football player is comprehending the concept of accepting responsibility for yourself. You are faced with so much, so fast, that it's human nature to just let someone else take care of everything for you. You pick out someone you have faith in and let them deal with the mundane details of your life. You just want to concentrate on having fun and playing football.

In my case, I wanted to duplicate the structure I'd had in college. At Illinois someone was always handing me an agenda, so I always knew where to go and what to do. And if I had questions about academics, I could seek out a professor or hook up with a teaching assistant. Now I was in the real world, and everything was on me. If I wanted to know something, I had to research it myself. There were no tutors. There were no kindly professors. It was dog eat dog, on the field and off.

When it came to finances, I was at ground zero in terms of knowledge. So naturally, I did what most rookies do in my situation: I found someone who seemed to have the knowledge I lacked, and entrusted them with my money. I just thought, *Out of sight, out of mind.* Not having dealt with the wolves, I didn't know any better than to sign fiduciary agreements with the wolves. Luckily, there was this little voice that kept telling me *No* whenever I was asked to sign a power of attorney. A lot of guys do that and lose everything.

I have to say, NFL draft picks are like lambs being led to slaughter. For someone who is unscrupulous or someone with a criminal mind, there is no easier way to make money than to prey on young athletes. All you have to do is hang around, pitch them a couple of things they don't know about, and get them to sign an agreement. You have all these guys with millions of dollars who have no concept of financial dealings. Most kids coming out of college want to buy their first hot car. If you're a first-round pick, maybe you buy your mom a house. After that, you don't know what the hell to do next.

I know I didn't. I came from a middle-class family, so we always had enough to live on, but we weren't materialistic people. I didn't particularly covet anything or care about anything beyond the basics. It doesn't take a lot to make me happy; as long as I can get from point A to point B, I'm content. So after I took care of my loved ones, I was like, *Let someone else deal with this financial junk.* Like most rookies, I didn't take an active role in my own finances my first year in the NFL, so I had no idea what was going on. Meanwhile the money was slowly being siphoned off by my finanicial adviser, Don Lukens.

Today, the NFL has a program that explains about embezzlement and fraud and identity theft. Still, they're talking to kids who don't have a sense of how prevalent it is, or how deep it runs. It would not be an exaggeration to say that 95 percent of the rookies who sign decent-sized contracts end up dealing with someone who's looking to take their money. Even when they have a friend or family member steering them, who's to say that these people won't be taken in and victimized, too? It is the rare player who actually has a qualified person he can trust looking out for him, and doing a good job of it.

I once told someone that the first thing an NFL draft pick has to understand is that he's no longer a person. He's an Inc. The day my name was called by the Cardinals, I became a corporation. To be honest, it happened even before that, because I had essentially made up my mind earlier that spring about who would advise me.

For a cat in my shoes, this is how it goes. It's draft day. Your name is called, you walk across the stage and shake hands with Paul Tagliabue, you smile for the cameras, you do interviews, you are on top of the world. From that day on, reality arrives, whether you acknowledge it or not. If you don't, these dudes can sniff you out like fresh meat. And before you know it, you have a "team" around you.

You have an agent who is deep in your pockets, selling you on a dream. These guys tell you you'll be in commercials and you'll get endorsement contracts. If you get Rookie of the Year, they say, you'll be the hottest thing on the planet. You sign with someone because you have faith that he'll work hard for you. Then you find out that he's spent four or five hours hammering out a contract, and lunching on 3 percent of that. You don't realize that your deal is essentially done based on where you're drafted. You can muscle a couple of dollars here and there, but nothing that would cover that commission.

Then you're dealing with a financial guy. You hope he's legit, but often he's not. The pitch he gives is, *Sim, in five years your whole estate will be set up and you'll be able to determine your income twenty or thirty years from now. You'll know everything about money if you work with me, I'll fly out every month and go over your finances.*

Well, of course, any young man will buy into that. What you find out later is that he's been funneling your money through his financial services company, taking a slice of every transaction. Then, every so often, he'll show up with a three-hundred-page document. You have twenty minutes to sign a bunch of forms, and he might slip one in there that's basically been drawn up for his own benefit. You're young, so you do it. You make the worst kinds of mistakes. You trust the man with the phatter ride than you, that's living in a bigger house than you. You think, *Why would this man steal from me? He doesn't have to steal for a living.*

Welcome to the world of white-collar crime! Young guys are easily taken in by these dudes because they don't know who *not* to trust.

Remember, in my case, up until this point the people I knew at this level were professors, people who were on my side. These wolves in sheep's clothing know that, and they do a great job coming off like folks in your life whom you've trusted and who did right by you.

In a sick way, this is a very accurate introduction to the life you will be leading in the NFL. There are two constants in pro football: The first is that people and situations are rarely what they seem. The second is that you're entering a world where hundreds of guys are basically making a living by identifying and then exploiting your weaknesses. I'm talking about a player's opponents. Yes, this happens in college, but it's still a game. In the NFL the man across the line is looking to take food off your table and put it on his.

So you're on your own for the first time in your life. You're winging it. You're learning as you go. It's exciting. You don't realize all this stuff is happening behind the scenes, but for now you probably don't care. For every success there's a smile and for every failure there's a frown. But you keep it moving, you keep pursuing your dream, because that's what life is about. I was excited about the prospects of finding my own way, becoming truly independent. I saw it as the first steps toward becoming a man.

Once the season starts, a rookie tends to look to his teammates for clues about what to do and how to act. I thought there would be someone who would show me the ropes, who would tell me where to go grocery shopping and point out the places to stay away from. I was expecting suggestions about whom I should hire to decorate my apartment. I thought I would develop a good group of friends, like I had in college. Almost like a fraternal order. And we would look out for one another.

Well, no one was reaching out to me. So I tried to observe some of the guys on the team. I looked at the big ballers, the cats with the big contracts, and the first thing I noticed was that they all had a hundred thousand dollars' worth of suits in their closets. So I'm like, *Okay, that's what it's about. Being a pro football player is about a hundred thousand dollars' worth of suits.* I went out and found someone to custom-design a wardrobe for me, and I spent a hundred grand, because I thought that's what makes you a professional.

So now I'm a suit guy. I got this stuff in my closet, and every jacket I try on comes up on my forearms whenever I move. Doesn't seem right to me, but I assume this is the new look. Mind you, I never really wore a suit except for Easter when I was a kid. I got on the plane for our first game and everyone started laughing at me. *Hey, look! Sim's got his little brother's suits on!*

I cringe whenever I think about this episode. I thought of myself as the big NFL millionaire, but in reality I was the same kid who wore the cap and gown at graduation, only now I could put two extra zeros on any check I wrote and not feel the pinch. I realized that I was just one of those cows you see following the other cows out to the pasture. I didn't know what the destination was, or even question why everyone was going this way.

The lesson of the suits turned out to be worth every penny of my hundred grand. Right then and there, I had an epiphany. All this external stuff is bullshit. It's smoke and mirrors. What matters in the NFL is how you play, and the depth of your commitment to the game. So almost immediately, I began to distance myself from the bullshit.

Okay, the next thing high draft picks think about doing is starting their own business. The NFL has a program that supposedly helps people create a career for themselves outside football, which is a great thing. The only problem is, when you decide on the business they don't send someone around to say, *Okay, here's what you need to do, here's how you have to set up the company, let's work on a business plan.* There's nothing that's hands-on, and man, that's what you really need at that point.

One of the things I thought I would get from my teammates (and didn't) was recommendations about good business advisers. I literally expected to get a list of contacts. *Here, you want to go into the record business? Talk to these people. They're the top people we do business with.* Needless to say, there is no such list. You are on your own, young man.

Looking back, I'd say my biggest problem as a young businessperson was that I liked everybody. I'm still that way. I find people interesting. I am curious to know what makes them tick, what makes them special, and what makes them different. Why do people do what they do? I'm fascinated by this. And the more I get to know people, the more I typically like them. This is a perfectly good way to run your life, but it's a horrible way to run your business.

Take my first agent, Roosevelt Barnes. I love him to death and to this day I'd do anything for him. From a business standpoint, I probably should have fired him years before I did, but I liked him too much. He was my agent all the years I was with the Cardinals. I didn't drop Roosevelt until I went into free agency. At that point I felt he wasn't going to help me from a business perspective, and I wanted to remain friends with him and go to his house for Thanksgiving and continue the relationship we had as friends.

I thought it would be cool to get into the record business, so I did. Did I know anything about it? No, not really. I reasoned that if I encountered a bump along the way, I could throw money at it and it would smooth out or go away. That's how young dudes with big contracts think. They see money as being the answer to everything, a way of removing the obstacles that are preventing them from fulfilling their needs and achieving their ambitions. You don't have to be poor or uneducated to think this way, either.

Take me. I didn't grow up in poverty, but I didn't grow up with money, either. My family had some nice things, and we owned a big house, but I knew there were nicer things and bigger houses and better neighborhoods out there. What was keeping us from that life? Money. So naturally, the first time I got my hands on some serious cash, I viewed it as a cure-all. Whatever I wanted to do, I now had the money to make it happen.

I knew that if you don't have a good education and strong values, money is likely to lead you down a precarious path. But I had those things, so money just seemed like the missing ingredient. It was a tool. I spent my money with confidence. What I eventually learned is that having an education and a good value system is meaningless if you don't bother to apply it to your financial decisions. My brief experience in the record business taught me that.

It also taught me that patience is everything. Just because you have the financial resources to make things happen fast, it doesn't mean you should rush into your decisions. What may feel like power isn't power at all. Power is having the knowledge and patience to make the right decision every time. This can be tricky when you're getting into a new business, because you may have the passion for it but not the experience. You're in a position, therefore, where you have to trust other people's expertise. I thought that finding those people, again, was just a matter of paying enough for them. I was wrong.

Eventually I learned not to listen to people who tell you, *This is what I can do for you.* Instead I look for people who have a strong sense of self-respect, who set goals for themselves, and who understand how to reach those goals. I want skilled, professional people who have a desire to be successful. I want people who understand my expectations, and who are as passionate and dedicated to meeting those expectations as I am.

I learned the importance of knowing your shit, too. You want to be in a new business? You study and research and ask questions. You stay at home and read until you fall asleep instead of partying all night. Before you put your money out there, you invest your time, your sweat, your hope. You make sure the chemistry's right. There's no need to go into business blindly, and there's no reason to put your faith in something you haven't fully evaluated with your intellect. Once it's in motion, that's when you have faith that it will work. But you don't start it unless you have seen enough to make you believe it will work. You don't place your faith in people you know nothing about, or who have no track record. You find out what they've done, determine what they can do for you, and then have faith that they will be successful in a similar role.

I also learned how important it is to be aware of what's going on in your business, because that's the only way you can know what's *not* going on. I need to know people are doing what they say they're doing, and what they're supposed to be doing. I need to see measurables. I need to see productivity. I don't want to hear excuses and I don't want to listen to someone who makes up shit and expects me to believe it.

I don't mean to sound hard-hearted, but aren't these the same criteria applied to me in my profession? I am judged on the number of tackles I make, the number of sacks I make, and the number of records I break. My employer sets a bar for me and I set my own bar even higher. I simply turn that around when it's my company and I'm the employer.

My advice to these young guys getting the big contracts is: If you take these first steps, then you have put yourself in a position to succeed. If not, you'll soon find yourself in a position to fail. If you do everything right and it pans out, that's great. If it withers and dies, it wasn't meant to be, and you move on knowing that you did everything you could to make a go of it. These are all lessons I now apply to my various business ventures and, to a significant degree, my own life. I tell you this now because I learned them from the mistakes I made in my first business, Juggernaut Entertainment. Like the suits, however, when I look back at the experience, I think the lessons came at a bargain price.

I had never entertained the thought of getting into the whole rap genre, but my oldest, dearest friend, Bennie Morrow, was a talented freestyle rapper and he got me excited about the idea. We didn't know what we were doing, but this was Bennie, and I'd give the guy a kidney if he needed one. I feel blessed when I see my friends happy and realizing their ambitions in life. If all it would take was a small investment, there was no question I was in. I remember telling Bennie, "I'd spend my last dime seeing you become what you want to become."

Juggernaut was basically Bennie, my cousin John Anderson, and myself. There was plenty of talent, plenty of money, and plenty of ambition in our little group, but we had no idea how to run a business. Our biggest problem was attention to detail. I thought among us we would cross the t's and dot the i's, but that didn't happen and we missed some great opportunities and wasted a lot of money. We needed to be workaholics and we weren't. I should have been the guy cracking the whip, but how do you do that to your two oldest and best friends?

Two friends from college, Sean Green and Danny Sanders, were also involved. They worked hard, but we were in over our heads and eventually we just ran the business into the ground. As I suspected, Sean had a great mind for business. He did such good work for Juggernaut that I promised him, one way or another, I would find him a great job. I didn't want him drifting back to his old crowd. I found him a job with American Express, and he flourished there. He also hooked me up with a great financial guy, Jonathan Miller.

The good thing about the Juggernaut experience was that it pushed our friendships to the limit. We all got frustrated and pissed at one another, yet never did it diminish the bond we had. I feel bad because Bennie had skills. We just never found the right way to get his career off the ground. But as I said, the upshot of that experience is that it demonstrated to my friends how committed I was to our relationships, and how strong our friendships are. It also brought to light the importance of recognizing the strengths and weaknesses in the people you love, and how they translate into business. It's just like football—you don't play a guard in the backfield and you don't put a cornerback at nose tackle. You find a position where talent is maximized and people have the best chance of succeeding.

Sometimes I think the Cardinals could have used this advice. We opened the 1996 season on September 1 against the Indianapolis Colts, in the RCA Dome. Our head coach, Vince Tobin, had been the defensive coordinator for the Colts, so we felt we could score against them. Our quarterback was Boomer Esiason, a former MVP and a very smart guy. We also had Larry Centers, a back who could run the ball and catch it, too. The question was, could our defense contain the Colts? They had Marshall Faulk, a great runner who had gained 1,000 yards in both of his NFL seasons.

On Indy's first play from scrimmage I put a move on the tackle and broke into the backfield just as their quarterback, Jim Harbaugh, handed off to Faulk. I nailed Marshall for a 2-yard loss. That play was a monumental moment for me. Not only did I make an impact play on the first down of my pro career, but I did the thing that everyone said I couldn't do, which was stop the run from my new position, defensive end. I like to think that, at that moment, I served notice on the league that I was going to be a special player.

Being a special player meant something different in the NFL than it had in college. With the privileges that come with stardom, there are some basic responsibilities, and I was pretty clueless about them. At that point in my life, I had no idea what it meant to be a professional. I thought because I was so good so young, I didn't have to do the things the others did. I failed to grasp, for instance, how important it was to be on time. This was never a strong point for me, but in college they let me slide. In Arizona the coaches would go berserk when I sauntered into a meeting twenty minutes late. I had no concept of how offensive that was to the team structure.

One of the transitions you have to make from college to the NFL is time management. You've already made the adjustment from living at home as a teenager to living on your own at college, so you think you can handle the next jump. But at least in my case, it was impossible. I swear, every day I would do everything I could think of to get to practice on time, and still I would be ten minutes late. Part of the problem was that I continued to keep the hours I did in college, staying up all night with my boys.

Well, right away, people started talking about how I was a "problem player." My response was, "Man, I work harder than anyone on this team. How is that a problem?" What I did not see was that if you want to be The Guy, you have to be consistent and do all the little things off the field that the team expects. I was proud of the fact that I respected the game's traditions and had a throwback mentality. But by the same token, I saw myself as a twenty-first-century–type player. What did that mean? Fuck if I know. But I was young, I worked hard, and I had the talent to overcome any situation. If they wanted to call me a problem, fine. If I kept going out there on Sunday and destroying people, what could they do to me?

Obviously, I had some maturity issues.

My relationship with Vince Tobin was a perfect example. I was the kind of guy who always did what the coach said, who respected his wisdom and experience in matters pertaining to football. In dealing with my disciplinary issues, Tobin chose to earn my respect through subtle intimidation, and I guess I wasn't getting that signal clearly. I wasn't the least bit intimidated; I felt like we were on the same level—he needed me and I needed him. That was probably a mistake on both our parts, because we would sit and talk and accomplish nothing.

Here's an example. Tobin called me into his office early in the year and told me I was undependable. My response was, "How can you call me undependable? Okay, I have a problem waking up and getting out of the house in the morning, but I'm the guy you drafted to take the Cardinals to the next level, and I'm working my ass off in practice and getting it done on Sundays." And in terms of the little things, I may have been a rookie when it came to waking up, but I was also the kind of cat that would stay after practice for an hour and a half by myself.

Tobin also told me to stop predicting I'd win Rookie of the Year, that I was putting too much pressure on myself. I told him, "That's what I believe, Coach. Why should I stop saying that? If people ask me how I'm going to do this year, I feel I should tell them the truth." At that time, I didn't see the point of giving a soft answer, of mumbling some cliché so I could look humble.

Finally, he said, "Sim, I'd appreciate if you'd stop saying you're going to be Rookie of the Year, and please start making it here on time. This is not as easy a life as you think. You have to respect the game—you have no idea how hard it is—and that starts with these little things."

I said, "I do know how hard it is. That's why I work so hard."

Anything Tobin said, I had an answer to. It wasn't that I didn't hear what he was saying—I just couldn't understand it. He was selling, but I wasn't buying. I would listen and say, *Okay, okay,* but I just wanted to get out of there. The next morning, he sent someone to knock on my door to make sure I got to practice on time. And the next day, and the next, and the next.

That first year in the NFL, I'll be honest, I had no idea what I was doing. I was aware of the fact that teams were watching me and trying to find my weaknesses, because they would try different shots on me every week. But my strengths outweighed my weaknesses to such a degree that I could usually get by on instinct. I was beating guys on effort, physical talent, and great conditioning. I had no clue how I was getting past them, but I know I was driving them crazy, because I never used the same move twice. All that film of me was going to waste.

Reporters would ask me to analyze some of the plays I made, and I couldn't do it. I didn't have the experience to understand why I was being so successful, or the vocabulary to describe what I was doing on the field. Sometimes I wouldn't even remember a play they asked me about. That first year was a blur.

As for getting along with my teammates, that was kind of a blur, too. Fans assume that the veterans might help out a guy who could be an impact player, explain things during games or in practice. But on the Cardinals, this was not the case. We had some talent on that defense—Aeneas Williams, Eric Hill, and Eric Swann were Pro Bowl players. But they were not helping me out. Between the lines, there was no one to lean on.

Personally, I liked Aeneas. He worked as hard as I did. Just watching the level of his dedication from a distance helped me become a better player. He was the consummate professional. When I first saw Aeneas, I can't lie—I couldn't understand how he could be as great as he was. His talent level didn't jump off the board. But then I got to know him and it became clear. He was very focused, and his approach to the game was very structured. That told me that a lot of NFL football is played between the ears.

I couldn't understand why Swann was so good, either. He had talent, no doubt. But he always seemed to have a lot on his mind besides playing football. He seemed to play without passion—or at least his passion was not obvious. I'm sure Eric was passionate, but not in a way that I could see. I had actually met him in Champaign before the draft. He came over with his agent, Rocky Arceneaux, whom I had met earlier. He had heard a lot about me and wanted to check out what all the hoopla was about. I don't think he ever dreamed we'd be playing on the same line. He was cool when we met, but once I got to Arizona, I sensed a lot of jealousy on his part. It wasn't the kind of overt jealousy that you can see and understand, like when the seniors objected to my starting as a freshman. In Eric's case, someone would write something complimentary about me, and he would get angry at me. The irony is that I wasn't enjoying the attention I was getting. It was a distraction.

Eric was having problems with the team and wanted to be paid more. He felt he wasn't appreciated, and that he wasn't being used properly. So when I showed up and started to take some of his thunder away, that was not a healthy thing. We were both good players, so we clicked on occasion. But mostly we clacked. I was so young, I didn't understand why there was a conflict. He was a tackle and I was an end—we didn't even play the same position. His attitude would have been understandable if we were fighting for the same job, but we weren't.

I soon came to realize that the most dramatic difference between the pro and college games was that, in the NFL, you go about your business, maintain an even temperament, and you don't worry about your rapport with your teammates. I would arrive at the locker room on game days all charged up, bouncing around, and guys would give me some sharp looks, as if to say, *Sim, why don't you calm down.*

It was troubling to me that this was the way we were supposed to prepare for a game. This is football. This is the game we all grew up playing. We've reached the highest level, and every Sunday should be a celebration of that. It's not a job—we're grown men living a kid's fantasy.

I really dig the history of sports. I've been like that my entire life. When I began to have success in the NFL, reporters would ask me if I realized the historical context of my achievements, and they were surprised when I demonstrated to them that I did. I made it my business to know about the people who'd played defensive end before me, and I can tell you more about cats like Deacon Jones, Carl Eller, and Reggie White than you probably know. The more I learn about those who came before me, the more it crystallizes my own career. Most athletes don't know shit about the history of the sport they play, and that's a shame, because it diminishes their appreciation of their own situation. Also, it's disrespectful to the greats of the game. The difference between a ghost and a legend is people remembering you. How will today's players feel if they're forgotten? Well, it starts by respecting what came before you.

That doesn't mean comparing yourself to players from other eras, which is something the press is always asking you to do. You might be able to do that in a sport like baseball, but in football I think you short-change the game when you try to say a player today could have kicked ass against players from, say, the 1950s. The history of football is a continuum. As players get bigger, faster, and more athletic, the game evolves and the balance of power shifts. You have eras when defense dominates and eras when offense dominates. You have eras when the running game is the key, and eras when the passing game is the key.

The one constant is speed. Speed is everything, and that holds true in any era. Deion Sanders could run rings around Night Train Lane, but in his day Night Train was every bit as good as Deion because he was more athletic than the receivers he was covering and the runners he was tackling. Brian Urlacher is twice the athlete Dick Butkus was, but Butkus was even more dominant in his era than Urlacher is now. Deacon Jones is my height and weight, but from what I can tell he wasn't as quick and agile as me. Back in the 1960s, however, he was unstoppable. The dude had two hundred-something sacks before they even officially counted them. Guys who ran 4.6 40s twenty-five years ago would now have to run 4.2 40s just to qualify at their positions—and that includes the Hall of Famers. I think each era is like its own snapshot of football evolution, and should be preserved that way. The men who were giants in their time are still giants in my eyes. They had as much courage and valor in their day as we do in ours—if not more. I love the folklore and the legacy of the old players, and one day I hope people accord me that same respect.

As a football fan, I'm always interested in the player who stands out in his era. I've spoken to Jim Brown, and I've looked at his rushing stats. He was the best runner anyone had ever seen, and is still considered by many to be the best player ever. To me, the most interesting stat is not how many yards Jim gained. It's his height and weight compared to the guys on the other side of the ball. He was fast enough to get by the defensive linemen of his era, which meant he was taking on linebackers in the open field. Well, he was bigger than almost every linebacker in the league at the time. And forget about the defensive backs. It took three of them to drag him down. I always wanted to be that guy. The Jim Brown of defensive linemen.

I was able to sit down with Jim once at a restaurant, and our meal turned into a five-hour conversation-slash-jousting-match. We talked all night about the passage of time in football and how the game has changed. We discussed what it means to be a man, what power is, and the qualities that make a leader. What a night that was. We did a lot of mental sparring along the way, because I have my own opinions about the important things in life, and some of his views are pretty unique, too. Jim listened very intently to what I had to say, and I had a very open mind to what he was saying, because it comes out of a long and extraordinary life experience.

What an opportunity that was to get a glimpse into the mind of the man whom many people consider the best football player ever. It was the same kind of conversation I'd wanted to have with Joe Greene, the Cardinals' defensive line coach, the entire time I played in Arizona—and why it hurt so much that he thought I didn't respect the history of the game. There is nothing I respect more.

Mean Joe Greene. This was by far the most complex relationship I had with anyone on the Cardinals. He was a legend, and even though I was a Bears fan as a kid, I had followed his career. One of the first things I said to Joe was, "Man, I had your football card!"

I knew Joe had so much to teach me, and I was really looking forward to learning from him. Ultimately, my goal was to see things on the
field the way he saw them, both as a Hall of Fame defensive player and
as a modern NFL coach. And secretly, I wanted to forge a father–son relationship with Joe. So to say my expectations were high was an understatement. In my mind, my relationship with Joe would be more
important than the one I had with my head coach. I wanted to nurture
that relationship, so when he said, "Come in early and watch films," I
dragged my ass out of bed and made sure I was there at seven. He was a
former player with world-class ability, and I was a current player with
world-class ability, so I wanted him to feel like I was embarking on the
same journey he had taken through the NFL, and that he could be my
guide. Theoretically, this is what great players who become coaches are
supposed to do. Their busts are up in Canton, their legacies as superstars
are secure, so they are free to establish their legacy as a coach by turning
out superstars of their own.

I let Joe know that I was willing to share my glory. If he made me a
great player, I was not going to take all the credit. At first, he seemed
open to this idea. And I was happy because I thought I'd re-created the
kind of player–coach relationship I'd enjoyed in high school and college.
But Joe is a moody person. Sometimes he'd be up, and sometimes not.
And I never knew why. I had never dealt with a guy like this.

Compounding the problem was the fact Joe thought there was a
generation gap between us. At times he just didn't understand me. He
thought I acted like a thug—not because of anything I did or said, but
because I wore some trendy hip-hop stuff and had my headphones on
all the time. I came to practice with my headphones on, and left practice
with my headphones on. I listened to music constantly.

One day on the field, before practice, for no reason, Joe decided he
was going to pick a fight. "What's up with you?" he said in a disparaging
kind of way.

"I don't know," I replied. "What's up with you?" When he didn't answer, I asked him how he was doing.

"What the hell you mean, How'm I doing?" he said. Joe liked to
mess with you sometimes, and I thought this was one of these times. I
started laughing. But he was angry. "What the hell's wrong with you?

You walk around here like a damn fool, with your headphones on like you're passing through the damn 'hood.'"

I said, "Whatever, man."

"I'm serious," he said.

Well, we both began saying stuff we shouldn't have, very disrespectful stuff. And we almost came to blows. After that, we didn't speak for two weeks.

What finally brought us back together was when he found out what I was playing on my "damn headphones." I listened to a lot of old-school music, as well as jazz. But Joe saw me chilling and figured it was Tupac or Biggie. Yeah, I was listening to those guys, but I was also listening to a lot of the same music he did. Well, Joe found out that I was listening to John Coltrane and Charlie Parker and he got all interested.

"What do you know about those guys?" he said.

When I answered, I could see it kind of took his breath away. After that, we talked about music a lot. We would have great conversations, comparing different bands and musicians and styles. We had a different language besides football we could speak, and after that we were cool again. But on the balance, we were almost always in conflict over something my rookie year.

Did Joe see me as a modern version of him, getting the accolades he once had? Was Joe envious of me? Of the money I was making? I'm still not sure, and anything I say will probably exacerbate the problem. But at the time I was too young to absorb the complexity of what he was feeling, so it always took me by surprise and hurt me. It was like running with a guy who doesn't have your back.

Joe may not be considered an all-time great coach, but on the whole I'd say he was a very good coach for me. We worked together for five seasons, and during that time he taught me how to play the game freely. The top athletes in different sports tend to see the game unfold at a slightly slower speed than everyone else. I can't tell you what the brain science behind it is, but I know it's true. If you experience a play at a slower rate of speed, then you have an extra fraction of a second to react or make a decision, and it looks like your body is moving slightly faster than everyone else's. Joe played the game at this level and so do I. Every so often, he would tell me that I was slowing down, and remind me that it was okay to play fast, without inhibition. To have someone on the sideline who understood that was major, and I appreciated that big-time.

I love Joe to death to this day, and would never say anything to diminish his greatness or his legacy. I have nothing but respect for him, and if he needed something I'd be there for him in a heartbeat. The conflicts we had were always puzzling to me, and over the years it probably didn't help that I tended to laugh them off. But that's the kind of cat I am. I let shit go.

Anyway, that first year, I kept expecting Joe to impart to me those little techniques he had used successfully as a player. But outside of discussing what our schemes would be against the teams we were playing, he didn't give me that much one-on-one instruction. I think he could see I was having success and didn't want to mess with my head. I was dominating veterans on raw ability. There was time to refine that ability later.

The season opener—and the season, for that matter—started to go downhill after I tackled Marshall Faulk on the first play of the year. Jim Harbaugh threw for two touchdowns, one late in the game, and we didn't score our first touchdown until the end of the fourth quarter, when it was too late. We lost 20–13.

Our home opener was the ESPN game on Sunday night against the Dolphins. It was hot as shit in Sun Devil Stadium, but we were ice cold. Everything went wrong—we had a punt blocked, we fumbled, we had a bunch of penalties—and that was in the first quarter alone. You can't do that against Dan Marino and survive, and they were up 24–0 at the half. They won 38–10.

It got worse the next week in Foxboro, when we let the Patriots trample us. Curtis Martin scored three touchdowns, and Drew Bledsoe was on fire. At halftime they had more first downs than we had offensive plays! It was embarrassing. We lost 31–0. That was it for Boomer Esiason. He wasn't moving the team, and Vince Tobin decided to give the QB job to Kent Graham. Kent did a good job for us as the starter. In our next game, at the Louisiana Superdome, the defense was tight and the offense began to make some progress. LeShon Johnson, whom I rememebered from Northern Illinois in the early 1990s, made two long touchdown runs and finished the day with 214 yards. We had our first win—my first NFL win—28–14.

LeShon did it again the next week in a wild game. We were playing the Rams at home and Tony Banks threw three long touchdown passes to give them a 28–14 lead going into the final fifteen minutes. Graham threw TDs to Larry Centers and Frank Sanders to tie the game with eleven seconds left. In overtime LeShon took a handoff and went 66 yards, down to the 8. Greg Davis kicked a field goal to win it 31–28.

We traveled to Dallas after a bye week to play the Cowboys in our first conference game. Michael Irvin was coming back from a suspension and Emmitt Smith was looking for his hundredth career touchdown, so there was a lot of buildup. It was a defensive battle all the way, and we ended up with just a field goal. Emmitt scored twice, including a short run up the middle with two minutes left, and that was the game, 17–3.

We won our third game in four tries against the Tampa Bay Buccaneers when we returned home. Graham moved the ball on three long drives for 13 points, and that's all we needed, because our defense was dominant. We won 13–9. The following week we were home again against the Jets, who hadn't won a game. We were counting on a victory, but that's when Adrian Murrell decided to bust loose and run for 200 yards, and we lost 31–21. Our record was 3–5, and with eight teams ahead of us for playoff spots, the math didn't work in our favor. The season was starting to slip away.

We went up to New Jersey to play our first game against the Giants, the team whose uniform I had hoped to be wearing. One look at the crowd and I remembered why. They had the same record as us, but there were like forty thousand more people in the stands than at our last home game. And the fans were into it, too. I felt like we were going to have another good day on defense. The Giants quarterback was Dave Brown, and in the first quarter I nailed him. He had to leave the game, and Danny Kanell came in. We held the Giants to two field goals until midway through the fourth quarter, when Kanell threw a touchdown to Thomas Lewis. The defense did a nice job, but unfortunately, we had zero points—Kent Graham had also left the game in the first quarter, with a knee injury. Boomer came back in but we went nowhere. We scored with forty seconds left, but the game was over at that point and we lost 13–7.

We traveled to Washington to play the division-leading Redskins with a new kicker, Kevin Butler. What a trip! Butler was the kicker for

the Bears when I was a kid. And what a game. Esiason was hitting receivers everywhere, and he finished with 522 passing yards, one of the
greatest days in history. The game went into overtime tied 34–34. Butler
missed a field goal that could have won it, then Washington's kicker, Scott
Blanton, made one from 38 yards. But there was a holding call, and he
had to rekick from 48 and missed. There was less than a minute to play in
OT when Butler missed again, but the 'Skins were called for offsides and
we got another shot from 5 yards closer in. This time Butler made it.

The Cardinals were tired and happy in the locker room, but I was
pissed. This was the one game where the other team got the best of me.
I was being doubled by two linemen who were literally drive-blocking
me, like you see them do when they move the big sled. I had been double-teamed in pass protection my whole career, but this was the first
time I had seven hundred pounds of prime NFL beef coming after me
the instant the ball was snapped. It surprised me, and on a number of
plays they were able to move me off the ball. Joe Greene pulled me aside
with some words of fatherly advice: "You can't play that way anymore or
you'll be sitting on the bench."

That's all he needed to tell me. The next time we played Washington
I dominated the shit out of them and had two sacks. We won, 27–26,
when Butler kicked a field goal with no time remaining. Those two
losses to us kept the Redskins out of the playoffs.

Anyway, that was the pattern throughout my rookie year. If someone did something well against me the first time we met, I would make
sure they couldn't do it the next. In between the two Washington games,
we beat the Giants and Eagles—scoring more than 30 points three
weeks in a row—but then we started turning the ball over and got killed
by the Vikings. We had another good defensive struggle against Dallas,
but they beat us again, 10–6.

A week after that second Washington game, we played the Eagles
again. I needed one sack to tie Leslie O'Neal for the NFL rookie sack
record. Ty Detmer was Philadelphia's quarterback, and I was on top of
him all day. But every time I got to Detmer, he got the pass off. I was literally all over his back, but he kept throwing the ball away. It was a fun
game for me, because I was causing a lot of havoc, but frustrating because I needed to make a tackle that actually showed up in the numbers.

I finally dragged Detmer down, but we lost 29–19. That was the last game of the year. A win would have given us an 8–8 record.

After the season, I was voted Defensive Rookie of the Year by the Associated Press and a couple of the football weeklies, and NFC Rookie of the Year by United Press. Eddie George, my old nemesis from Ohio State, took most of the offensive rookie awards.

I thought this recognition would translate into some commercial opportunities, but nothing was happening. My agent didn't seem to be making any progress, so I sat down with a marketing firm. I'll never forget, the woman explained that I'd have to become "larger" before those opportunities came about. I was like, *Larger how?* What more could a first-year defensive player do than be named Defensive Rookie of the Year? I thought if you did good things, good things would come to you. Well, nothing was coming.

Some people suggested to me that maybe I would benefit from some bad press. As we know, the "right" kind of bad press can go a long way. I didn't like that idea at all. What about recognizing hard work? What about building an image around professionalism? Why couldn't I be sold as someone who respects the game and does good things?

What this lady was essentially saying was that I had to create a personality big enough to get noticed above all the other personalities in football. *Wow,* I thought, *this is crazy.* It was a real learning experience. I recognize that anyone who performs for the public whores himself to a certain degree, but it was important to me to maintain a certain standard. Later, when I began my clothing company, I was glad that I hadn't turned myself into some cartoon character just to draw attention. My serious, dedicated, professional side became a great selling point in what would turn out to be my first business triumph.

5

I hated the 1997 season.

For me, as a person and as a football player, it was profoundly disappointing. By the same token, it was also very illuminating. All my life I had wondered how in the world an athlete in his prime years could have a superstar season, then follow it up with a horrible one. Well, now I know.

From the perspective of an Arizona Cardinals fan, 1997 must have been a frustrating season, too. If you could wave a magic wand and change the outcome of maybe a dozen plays that year, we would have had one of the best records in the NFL. Instead, when we had completed our final down, we had one of the worst records. Although I don't particularly relish the thought of recounting this miserable year, I will because, if nothing else, it was an instructive season.

The anatomy of a season gone wrong begins in January 1997. I had just finished my rookie year, and literally had nothing to do. In college, you hit the books, stay in shape, whatever. One spring at Illinois I even ran track. It was like a routine. Well, they say an idle mind is the devil's workshop, and that spring I got it in my mind to try my hand at professional basketball.

The idea began germinating, you'll recall, during my holdout the previous summer. Had the Cardinals not acceded to my salary demands, I really did intend to play hoops. People had been trying to get me into basketball since high school, because there was a time when I was as good a basketball player as I was a football player. And I've always genuinely liked the game. To this day, I incorporate basketball into my off-season workouts. It exercises muscle groups in ways no football drills can, it helps with my explosiveness, balance, and overall body control, and of course it doesn't hurt that I can shoot the lights out. I play five-on-five, three-on-three, one-on-one—each variation offers something different. I can drive the lane and dunk, or pull up for a 3-pointer.

I'd always wondered what would have happened had I committed myself to basketball as deeply as I had football. In the spring of 1997 I decided to find out. I dedicated myself to improving at basketball; my goal was to become at least 50 percent better. The Cardinals knew nothing about this, but word started circulating in the hoops community and I was invited to try out for Philadelphia of the U.S. Basketball League, a pro league that operated in the spring and summer.

Even though the USBL was considered a minor league, there was major talent on the floor. Guys who were stars in college, overseas players—basically anyone with a game who hadn't established himself in the NBA. I got out there and kind of surprised myself, because I was bringing it against these guys. I was scoring, rebounding, blocking shots. The guys knew my name from Illinois, and they assumed that I had played on the basketball team. They'd say, "Yeah, Sim, I remember you. You were great at Illinois."

Of course, I hadn't played organized ball in almost ten years. One year at Mount Carmel I went out for basketball and made the team, but I quit before the season started. I found that I didn't love the game like I loved football, and knew I'd have problems committing to it.

Well, I made the team in Philly and it was still a big secret. Then *NBA Inside Stuff* found out and sent a film crew to practice. I didn't have a problem with this, because I knew the Cardinals would eventually find out, and there was nothing in my contract expressly forbidding it. What irritated me was that *NBA Inside Stuff* treated me like a novelty act. They slanted the story so that it looked like I was trying to draw attention to myself, when all I was doing was trying to have fun and explore a part of myself—to succeed and excel according to my own standards. I guess it was naive of me to think I could toil in anonymity after becoming a star player in my rookie NFL season, but I wanted this basketball experiment to be a personal thing, and it quickly became public.

I was so pissed that I almost walked away. In fact, I had decided to quit. But then the Cardinals found out and they were outraged. The GM called me and said, "Simeon, I want you to stop this madness. If you get hurt, you could lose your contract. We're not going to put up with this."

Now I was doubly pissed. No one owns me. No one tells me what I can and cannot do if I'm doing it on my own time. So just as I was about to slip quietly away from pro basketball, I decided to stick with it. I played around thirty games and really enjoyed myself. I was able to explore one of my dreams, and immerse myself in a different culture, and in the end I cured myself of wanting to be a two-sport athlete. I also gained a lot of respect for my teammates. For the most part they were on the fringes of pro ball, with very little chance of making it to the NBA. But they sacrificed everything to play the game they loved. They were as passionate about basketball as I was about football.

My brief career as a pro basketball player also made me appreciate what I had accomplished as a pro football player. I was riding chartered buses with guys whose only dream was to wear an NBA uniform, and most of them knew that dream would never come true. It got me thinking how many people I knew, in high school and college, who had that same dream about the NFL, and how in some ways I was living their dream.

When I came to camp that summer for my second NFL season, I was electric. I was playing great football. I was lightning-quick, strong, in better shape than anyone else on the Cardinals. This was the first year, remember, that I had trained with the team in the preseason. We were in Flagstaff, which is way above sea level. After a few days I started to feel sick. I thought it was because of the altitude. The Cardinals immediately said it was because I had played basketball. That was bullshit, of course. I had given myself a good six weeks of recovery time between the USBL and training camp.

The doctors couldn't figure out what was wrong. They thought it was a viral infection, or possibly mountain sickness, whatever that is. I spent time in the hospital, including three days in the ICU. They even gave me a spinal tap. It was no fun. Meanwhile, I was losing weight like crazy. Normally I start the season at 260, but I had trimmed down to

250 or 255 and felt great. In no time, however, my weight sank to 230, which is a problem if you are a defensive lineman in the NFL.

After a few weeks I began to feel better, and decided I was ready to return to practice. I still had that gung-ho college mentality. Even though I was thirty pounds underweight, I went out and started playing at full speed. This was stupid, because I had lost some muscle mass, and I fucked up my left shoulder on a play that wouldn't have caused a bruise under normal circumstances. I recovered a fumble in a preseason game against the Rams, a bunch of guys jumped on top of me, and I felt this flash of pain. Afterward I was diagnosed with a slightly separated shoulder and nonpermanent nerve damage.

I have to say, I wasn't pressured by the team to play after I felt sick, and even as opening day neared, the Cardinals did not push me to get back in the lineup. That was all pressure I put on myself. Man, I wanted so badly to prove them wrong about basketball, and I wanted to show that I was a team guy, impervious to illness and injury. There wasn't enough time to restore the muscle mass I had lost in Flagstaff, so to get my weight up I just ate like a pig until I was up over 250 again. When the year began, I actually had a stomach—something I'd never featured before—and I could barely lift my arm because of the pain. I was a mess.

All of this was taking place against a backdrop of high hopes and internal intrigue. The Cardinal defense had the makings of a dominant unit. The only shaky area for us was our defensive backfield, but it looked like Aeneas Williams would have plenty of help back there. I was probably too young to know better, but to my mind we had the right mix of personnel to become a playoff team. Mentally, all the players felt we would be the team to beat in the NFC East. We were convinced we would reach the next level in 1997. It was an exciting time to be an Arizona Cardinal.

The big news of the preseason was the arrival of Jake Plummer, our top draft pick out of the University of Arizona. "Jake the Snake," they called him. Boomer Esiason was gone and Kent Graham was given the starting job. But the feeling around Phoenix was that he was just keeping the spot warm for Plummer. Jake would get to sit for a while before he was expected to make an impact. On the other hand, much hinged on my performance.

The team had seen what I could do as a rookie, and projected me as even more of an impact player in my second year. This enabled the defensive coordinator, Dave McGinnis, to develop new schemes, assuming that I could shut down my part of the field. I didn't mind the extra responsibility, but I was nervous about how long it would take me to return to full strength. Although I was still too young to understand how other teams would react, I sensed that if I showed any kind of weakness, our opponents would start running everything at me to knock me out of the game. Pro football is a dog-eat-dog proposition, man, and I had no interest in becoming a can of Alpo. I just knew that I had to play really, really well.

This was not going to be easy. In our first game, against Cincinnati, there were times I felt like someone who had just been discharged from the hospital and tries to do everything he normally does. I lacked my usual strength and stamina, and trying to push myself just made things worse. This was the first time in my life I had started a football season in anything other than peak condition. And I had never had to deal with any kind of health issues.

We lost that first game to the Bengals when they scored three times in the fourth quarter. We were actually ahead, and had a chance to run time off the clock, but Larry Centers fumbled and gave them the opening they needed. I struggled to play up to my usual level, and afterward I can honestly say that this marked the first time I truly respected football. Things had always come so easily to me, and I had so much love for the game, that I'd never appreciated how much football demands from you as an individual. For the first time in my life I'd come up short, and it was humbling to see the result.

The Bengals were down late, everyone in the stadium knew they had to throw, and it was my job to make the great play. The Cardinals had brought me in to take charge in these situations. This was Simeon Rice time, and I failed to capitalize. My frustration was compounded by the fact that our defense played very undisciplined in the waning moments of that game. Jeff Blake was completing his passes, and we were letting them stop the clock and get out of bounds. They would run the same play over and over and we couldn't stop them. I was like, *Oh my God, what are we doing?*

But what could I say? I wasn't getting the job done. I had done it the year before, so I half expected to do it again in this situation. But not being 100 percent, I was coming up short time and again. Unfortunately, I wasn't mature enough as a player to recognize what was going on. I didn't know how to adjust, to allow for my weakened condition and do certain things differently. Later in my career, I learned how to compensate and play an effective game when I wasn't at full strength. But not on this day.

So what happens a week later? We play a great game against the Cowboys and beat them 25–22 in overtime. I was feeling better and was up for my battle with Mark Tuinei. I'll never forget how much respect he gave me. Tuinei was a Pro Bowl veteran and I was a young kid, but he was telling everyone how I was going to be a great player. He fought really hard and won some, and I fought really hard and won some. But as the game wore on, I got the upper hand and I closed that game out. They had no answer for me.

Beating the Cowboys was a big, big deal. To Arizona fans, that was like winning the Super Bowl. To us, it was one of the hurdles we had to overcome in order to be taken seriously. We got caught up in the excitement and really felt like we were going somewhere.

That made what happened in our next game really crushing. We played the Redskins tight all day, and I forced what should have been the pivotal turnover in the fourth quarter. Stephen Davis was carrying the ball, and I tackled him and stripped him. We recovered, but the referee ruled that he was down when the ball came out. I saw video after the game, and it was definitely a fumble. They were deep in their own territory at the time, so that would have been the game right there. We regrouped and made a goal-line stand late in the fourth quarter that forced overtime, but we fumbled at the beginning of OT and lost 19–13.

Three weeks. Three close games. One win. You'd think we would have been discouraged, especially since we were going into a bye week, but to a man everyone on the Cardinals felt we were on the verge of a big run. We talked a lot about getting the details right, doing the little things in tight situations. This is what we needed to change in order to get over the hump and become a winning NFL team.

If anyone needed an illustration of this fact, our next game, against the Buccaneers, provided a vivid one. Our defense was dominant all day.

Aeneas Williams made a great interception in the third quarter that gave us the lead, but when we had a chance to close Tampa Bay out, Aeneas went for another pick instead of just tackling Karl Williams and they scored to take a 19–18 lead. It went right through his hands and Karl caught it. He's still running today. Game over. No disrespect to Aeneas, who is one of the all-time greats, but it was fourth down. All he had to do was cover the guy. But he went for the stat instead of the tackle. And once again, we were done in by the details. Unlike our other two losses, we were seriously pissed about this one.

Kevin Butler actually had a chance to win the game, but he was too far out of his range and missed. It was a tough year for Kevin, who was thirty-five and nearing the end of the line. He was a guy I rooted for as a kid, but he missed a lot of field goals in 1997, so I had some mixed emotions about that. In our next game, however, he was money—he drilled four straight against the Vikings, and it looked like we would finally get our second victory. But with a minute left, he missed his fifth attempt. Instead of leading 22–17, it was 19–17, and Brad Johnson—who would be my quarterback in Tampa Bay years later—took Minnesota down the field. Then Eddie Murray, who was forty-something, made his kick to win 20–19.

After losing three of four close games, to lose yet another was really deflating for us. We didn't feel like a 1–4 team, but I can't say we felt like a 5–0 team, either. Still, if we had seen to the details, that's what our record would have been.

We finally got our asses kicked the following Sunday, when the Giants came to town. Jim Fassel, Arizona's old offensive coordinator, was now New York's head coach. They were better prepared than we were and flat-out beat us. At the time I didn't think Fassel would have any particular advantage coming back against his old team, but they did beat us twice that year, so maybe he did. All I remember is that they put a pounding on Kent Graham and knocked him out of the game. Our number two guy was Stoney Case. He went in and couldn't do anything either, and we lost 27–13.

That game was memorable for another reason. Everyone on our front four got hurt that game, myself included. I'd never seen that before. The fans probably thought we were begging out of the slaughter, but we were all legitimately injured. I don't think we were 100 percent as a group the rest of the year, and that basically spelled our doom.

We played the Eagles next. Graham was still hurt, so Case started. Stoney was a nice guy, but he was looking at a best-case scenario of being a career backup, and in this instance we all knew that Jake Plummer was our quarterback of the future. Kevin Butler had lost his job, so we had a new kicker, too, named Joe Nedney.

Nedney had a decent leg, and he made some big kicks for us during his career. His story was typical of most NFL kickers. He played college ball in his hometown for San Jose State and had a good career there, but went undrafted in 1995. The Packers signed him that spring but cut him in camp when they kept Chris Jacke. A field goal here, a touchback there, and maybe Joe would have been kicking for the Packers in the NFC Championship game—that's how fine the line can be when you're a kicker in the NFL.

Oakland took Nedney off the scrap heap, but he didn't show them anything and he was released a week later. Finally the Dolphins signed him as insurance for Pete Stoyanovich, but Stoyanovich held the job all season and Joe never got in a game. Still, he showed enough that the Dolphins felt confident enough to trade Stoyanovich for a high draft pick, and Joe Nedney was the Miami kicker for all 1996.

Alas, he didn't survive training camp the following year. The Dolphins brought in Olindo Mare, and he beat Joe out. The Jets claimed him off waivers to compete with Joe Hall, but that experiment ended quickly. After the season started, the Dolphins reappeared to sign him, but cut him after one game. Joe became a Cardinal on October 15. When you hear stories like that, it makes you wonder how guys handle it. Thank God I'm not a kicker.

The Eagles game was crazy. They were starting a new quarterback, too, Rodney Peete. Rodney had been around a while, so he was a known commodity. He was in his thirties at this point, but could still move around and create opportunities with his speed. Our guy wasn't making anything happen, so in the fourth quarter Vince Tobin sent in Plummer. Well, he was damn brilliant. Jake kept hitting third-down conversions and led us to a touchdown on a long pass to Kevin Williams on third and 11. With time winding down and the Cardinals up 3, Peete scrambled and set up the tying field goal to force overtime—our third of the year. Rodney beat us in OT with a pass to Charlie Garner, who made a long run to set up a field goal by Chris Boniol for a 13–10 final.

Seven games, six close, one win. Shit! I still can't believe we started a season like this. I was starting to drag, but I still went out with enthusiasm each game because I loved football. The mood among the other players was mixed, but hey, you have to be a man, suck it up, and move forward. A few guys packed it in, but most of us were looking forward to a comeback in the second half. The coaches, on the other hand, were going crazy. They were all fearing for their jobs.

As dismal as our season had become, people in Arizona were still upbeat. Jake Plummer had shown enough in his first action to get people excited. He was the future of the franchise, the man on whom the fans could pin their hopes. The players knew better. It would be a while before Jake settled in, and in the meantime he would have to take his lumps with the rest of us.

Fans looking for a light at the end of the tunnel got it against the Oilers the following Sunday. Only it wasn't Jake. It was a freight train named Steve McNair. He was in his first full year as a starting quarterback, and this was easily the best game of his young career. They beat us 41–14, and I have to admit I was impressed. I had him in my crosshairs a bunch of times, but he was fast enough and powerful enough to break out of my tackles. I had never played against anyone so hard to bring down. Poor Jake, meanwhile, had Oilers on him almost every time he dropped back.

Plummer was still struggling the following week in a rematch against the Eagles, who did everything short of handing us the game with stupid penalties and careless turnovers. The outcome was still in doubt in the fourth quarter, however, so Vince Tobin sent Kent Graham in to seal the deal for us. Finally we had win number two. We were 2–7 instead of 7–2, based on maybe six or eight plays that didn't go our way. That's how thin the margin between winning and losing can be in the NFL.

Despite his problems, Jake got the start against the Cowboys the following week. He was unable to do much, but this time it wasn't his fault, it was the offensive line's. I don't know how many sacks Dallas got in this game, but if you told me twenty I'd believe you. It was a debacle. They outplayed our guys in every facet of the game—mental, physical, emotional—and we had no effective way to adjust. It was embarrassing for everyone. The final score was only 24–6, but we took one hell of a thumping that day.

Jake finally had a big game against the Giants in Week 12, racking up almost 400 passing yards, but Jason Sehorn made a couple of clutch plays and New York scored 9 points in the fourth quarter to win 19–10. I thought we had exhausted every possible way to lose at this point, but I was wrong. The next week, against the Ravens, our linebacker Mike Caldwell was whistled for an unnecessary roughness penalty that kept Baltimore's final drive alive and enabled them to tie the game. Imagine our surprise when, instead of losing, we actually won. Plummer threw a couple of balls to Rob Moore with time running out, and Nedney split the uprights for a 16–13 victory.

I'll bet fans wonder what the huddle is like after someone commits a dumb-ass foul like Mike did. Well, Mike felt like crap, I can tell you that. But for everyone else the goal is to get the guy's head back in the game. So we didn't scream at him, we didn't act all defeated. In those situations you watch everyone's back, you pull together. You know Mike's going to hear about that play all week from the coaches and the press, so why let it prevent you from getting the job done on the field? Besides, there are a million little things that happen in a game that get you to that point, so where do you start laying the blame? You definitely don't start in the huddle.

Next up were the Steelers, and—what else?—it's another nail-biter. It was 20–20 at the end of regulation, which was not good news for us. Jerome Bettis was on top of his game that day, and he ran it down our throats in OT. My shoulder was killing me at this point, and I was in constant pain.

We lost to the Redskins and Saints after that, and in the New Orleans game my shoulder hurt so badly I literally couldn't put my hand down to get into my stance. The last three games, in fact—we finished the season with a comeback win over the Falcons—I don't think I played that much. It's amazing that we won that final game, come to think of it. In the locker room beforehand, everyone was ready to pack up their shit and go home. The Falcons were 7–8 going in after starting 1–7, so they were red-hot.

Mike Caldwell redeemed himself in this game when he made a great play on Jamal Anderson to get us the ball back for our winning drive. Our defense kept Atlanta out of the end zone three times late to preserve a 29–26 win, just our fourth of the season. After the game, no one sat around reminiscing. There was no group therapy. No one had any profound reflections on a 4–12 season. We just got the hell out of there.

What a weird year it was, 1997. In eleven of our sixteen games, the outcome was in doubt right until the final possession. We won four of those contests and lost seven. We did not have a single easy victory. Even when we outplayed our opponents, we managed to open the door for them to come back. The players were exhausted, the coaches were exhausted, and the fans were exhausted. Had we gone 12–4, it would have been what they call a "good tired." But there was nothing good about how we felt that day.

We lost in every way imaginable. This qualifies me to answer a question players get asked fairly often: Would you rather lose a close game that turns on a single play, or lose a blowout? My answer is that a loss is a loss, so the score is unimportant. The better question is, Would you rather lose a game when you play your best or when you've given up and you're half-assing it? The answer to that question is that you want to play your absolute best—or at least try your hardest—in a loss. It might be more disappointing, but at least you're likely to learn something from the experience. You can assess a loss more accurately if everyone plays their heart out, and makes the necessary adjustments.

Someone observed after the Atlanta game that we should consider our Week 17 win a silver lining in a season of anguish. That may be. But as if to prove that every silver lining is surrounded by a dark cloud, the victory cost us the first pick in the draft. Indianapolis finished 3–13 and selected Peyton Manning.

As disappointing as my second season for the Cardinals was, it was an All-Pro campaign compared to what was going on in my personal life. The business I had started in 1996, Juggernaut Entertainment, was doing terribly. It was hemorraging money with no end in sight. We had gotten it off the ground, but we lacked the experience to know what to do next.

Athletes like to say they can shut out all the off-the-field stuff, but the fact is that problems like these are constant distractions, and they don't get better if you ignore them. You don't have to have perfect harmony in your life to play great football, but you do have to have some semblance of order to enable you to concentrate on your profession. I didn't realize it at the time, but I had broken my own golden rule: *If it doesn't improve or enhance your ability to play football, don't do it.*

It was also during this time that I started to become aware that my financial guy, Don Lukens, was stealing from me like a motherfucker. I could have kicked myself. Don had called me out of the blue during rookie camp in 1996 and said, "Why don't you and your friends come out here to LA?" He wanted to pitch me on financial and estate planning, and I figured *Why not take a free trip?* I never intended to sign with Don, but once I got out there he was so big, and showed me so much wealth, I was overwhelmed. I wanted to be successful. I wanted to have this lifestyle. I was young and naive and no one was there to advise me. I figured this guy looked the part, so he must be legit. But I was sadly mistaken. It was all a mirage created to deceive me. I was lucky. Don broke some of his other clients. I was one of the first people to get suspicious, so I still had plenty left. He ended up doing time, but not enough to make up for what he did.

Some bad shit, right? Well, that wasn't the half of it.

I was embroiled in a court battle over the status of my son, Jordan, who I love so much. This brought up emotions I had never dealt with in my life, and it made me crazy. I had always envisioned a form of joint custody where I was involved in raising the child, not just supporting him. I told Jayna that together we could provide everything he needed, and initially she agreed. But things got volatile and eventually turned ugly.

I think Jordan's mother believed I would eventually marry her, and when it became clear that this was not going to happen she sued for custody. I didn't realize until we started hiring lawyers and getting into this fight how draining it would be. I had never dealt with anything like this, and it just wore me out. I had to fly up to Champaign several times during the 1997 season. It was utter madness.

At one of the hearings, I saw my father cry for the first time. The other side was trying to paint me as a real bad guy, and dragging the family's name through the mud. After all he had accomplished, after all he had done to make sure his family was raised right, it was incredibly painful to see Henry suffer in this way.

For a while I tried to lose myself in the women and the celebrity status I now had. I was a real playboy, and I would fly out to the coast and do the whole party thing, with Tommy Bennett, my one close friend on the team. I have never been a party guy in the sense that I drank alcohol or did drugs. But I had definitely developed an appetite for women. In college I began to realize that I was the type of guy women really responded to, and I took advantage of that the way you would expect a young man to—especially a young man who hadn't given women a second thought in high school. As a professional athlete, I had a much higher profile, which increased both the range and quality of women available, plus I now had the financial wherewithal to go anywhere or do anything I wanted.

Let me tell you, for a young man of twenty-three, that's the definition of power. You can feel it coursing through you when there are females in the room, and other people can feel it, too. For a while I really got off on manipulating people, which isn't my personality at all. All my life people had been saying they saw something special in me, and it finally occurred to me that I could dangle that thing like bait to attract women. I knew exactly what to say, exactly what ladies wanted to hear. They were responding to my light, my potential, my good-boy image, and I was playing them. All I wanted was pleasure, and I knew exactly how to get it.

It was like I'd stepped over to the dark side, testing the limits of my power, totally uninterested in the end result or the damage it would cause. I was having fun, but I was toying with the trust and emotions of a lot of good people, and causing a lot of tears and heartache. These were doctors, lawyers, models, all very upstanding women. It was intense. I was seeing a lot of women at the same time.

Eventually, though, it just crashed down on me. It was a case of absolute power corrupting absolutely. And added to all the other *oh-shit* situations in my life and my career, this just sent me right to the bottom. I shut down. I was like, *God, get me out of this and I'll never do it again.* I couldn't talk to anyone. I would go for weeks without having a real conversation. When I thought about all this horrible stuff going on in my life, I would become almost catatonic.

Compounding the problem was that my on-again, off-again relationship with the one person who really understood the nature of my being, was off-again during most of this turmoil. I met Quiana Whittler at the University of Illinois, and we dated for a good portion of the next seven years. We went through a lot together, and there was even a time where we discussed the possibility of marriage. Quiana was such a loving person, so honest and nurturing, that in the end I felt I just couldn't do that to her.

You have to understand were I'm coming from. To me, the gold standard of marriage is what my parents have. When my father looks at my mother, it's like he's seeing her for the first time—*every* time. Well, I want to feel the same way about the woman *I* marry. And during all those years Quiana and I were together, there were always three major issues that prevented that from happening.

The first was that I had a wandering eye. I was always curious about what other women would be like, and that created a lot of conflict within me. How, I wondered, could I feel so strongly about Quiana yet still have these feelings for women I hardly knew? The second was that I sensed there was this whole wide world out there I needed to explore, and I did not see her being a partner in that experience. I loved meeting new people, and I was certain that these situations would lead me into cheating. So again, as I looked forward, I didn't trust myself to maintain the relationship.

The third issue was about football. There was no way I could comprehend being married and playing football at the same time. I could not envision bringing marriage into my football, or football into my marriage. I know other guys have pulled it off, but with the way I approach the game, it was not going to work. My commitment to football superceded my commitment to Quiana, and regardless of how long we were together, this never changed. Everything I had I gave to my sport, and that didn't leave much for her. To Quiana's credit, she refused to accept me on those terms, but she was a patient woman who was willing to put her life on hold until I changed.

Unfortunately, I never gave Quiana the commitment and honesty she was looking for, and it was unfair to ask someone to wait around

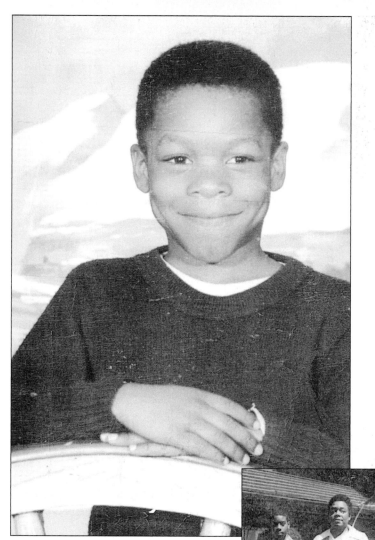

Me at age five: young, handsome and already the captain of my own destiny. (Courtesy of the Rice family)

Henry Rice unleashes his sons on an unsuspecting world. Check out those pants! (Courtesy of the Rice family)

My folks, Henry and Evelyn Rice. (Courtesy of the Rice family)

The Rice girls circa 1995: Yashia, Tonica, Nianna, and Sonya. They hate this picture. (Courtesy of the Rice family)

Mt. Carmel's football brain trust, Frank and Dave Lenti, hug their father, Frank Sr., after we beat Fenwich 27-0 in the 1991 state playoffs. (Courtesy Mt. Carmel Academy)

The University of Illinois's Mt. Carmel connection: Pete Gabrione, Bobby Sanders, Charles Edwards, Jasper Strong, Toriano Woods, Ola Ali, Matt Cushing and me. (Courtesy University of Illinois; photographer Mark Jones)

The famous "Ninja Turtles" defense. That's me on the left, coming out of my shell

(Courtesy Mt. Carmel Academy)

Lou Tepper's 1994 linebacking corps: Kevin Hardy, Dana Howard and me; John Holecek takes a knee. (Courtesy University of Illinois; photographer Mark Jones)

Yours truly about to drop Scott Dreisbach of Michigan. I finished my college career with 44.5 sacks. (Courtesy University of Illinois; photographer Mark Jones)

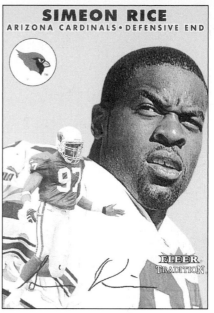

SIMEON RICE
ARIZONA CARDINALS • DEFENSIVE END

FLEER
TRADITION

My man, Ty Douthard, in action. (Courtesy University of Illinois; photographer Mark Jones)

As an aficionado of football cards, I think this is one of my best. I like the old-school feel.

One-on-one basketball is still a major part of my conditioning program.

(Courtesy Cliff Welch/CliffWelchPhotography.com)

until I could. For years, I tried to rationalize that this type of situation was what a man of the world, a football star, should expect. (My childhood role models were James Bond and the Fonz, so I wasn't exactly evolved in this department.) Eventually, it got to the point where I couldn't even bullshit *myself* anymore. I felt I was living a lie, stringing Quiana along, and that felt improper to me. We both just needed to grow, and we respected each other enough to let go.

As for the myth of the troubled athlete finding refuge and fellowship in the locker room, well, it's just that: a myth. The last thing I wanted to do was engage my teammates. I got through the practices and played my heart out during the games, but I was totally detached from the team itself. There was one stretch where I don't think I uttered a word for an entire month. When things started to go against the Cardinals, Joe Greene gave a speech criticizing the lack of communication on the club. Joe, who wasn't exactly the great communicator himself, made this statement in a general way, but everyone knew he was talking to me. At that point, I felt like everything in my life was out of control.

Joe was a good man. And despite our differences over the years, I know he was just trying to draw me out. He knew there was something serious going on in my personal life, but he didn't know what. Maybe he thought I would open up to him, or that someone else would clue him in that I was embroiled in a custody battle, or that my accountant was ripping me off, or that my record business was in the toilet. But that wasn't going to happen. Tommy was the only player who knew what was happening, and I only told him a fraction of it. And Tommy wasn't going to say anything anyway.

The only time I felt like I could think with any clarity was when I was with Ina. I would come home, she would be there, we would hang together and fool around, and I would forget my troubles for an hour or two. Ina was an English mastiff puppy.

The lesson of 1997 for me was that someone who comes from stability, someone who functions best when his life has some semblance of order, cannot excel in an environment of personal havoc and disorder. I didn't believe it until I lived it, because there are a handful of athletes who seem to thrive under these conditions. Look at Deion Sanders. Every day in that man's life was crazy, yet he was at his best on and off the field without fail. I had always heard that "personal problems" could turn an All-Star into a benchwarmer in one season, but I never appreciated how true this was until my second-year struggles.

Why did I choose this path? I have a couple of theories. There's the obvious one, which is that I was just trying to drown out my other sorrows in female flesh. But I must say that there was also a part of me that was simply interested in seeing how far I could go, how much I could get away with. That's my nature, after all. When I extend my performance to its limit, I always try to go a little farther. If I make two great new moves in a game, the next game I see what happens when I combine them. Sometimes it works and sometimes it doesn't. But the process is very intriguing to me regardless of the outcome.

Ah, but the trick is to push that envelope while staying within your game—doing what you already do well, while exploring new ground a little bit at a time. Looking back, my insatiable quest for off-field conquests in 1997 was very much within my personality. The problem was that I had less-than-honorable intentions, and that's not who I am at all. It was a game to me, and in this case I ended up on the losing end. Unfortunately, so did a lot of people I hurt.

After that year, I swore off women. At least I swore off relationships. I needed to slow down and assess my life. Tommy and I stopped flying to LA on Mondays, and stopped going to parties together. And I decided to pull the plug on Juggernaut Entertainment.

Finally, I had to be honest enough to recognize that, one way or another, all of the bullshit that had come into my life was bullshit I had allowed in through my actions or inactions. I needed to refocus myself on football.

And I did. After the season, everyone wondered whether I would play basketball again, and I made it clear that I wouldn't. That was not as easy a choice as you might think, because there were some scouts who said I had a shot at making an NBA roster. That was tempting, but I wasn't about to start the whole cycle of distractions again. I kept telling myself, *You're building a Hall of Fame football career. That's the goal now. Stay on track. Live the dream.*

Actually, that was the easy part. Honestly, the women part was something with which I continued to struggle. It was difficult for me to limit my entanglements. I wasn't satisfied with meaningless encounters; I always felt compelled to invest some emotion in what I was doing.

One of the few positive developments during the 1997 season was that Tommy cracked the starting lineup. He was a big defensive back out of UCLA whom the Cardinals had signed as a free agent after the 1996 draft. Tommy made the roster that summer and played great on special teams. The two of us were really tight—as tight as I was with my childhood friends. I can't even begin to tell you how close we were—like brothers. We had some good times, but as I was to discover, football friendships are radically different than you think they are.

Tommy was a physical pass defender whose cognitive skills helped him make big plays. It looked like he was going to have a nice career. He certainly spent money like he was expecting to be around for a while. He was making damn near the minimum, and by the end of the season he'd be flat broke. He didn't drink and didn't get wasted when he was with me, but I saw some things that worried me he might be a little self-destructive. Tommy didn't want to hear about it, though. He never wanted help, never wanted anything he thought was a handout, never had any humility. People were always surprised how intelligent Tommy was, but he could be stupid as hell sometimes.

In 1998 the Cardinals drafted Pat Tillman, and in 1999 they moved him into Tommy's slot. Tommy was the better player in camp, but the Cardinals wanted Pat in that spot. Basically, they banished my friend to the bench without a decent explanation, and he didn't know how to handle it. This is when his self-destructive tendencies came out. He started hanging with a different crowd and got into all types of shit. By the 2000 season Tommy was out of the league and he had severed our relationship. I remember telling Bennie Morrow, "When the shit hits for Tommy, he's going to realize I was the best friend he ever had. I just hope he still believes I'll always be there for him."

In the spring of 2004, a day after Pat Tillman was killed in Afghanistan, I heard from Tommy. After he left the Cardinals he wouldn't return my calls. I contacted his mother and she said he was doing badly, but wouldn't say much more. In all the years since, I had only talked to him once. Tommy had hit rock bottom and was reaching out for help. He was in Phoenix, he was hungry, and he needed something to eat. I didn't know how to handle it—he was the first friend I've had who ended up on the street.

The more I thought about it, the more I got pissed. I was pissed at Tommy, because he'd been so resistant to asking for help and now he was damn near beyond help. I knew the deeper I got involved in helping him, the more I would expose my life to whatever or whoever had helped bring him down. You'd think a famous athlete with money in the bank could reach out in these situations without hesitation, but just the opposite is true. And that's incredibly frustrating.

I was also pissed at the NFL. The league positions itself as the ultimate achievement for a football player, but it sells the dream without revealing the consequences. Like just about everything else in pro football, there's a lot of illusion. Obviously, if you get cut in high school or college or even in a pro camp, that's one thing. If you can't play, that's life. You move on. Once you make it to the NFL, there are all kinds of programs to make sure you have your shit together and understand your responsibilities, but that's more for the protection of the league and the teams than the players themselves.

When players leave football, it's rarely on good terms, and it's at a time when they are confused and angry and vulnerable. They may be suffering from low self-esteem. They may also be in physical pain, because often it's an injury that hastens their departure from the game. It's not a pretty picture, and it's no way to start a new career. If ever there were a perfect chance for the NFL to establish a program, it would be at this point. I'm still not sure exactly what happened to Tommy, but he was focused and intelligent, and unquestionably an asset to society. If he'd had the benefit of some kind of "football aftercare" or had a debriefing or a reentry program or something, things might have turned out differently for him and a lot of other guys I've heard about in similar circumstances.

Opponents of a plan like this would probably say that the league cycles through too many players each year, and that the guys who drift off are "fringe" athletes anyway. I may not understand the economics or the organizational hurdles involved, but I do know a couple of things about NFL players. Number one, every man in the NFL is an extraordinary human being. Each possesses the skills and desire to beat out hundreds of other guys who would give their left nut to play one down in the pros. So the idea that a so-called fringe athlete isn't worth the effort—or hell, that any human being isn't worth the effort—is a load of crap. Number two, pro football players may go down hard, but if you get them on their feet they'll do the rest. This is true on the field, and it's true after they've hung up their uniforms.

By the way, the superstars aren't immune to the problems that plague ex-football-players. Take Mike Webster, the anchor of the Steelers' offensive line during the 1970s. He played in four Super Bowls for Pittsburgh and went into the Hall of Fame during the 1997 season. He was a tough little guy who became a great player. Joe Greene used to beat the shit out of him in practice for years, and then one day he figured out how to turn the tables on Joe, and now Webster's a football immortal.

Well, not really, because Mike Webster is dead. He never got his life together after football. He drifted away from his family, he was arrested for forging prescriptions for drugs to treat injuries he received in the NFL, and two years after he was inducted into Canton he was found living on the streets. A year after that he passed away, at age fifty.

My Hall of Fame career, meanwhile, needed to get back on track. After a great rookie season and a troubled second year, I knew heading into 1998 that all eyes were upon me. The troubles of 1997 weren't all behind me yet, but I had taken positive steps to eliminate them, or at least bring them under control. The most important thing I did between the two seasons was get in touch with my spiritual side. I'm not talking about becoming a born-again or anything like that, but I was raised with strong Christian values and it seemed like a good idea to revisit them. Not to sermonize, but there is a lot to say for having stability in your life, and in my case all I had to do was return to the basics of my upbringing to find a more certain path.

I saw 1998 as the year I would emerge as a recognized All-Pro-caliber player. I'd given the league flashes, and now the challenge was to deliver a season of sustained brilliance. As for the Cardinals, in my mind I had no doubt about what our goal was for 1998: We were going to stay healthy, we were going to make plays, we were going to ambush the teams that didn't take us seriously, and we were going to make the playoffs.

For me, the process began in February. After giving my shoulder the rest it needed, I spent the next several months working out like a madman. This is when I developed the routine I still follow today: a program of weight training, agility exercises, road work—often in the mountains outside Phoenix—and some basketball.

Nothing monumental happened during this time, yet I had the sense that I'd crossed into a new phase of my life in terms of maturity. I really felt like a professional, like football was my job. I got better at cutting out distractions, and developed a better radar for looming troubles. I totally accepted the fact that my troubles weren't random occurrences that had befallen me; in one way or another, I had initiated all of them. I resisted the temptation to say, *Well, I just had a run of bad luck,* and found that taking responsibility actually gave me a better sense of control in my life—something that had been sorely lacking. Also, I learned how to draw strength from my friends and my family. In short, I was experiencing a kind of harmony. It made the prospect of a new season really enjoyable.

With two years under my belt, I could look around the locker room and assess our talent with some degree of accuracy, and what I saw I liked. Jake Plummer had a feel for the NFL, and obviously he had talent. Rob Moore, whom Arizona had acquired from the Jets the year before I joined the team, was coming off a league-leading season as a receiver, and Larry Centers was a great pass catcher out of the backfield. We had picked up another ex-Jet, Adrian Murrell, a guy with a knack for breaking off big runs, and signed Mario Bates, a short-yardage runner, from the Saints. We also drafted Michael Pittman, a talented dude out of Fresno State.

The offensive line had been a weak point in 1997. Opposing teams had sacked our quarterback more than seventy times. We picked up Lester Holmes, a solid blocker from the Raiders, and we already had Lomas Brown, who never gave up a sack while I was on the Cardinals. We also had a new offensive coordinator, Marc Trestman, who was installing a West Coast Offense to make better use of Jake's mobility, so there was no way he was going to get hammered the way he had in his rookie year.

Let me just interject that it's all good to put in a new scheme, but it's never really about the scheme. That's just an illusion; it makes it seem like coaches have some mystical understanding of the game that they don't. The execution of the scheme is everything. If you've got guys who can execute, I don't care if you're running the wishbone or the flying wedge, it's going to be effective. You can be a genius in the West Coast Offense, but if you don't have the personnel, you end up looking like a dunce. Luckily, we had the athletes to make this system work, so the fans had a legitimate reason to be excited about our "new look" on offense.

The defense, however, was Arizona's true strength in 1998. The team's first-round pick was Andre Wadsworth out of Florida State. The Cardinals were holding the second spot in the draft, which was going to be used on either Peyton Manning or Ryan Leaf, and since we had Plummer we swapped picks with the Chargers, who were sitting at three. We got a second-round pick, which we used on Corey Chavous, plus we got Patrick Sapp (no relation to Warren) and Eric Metcalf, who was no longer a top-tier receiver but was a very good return guy. Considering what happened to Leaf, I'd say we got the better of that trade.

Like me, Andre came into camp after a long holdout. So for most of the summer you heard how good he was, and how he could be as good or better than me. I may have come to the Cardinals with higher expec-tations, but because of these comparisons Andre came in with a lot more hype. I know the team was saying *Andre might be better than Simeon* to get fans excited about the coming season, but it did piss me off a little. This was my third season, I was a young guy, and they made it seem as if I was already losing a step! In my mind, I was thinking that the league didn't fully appreciate just how fast I was. I honestly saw myself as being un-stoppable. So even though the comparison wasn't meant as a slap in the face, I took it that way to give myself a little extra incentive. If Andre came out with a blast like I had in 1996, then more power to him. We would be that much better.

Andre would team up with me and Eric Swann and Mark Smith, a second-year man out of Auburn who was ready to have a big year. It was not an exaggeration to say we had the best defensive line in the confer-ence, if not the entire NFL. We were solid at linebacker with Jamir Miller and Rockin' Ron McKinnon. We also added two promising young guys to our defensive backfield in Chavous and Tillman. They had Aeneas Williams to show them the ropes. The stars were aligned, and the defense was ready to sow its oats.

Head Coach Vince Tobin seemed genuinely excited, too. He knew knew our 4–12 record could have been 7–9 just by reversing the overtime losses. He also knew our division was weak. The Redskins, Giants, and Eagles were shaky at quarterback, and even though the Cowboys still had their big-name stars, the unheralded guys who had won games for them in the trenches were old, injured, or just gone. Hall of Famers are nice to have at the skill positions, and Dallas had Troy Aikman, Emmitt Smith, and Michael Irvin. But when the O-line and D-line start to go, that puts a lot of pressure on your so-called marquee players. We still figured to have trouble with the Cowboys, however, because they had Deion Sanders and Darren Woodson in coverage. They were the thorn in our side, no doubt about it.

I definitely had a sense that summer that everything was finally falling into place. I can only speak for myself, but I had a very strong feeling that I was in the right place at the right time. My goal as a player was to take this franchise that had taken me, turn its fortunes around, and help boost it to the next level.

As a team we definitely knew what we had going. And we knew what we had to do. We had to find a way to win the close games in 1998. We had to avoid giving up points early, which forced our offense to play catch-up. The defense was really, really strong, but to make that advantage work, we had to dominate opponents and keep them off the scoreboard until the offense scored.

Jake Plummer was good in the clutch, which gave the guys a lot of confidence. He was being compared to Joe Montana, but it was a little early to draw any serious parallels. The NFL likes to build stories around its young stars, to create a veneer of greatness. A lot of people felt it was unwise to put that kind of pressure on a young guy, but what fans need to know is that players rarely buy in to the kind of stories the league manufactures. Don't get me wrong—it's nice to get the added attention, and if there's a soup commercial or a deodorant commercial in it for you, God bless. But as soon as you actually start believing your own buildup, you're asking for trouble.

The NFL is the most successful marketing entity in professional sports. They know how to create a story, how to tell it, and how to make sure people hear it. We as players benefit from this kind of marketing—it generates revenue for the league, and we share in that. And I have to say, the league knows its audience. In Plummer's case, comparing him to

Montana touches on an underlying theme that football fans really enjoy. They're not saying Jake Plummer is the "next" Joe Montana; probably no one will be. What the story promotes is this idea that a successful player doesn't have to possess great physical attributes or a have a certain football pedigree (like Peyton Manning, who came into the league that year). What he lacks in God-given ability he can make up for with a blue-collar, lunch-bucket, nose-to-the-grindstone work ethic that can elevate him to championship status.

Isn't that just a different spin on the American Dream? I think it is. And for all those millions of fans out there who never had a silver spoon in their mouth, doesn't Jake the Snake embody a lot of who they are and what they hope to be? Your average man on the street isn't a superstar. He's the guy who doesn't have all the talent, all the skill, all the technique. He goes out every day and works with what he's got, and he makes it, sometimes in the face of insurmountable odds. That's a powerful message to send out every Sunday—a big connection you make with your fans. It may reduce football players to cartoon-character status, but the NFL knows if you give people what they want they'll keep coming back for more.

Is it fair to Jake Plummer? Dumb question. Life isn't fair. Is it accurate? Well, Jake did (and does) share some of those intangible attributes with Joe Montana. They have that same glint in their eye that gives you hope when another quarterback might not. To see that in a young player is a very exciting thing. It also fits very neatly into the league's marketing plan. Just when it's no longer cool to break out your number 16 San Francisco jersey, there's a number 16 Cardinals jersey on sale for $89.95. For the people who had been living vicariously through Joe and his jersey, now they can get their rocks off wearing Jake's stuff.

One reason players don't put too much stock in the league's image buildup is that the same powers-that-be can also start a campaign to tear a player down. For example, the David and Goliath story is a particular favorite of the league, and they use it on a lot of different levels. It's great to be David, but what happens if you're Goliath? That sucks. You can quickly find yourself in a no-win situation. If you are successful, you merely support the image of yourself as a big, bad monster. And if you lose, you look like an asshole who got what was coming to you.

Also, if you start believing the image football is creating for you, you run the risk of losing who you are. If you never live up to your hype, you'll think of yourself as a failure. If you achieve what was predicted for you, who's to say you couldn't have achieved more?

The networks, of course, are enthusiastic partners in this process. They take the ball from the NFL and run with it. In fact, they are under even more pressure to create stories, because they are often competing against one another for viewers. In the case of ESPN, the relationship is even trickier, because they are supposedly reporting hard news, too. Now, how can you create and perpetuate semifictional stories for the NFL and report NFL news without a conflict of interest, or at least a credibility issue? The answer is you can't. There is a saying around the league that ESPN takes great pride in turning a nobody into a some-body, and greater pride into turning a somebody into a nobody. More on this later.

An even weirder situation exists with *NFL Insider,* which is owned by NFL Properties. In general, it's a good magazine that profiles players and gives fans some perspective on the game. But there is a lot of news and opinion in the publication, as well. In 2001, *NFL Insider* wrote about me and stated that I had turned down a huge offer from the Jets, and that I would not have signed the same deal with the Bears that I had signed with Tampa Bay. Well, A) I never talked to the Jets, and B) I most certainly would have signed with the Bears for the same money and terms I did with the Bucs. Obviously, the writer never checked these facts with me. But there they are in print, for all the world to see. Normally, I would just laugh this off. Writers get their facts mixed up, or they have to make deadlines, or they just don't do the legwork. But this is an NFL publication, so presumably, someone from the NFL is checking the facts or at least approving the copy. My question then is: Was this Simeon Rice item NFL *news* or NFL *entertainment*?

The players all know the bottom line: Football may be larger than life when you're watching from the stands or sitting in your living room, but down on the field it's the same game you played in your yard as a kid. The offense tries to move the ball and the defense tries to stop it. Remembering this helps you stay grounded when you're surrounded by layer upon layer of illusion. This makes it a little easier to write your own story—and to ignore what they say on TV or write in the papers about you. Tony Dungy, who coached the Buccaneers my first year with them, put it very succinctly. He would throw everyone but the players out of the dressing room, slam the door, and say, "The only thing that matters at this point in time is the men in this room. We are the authors of this book— everybody else is just writing columns and filing stories along the way."

The story of the 1998 Cardinals began in Dallas. Call it a measuring stick, call it a grudge match, call it whatever, but it was a challenge we welcomed. The Cowboys never took the Cardinals seriously, and this literally dated back decades. I had played them four times and lost three times, and I couldn't stand those guys. They were so smug when it came to us. We would hear stories from their camp about how they didn't even practice hard before a Cardinals game. It was like an off week for them. Well, that was like someone calling you a punk.

Before I came into the league, I wasn't sure how I would react to situations like this, where one team had a tradition of beating the other. I figured, *Those were some other guys, not me. It's a new day, a new game.* Once I arrived in Arizona, that turned out to be the case. Except for this one exception. I had a big Cardinal head on my helmet now, and it made me despise the Cowboys. The trap you fall into, however, is feeling like you are part of a losing tradition. So my approach was, *Simeon Rice is on the scene, and my job is to change that.*

My approach didn't matter much on this day, because the Cowboys beat our asses 38–10. That was a lesson for us, a wake-up call. As good as we thought we were, this team dominated us in every facet of the game. Everything we planned went awry. Aikman, Smith, and Irvin was not a cliché—they were real guys who made real plays. The only good things I can remember from this game are that my friend Tommy Bennett made a nice interception and run, and that we could look forward to a second crack at the Cowboys, since they were in our division.

Week 2 found us in Seattle. The Seahawks picked off a couple of Jake Plummer's passes early and ran them back for TDs, and the game was all but lost before halftime. The offense never got it going, which was cause for concern. But we knew we could afford to be patient with it, because our defense was looking very tight. We just hoped the offense would catch fire sooner rather than later.

We showed just how good our defense was a week later, on a Sunday-night game against the Eagles. I sacked their quarterback, Rodney Peete, twice, and almost had him four or five other times. They couldn't do squat against us. Only problem was, we couldn't do squat against them, either. The game was scoreless in the fourth quarter, and then we traded field goals.

The pivotal play came when Ron McKinnon stripped Peete. The ball was loose, and there were two Eagles between me and the ball. I already had a head of steam, so I just basically bowled them over and scooped it up. I wanted a touchdown badly, but I was pretty exhausted at that point and someone ran me down after about 10 yards. We scored right after that and added a second TD for a 17–3 win.

Having a game like I did against the Eagles is a blast. When you put the QB on his ass over and over again, it not only means you're dominating the man in front of you, but also means you've disrupted your opponent's basic blocking scheme. From the point they realize that, it becomes a crazy, high-speed chess match. They adjust, I anticipate their adjustment and do something they're not expecting, they try to stop that, I go back to the first thing I did, and so on and so forth. This process is a fundamental aspect of every sport, but in football it plays out at an extremely rapid pace. Sometimes you actually get inside the offensive line coach's head, and you can guess everything he's about to do. When that happens they have to double- or triple-team you on every play or you'll bleed them to death.

We had our first win, our defense had given our future opponents plenty of interesting film to watch, and even though the offense was still sluggish, Adrian Murrell had played the kind of game we all expected, so everything about the Philly game was encouraging.

We traveled to St. Louis for a Week 4 matchup with the Rams, where I did battle with Orlando Pace, their great young left tackle. This was a nice win for us. We had them on the ropes in the first half, but Eric Swann got into a skirmish and kicked some guy. He got thrown out and the Rams got a first down and scored to keep the game close.

There is never a situation where you want to take a penalty like that. Contrary to what some fans might think, the other team doesn't think you're sending a message. They just think you can't control yourself, which is a weakness that can be exploited. You give them a first down, better field position, more confidence—and you might lose a key player, too. I've only been whistled once for this type of flagrant violation as a pro, and sure enough it cost my team a touchdown. In a playoff game, no less.

Against the Rams, Plummer and Murrell were moving the sticks and the defense was doing its job, but the game was still tied 17–17 in the fourth quarter. It turned for us on a pass interference call, which set up Joe Nedney's winning field goal. We would win a lot of close ones in 1998, and our kicking game would be a crucial component.

We had problems again in the first half of our next game, against the Oakland Raiders. We turned the ball over three times in the second quarter, including a horrible throw Jake made that Charles Woodson picked off in the flat and ran back for a score. We basically gave the Raiders 17 free points. It's a matter of pride for a defense to hold the other team after a turnover, to stop the bleeding, as it were. But honestly, when you get three bunched together like that, you can't helping thinking, *C'mon, offense, cut it out and play football!*

Believe it or not, a turn of events like this rarely causes friction between the offense and defense. They don't need us to let them know they're stinking it up; they're already thinking the same thing. The same is true when the defense gives up a bunch of big plays. You get angry, but you get angry as a team. I've always looked at it that way. If you're wearing the same uniform, you're in this thing together. Together you stand or together you fall. Besides, if someone really needs to be singled out, then that's the coaches' job. They're paid to get up in your face, if that's what it takes.

Although we lost the Raider game, it didn't turn into a blowout, like a lot of games do when one team puts points on the board fast. I'm not a believer in the concept of an "encouraging loss," because losses are always discouraging. But here was a game we could at least take something positive from. The Raiders spent thirty minutes trying to put us away, and we wouldn't let them. At the end of the game, they were up 23–20 and trying to run out the clock. Andre Wadsworth made a huge play to cause a fumble and get us the ball back. Plummer moved us down the field, into Nedney's field-goal range, but Tobin decided to get us in better position and called a pass to Eric Metcalf, who was supposed to catch the ball and get out of bounds. The Raiders allowed him to catch it, but then pulled him down in bounds. We were out of time-outs, so that was the game.

In those situations, I'm watching the game as a Cardinals fan, like everyone else. We were really excited to have a shot at winning or tying, and I really wanted us to score a touchdown. But when it got down to the nitty-gritty and we didn't try the field goal, I was like, *Oh no! What is Vince doing? You don't flirt with disaster like that!*

We did not want to start the season 2–3, but here we were with a losing record based on a game we definitely should have won. That extra W can be precious. Even though I had yet to be in playoff contention as a pro, I'd seen it happen with the Bears when I was a kid. One year they missed the playoffs by one win. Another time, when I was in high school, they made the playoffs on the last Sunday as the wild card.

Speaking of the Bears, they were the team we had to beat the following week. They were 1–4, but they had been in every game, so we took them seriously. We won 20–7 on a day when our inside linebacker, Rockin' Ron McKinnon, went crazy. He was in the zone. He could have had five interceptions, maybe more. He ended up with three, plus a fumble. It felt so good to see Ron have a game like that. He is one of the best people you could ever hope to be around. He was a tremendous teammate, gave you everything he had. Ron was floating on air that day, and it was great to see.

I should say that whenever a defensive player puts up interception numbers like that, educated fans should be aware of what's happening on the line in front of them. There is a direct connection between the game the pass rusher is having and the number of interception possibilities—particularly those that come a DB's way. Against the Bears, Eric Swann had an absolute beast of a game. He won the battle in the trenches single-handedly. He was so dominant that I had no choice but to take a backseat to him. I felt like a spectator at times. I remember coming back to the huddle thinking, *Wow, this dude is good.*

Next stop was the Meadowlands, where we had a chance to put the Giants in a permanent hole. Although they had gone 10–5–1 the year before and made the playoffs, they weren't as good as the Cardinals on paper. But we still had to take care of business on the field if we wanted a shot at the division title. Kent Graham was their starting QB, and it was nice to see him get another chance to start. The Giants' old starter, Dave Brown, was now our backup.

The Giants always had a solid defense, and on this day they made the plays and we didn't. They won 34–7, which made it fourteen losses in our last fifteen visits to Giants Stadium. Intellectually, you know that one game in one season has nothing to with games stretching way back into the 1980s. Intellectually, you know that the failures of the old players don't apply to you. But it's impossible to ignore a statistic like that. All week long, you get questions about it. All week long you read about it.

This is what I was saying about the Cowboys. Even though, among the Cardinal players and coaches, we talk about a history of losing in the context of a new beginning, a new mentality, a new mind-set, of turning the trend around, I think you are subconsciously acknowledging it, and somewhere I'm sure it lodges in the back of your mind. Seriously, when you say to yourself, *Okay, we're going out today and we're going to beat the odds,* doesn't that mean deep down you feel the odds are against you? And by extension, doesn't that mean you are connecting yourself to all the retired dudes who lost games when you were a kid?

It's an interesting question, though not one that NFL players care to dwell on. It's fun to go out and make history, but you don't want to believe that history is against you. You'd rather just deal with the opponent you're facing on the field.

We had a bye week in the schedule, which gave us a chance to get healthy before taking on the Detroit Lions. You definitely need a week of rest before playing against Barry Sanders. He's extremely hard to tackle—in that respect one of the best who has ever played the game. I'm probably the only defensive end in football who has ever run him down.

I had a hell of a game against the Lions. I was on top of their quarterbacks, Charlie Batch and Frank Reich, all day. Batch got the ball into our end of the field pretty consistently, but whenever the Lions got close we stalled them with an interception or a big third-down play. The Lions, meanwhile, were doing the same thing to us, keeping us off the board earlier. This was starting to look like an ugly game when Jake Plummer hit Rob Moore with a long TD pass to put us up 14–9.

The Lions came back and scored a touchdown, and Bobby Ross called for a 2-point conversion. Everyone in the building knew Sanders was getting the ball, but we managed to keep him out of the end zone to keep the score 15–14 instead of 17–14. We came back and Nedney kicked a field goal to give us a 17–15 lead, then Mark Smith sacked Reich to cause a fumble that our linebacker Tony McCombs recovered to ice the game.

I love a good goal-line stand, and the play we made against Barry set the tone for us the rest of the year. We knew we could be a dominant defensive line, and now the rest of the league knew it, too, because that play was aired over and over on all the highlight shows. To the average fan, it looked like Barry just couldn't get into the end zone. To players and coaches, it looked like the Cardinals had become a disciplined team that was confident enough to plug the gaps and make plays with their backs against the wall. And this was definitely the case. We were coming together.

The Washington Redskins were our next opponent. They were having a tough year, much like the Lions, so we knew we could wear them down and beat them if the game got close. And it did. Nedney won it for us again with a late field goal. Now, I know I said I watch these games like a fan, but that doesn't mean I'd like to see our team win nail-biters every week. Given the choice, anyone with half a brain in the NFL would rather crush an opponent than beat them in the closing seconds. Although you take a win any way you can get it.

This marked the second straight week I recorded two sacks, and I had a lot of tackles, too. I like to think of each sack as an individual masterpiece, a work of art where everything comes together in just the right way. But the truth is, the ones I get against bad teams, like the 1998 Lions and Redskins, are a lot easier to get than the ones against good offenses.

I didn't have too much time to pat myself on the back, because the Cowboys were coming up. This time we had a chance to tie them for the division lead, but again it was a disaster. Troy Aikman put the ball in the end zone on us four times in five series in the first half, and we didn't regroup until the second half, when it was too late. It turned out to be an exciting game. Jake Plummer led us on a comeback and almost pulled it out.

Almost unnoticed in the Dallas game was the fact that, in the second half, our defense was in complete control. We had solved the Cowboy offense, and they couldn't do jack against us. In a weird way, this was the turning point of our season. There were six games to go, and we knew that if we got the Cowboys a third time (in the playoffs) we would crush them. Beating the same team—I don't care who it is—three times in the same season is almost impossible in the NFL. For the rest of the year the prospect of a third shot at America's Team fueled our play.

The rest of the year was all about us. We were the masters of our own fate, not some other team playing in some other town. We were still in the playoff chase despite the fact that we hadn't done the things we knew deep down we were capable of doing. Now it was time to be focused and consistent. The Cardinal coaching staff picked up on this new mood in the locker room and did a fantastic job showing us what we were doing right, what we were doing wrong, and making us understand where that next level was and how we could get there.

This is the only way I can explain what happened in our next game, which was one of the wildest I've ever experienced. We traveled to Washington to play the Redskins and we went up 31–0 in the second quarter. Then the roof caved in. Trent Green threw three touchdown passes to Michael Westbrook, then they scored two more times. Larry Centers crossed the goal line for us in the third quarter, which meant we still had the lead, 38–35. Later we got the ball down to the 1-yard line on fourth down. The way the game was going, Vince Tobin didn't want to settle for a field goal and a 6-point lead, so we gambled and Plummer took the ball himself for a touchdown.

Sure enough, the Redskins came right back and scored. Pat Tillman made a nice play to recover their onside-kick attempt, but we couldn't get a first down and Washington took over on their own 31. Green's luck finally ran out when Kwamie Lassiter picked off one of his passes. We survived, 45–42. We found out later that if the Redskins had won, it would have been the greatest comeback in NFL history.

The Washington shootout illustrates one of the biggest illusions in football: the belief that you are "winning" a game. Just because the score has you ahead, it doesn't mean you're beating the other team. The only time the score matters is when it is mathematically impossible for one team to beat another, and that doesn't happen until the very end of most games. If one team is ahead and the other team refuses to give up, you're going to have yourself a ball game nine times out of ten.

All it takes is for one or two guys on one or two plays to relax a little and suddenly the entire complexion of the game has changed. The belief that you're winning changes the way you play—it's human nature—and it's at the root of almost every great comeback you'll see.

Something saps your energy when you think the game is over, and it's almost impossible to gain it back when the other team starts closing the gap. I'm always thinking, *We haven't beaten these guys yet, let's keep finding ways to stop them.* Understand that this is different from saying, *Let's keep doing what we're doing,* which is a trap teams constantly fall into. If you don't give an opponent new looks, they're going to figure out a way to beat you. That's what those guys with the binoculars and the headsets get paid to do.

In the Washington game we compounded the first deadly sin of overestimating ourselves with a second deadly sin: underestimating a good young quarterback, Trent Green. Look how he's grown into a fine quarterback since then. I personally almost decapitated Green a couple of times, and he kept coming back at us. A bad quarterback doesn't complete thirty passes and score 42 points on our defense, so he was already really good. I think that was the first year he was an NFL starter, and based on that season the Rams signed him to be their quarterback in 1999. You remember when Green got hurt in camp and Dick Vermeil started crying? Well, he had every right to cry, because he'd lost an excellent quarterback.

I played my A-game against Washington that day, so I was feeling extra good about our performance. Is it right for a player to be proud of his individual performance in a game that was sloppy and ugly like that one? The answer is simple. If you win, you feel great, and you have every right to feel great because you know that it might have been your outstanding play that staved off defeat.

Our record was only 6–5, but the way the NFC was shaking out we still had a decent shot at a wild-card berth. It was between us, the Giants, and the Bucs for two spots. The Bucs were playing the Bears, so that looked like a win, and the Giants were playing on the road on

Monday Night Football against the 49ers, which looked like a loss. The Cardinals were scheduled to play the Kansas City Chiefs, who hadn't won a game since, like, September, so we figured we would be in pretty good shape when the smoke cleared on Week 13.

Well, we were right about the Bucs and Giants, but wrong about the Chiefs. They beat us 34–24, and Rich Gannon was unbelievable in this game. His release was amazing. We were totally unprepared to defend against him. Gannon had been around forever. Hell, I remembered him playing the Bears when I was in high school. It was at this point in his career that he was finally putting it all together, and unfortunately he put it together on us. The Cardinals were now 6–6.

The next week, we had a chance to put some distance between ourselves and the Giants, and they beat us, too. This was a disaster. We had a comfortable lead late in the second quarter and then Shaun Williams, their top draft pick, intercepted a pass to set up a field goal that cut our lead to 17–10. The Giants scored 10 points in the third quarter to make it 20–17, then they stopped our offense twice at the goal line to put the game away.

We had put ourselves in a position where we absolutely had to win our final three games, against the Eagles, Saints, and Chargers. You never like to have your back against the wall like this, but in sports you know it's going to happen sooner or later and you're almost curious about how the team will respond.

Not to give anything away, but this had to be one of the greatest, most exciting endings to a season in league history. We went into Philadelphia and played an awesome game. Tommy Bennett got us going with a 70-yard interception return in the first quarter to give us a 10–0 lead, then Duce Staley made an incredible run for them to make it 10–7. We got down close to the end zone in the second quarter, but Adrian Murrell fumbled and the Eagles went all the way down the field for the tying field goal before halftime.

We made two nice drives to start the second half, but we were stopped on fourth and 1 at the 11, and the next time down Jake Plummer was intercepted by Troy Vincent. Early in the fourth quarter Irving Fryar made a hell of a catch for a touchdown, but we responded with a long drive and a touchdown of our own to tie the score 24–24.

With seven seconds left we tried the winning field goal, but Chris Jacke (Joe Nedney had hurt his knee a couple of weeks earlier) missed. In overtime, with our season hanging in the balance, Plummer connected with Rob Moore on two pass plays to get us into field-goal range, and this time Jacke's kick was good.

Moore was the perfect guy for this situation. He didn't draw a lot of attention to himself. He was a quiet, businesslike player, a big receiver who was very athletic and caught everything. He had great leaping ability, but he could also run the deep routes and get open. He had a nice year even though his hamstring wasn't 100 percent, and that's saying something at this level. Moore made plays even when the other teams knew exactly what was coming, just like Terrell Owens and Randy Moss did, only he didn't make headlines the way those guys did. There haven't been many guys like him in this league.

We had New Orleans at Sun Devil Stadium for our next-to-last home game, and this was a great battle, too. The Saints needed to beat us and the Buffalo Bills to have an outside shot at the wild card, so we knew this would be a fierce contest. We should have had at least four touchdowns in the first half but came away with only two field goals. All day long, either we screwed up or they made a great play to keep us from scoring. We had over 500 total yards of offense, but we still had to make a huge comeback at the end.

The defense kept us in it. Patrick Sapp killed one drive when he forced Kerry Collins to fumble. We also blocked a field goal. And we stuffed the Saints on a fourth and 1 at our 9-yard line. That preserved a 16–10 lead for us, but I'll be damned if Collins didn't put one last drive together and score on us with less than two minutes to go, giving the Saints a 17–16 lead.

Jake started on our own 8, and drilled two pretty passes to Frank Sanders. These were his ninth and tenth catches of the afternoon, and on the strength of this performance he would end up leading the NFC with eighty-nine receptions. A couple of plays later Jake scrambled 21 yards, and we sent out the field-goal team. Chris Jacke split the uprights for a 19–17 win. We were still alive in the playoff chase.

All of Arizona was buzzing that week. This was the most important game since the franchise moved from St. Louis, and people seemed to be split on how we would do against San Diego. The Chargers were one of those teams with nothing to lose, which made them dangerous, and they had a damn good defense, which made them doubly dangerous. This was the team that had anointed Ryan Leaf as their starter in training camp and then got caught with their pants down when he couldn't get the job done.

By this time they were playing Craig Whelihan, who had been their third-string guy for about four years. Natrone Means, their big back, was hurt on and off that year, which meant that Terrell Fletcher—basically a pass catcher—was now their featured runner. I had played against Terrell when he was at Wisconsin, and he had some skills. Their receivers were just a year or two out of college. This was a horrible offensive team. The Chargers had scored more than two touchdowns only once that year. Still, with so many unknowns, I sensed our coaches were nervous that some nobody would have a big game and make life miserable for us.

After two heart-stopping victories, we really could have used a cakewalk here. But it was not to be. Our defense was amazing and it had to be, because the San Diego D was solid. Kwamie Lassiter was the right man in the right place at the right time on this day, intercepting four passes, which tied an all-time record. His first INT set up a field goal that gave us a 10–0 lead; Murrell had scored on a short run a few minutes earlier. Lassiter's second pick came at the end of the half, and his third stopped a Charger drive in our red zone in the third quarter.

Kwamie was a tenacious defender. He was one of those guys who was always near the ball, and he could chase it all over the field. He had great awareness, too. One of his interceptions against San Diego actually hit the back of another guy's foot, and he had the presence of mind and concentration to pluck it out of the air. He was outstanding all year, but in this game—the biggest of his life to that point—he came through big time.

We missed a field goal right after Kwamie's third interception, but still had a 10–3 lead. San Diego started a drive but fumbled, and I fell on the ball. This time we made the field goal for a 13–3 lead. The Chargers were relentless, though, and they put 3 more points on the board to begin the fourth quarter. They came right back for more, but Lassiter picked Whelihan off again on our 7-yard line, and returned the ball 29 yards. Jake Plummer got us in field-goal position, but Chris Jacke missed again.

It turned out we could have used those 3 points, because here came the Chargers again. They got to our 20-yard line, but we pushed them back and they faced fourth and 20 from the 30. Trailing 13–6, they had no choice but to try a desperation play. Whelihan made the throw of his career, and Ryan Thelwell, a rookie wideout I had played against at the University of Minnesota, caught the touchdown of his career to tie the score 13–13. There were sixteen seconds left in the game and now we had to play a damn overtime against a hot quarterback.

Or did we?

John Carney kicked off and Eric Metcalf, our veteran return guy, made a great run across midfield. Eric was the son of Terry Metcalf, a Cardinals legend whom I'd watched run circles around the Bears when I was a kid. The irony on this day was that the Chargers basically gave him to us before the season in the Ryan Leaf deal. Anyway, Eric's run took nine seconds off the clock. Jake Plummer came in and threw a 10-yarder to Frank Sanders. We stopped the clock with a second or two left, and Jacke came on with a chance to put us in the playoffs. On this day, he had already missed a couple of crucial attempts, and this one was from 52 yards.

When your entire season hinges on a single kick, it's a matter of personal choice whether you watch it or not. Sometimes you're so exhausted or so emotional or so superstitious that you can't bring yourself to look. Guys who feel that way close their eyes, look at the ground, look at their teammates, or look at the crowd. No matter what—as long as you remember which stadium you're in—you'll know from the fans' reaction. I'd say about 70 percent of the players watch, but I'm telling you, there are a lot who simply look away. Personally, I watch all of the kicks, including the one against San Diego.

It was perfect. Next stop Dallas, for our date with destiny.

Now a little history. The Cardinals were originally from my town, Chicago. The Bidwell family owned them way back then, and the old man, Charles, died right before the 1947 season. That year they went on to beat the Eagles in the title game 28–21 for their one and only NFL championship. They lost to Philadelphia 7–0 in the 1948 championship game. That 1947 game was the last time a Cardinals team won in the postseason. Forty seasons had passed and not one win in the playoffs. That's sick.

The Cardinals moved to St. Louis in 1960, and they had some playoff teams around the time I was born, but they never won in the postseason. They made the move to Phoenix in 1988, and averaged about five wins a year. In 1994 they were 8–8, but the franchise's last winning season was 1984.

At 9–7 we had broken that string of futility. Now came the real challenge: winning in the playoffs. Our opponent was Dallas. We could not have been more confident. All of the intangibles were on our side. We had finished the season with three dramatic victories in tight, defensive battles. Each game ended with two minutes of pure passion for us. We had to look each other in the eye and ask, *How much do you really want this?* And we answered that question with near-perfect execution each time.

They say the playoffs are "Win or Go Home," but we had basically been in that frame of mind for a month by the time we played the Cowboys. The Cardinals were a tough, talented, resilient team at that point, and looking back I would not have been shocked if that particular club made it to the Super Bowl. Still, if you asked a hundred knowledgeable football fans who was going to win the wild-card game, with sixty-three thousand fans going crazy in Texas Stadium, I think ninety-eight or ninety-nine would have picked the Cowboys.

If I had to describe how the Cardinals felt heading into this game, the word that comes to mind is *prepared*. We knew the Cowboys, we respected the Cowboys, but we did not feel they could do anything to us we hadn't seen before. Coupled with how we'd run the table at the end of the season, we couldn't conceive of a scenario where we would not be in control. We knew we could win this game, and now it was a simple matter of doing it.

The week leading up to the game was exciting. We had won over a lot of doubters at the end of the year, and people who didn't normally follow football became swept up in the momentum. The Cardinals were actually competing with the big boys, and our die-hard fans thought, like I did, that we could go all the way. It's hard to describe how exciting it is to be three wins away from the Super Bowl. Once you're in the playoffs, you can let your imagination race and picture yourself playing for the championship. It makes you remember what you're playing for, what you're killing yourself for all season. You know that you have to focus on the task at hand, and you know if you win there's probably an even better team waiting to play you next. But the confidence we had was really exhilarating. It seemed like we could accomplish anything.

By game day you are so eager for kickoff to come that you can't stand it. You know what your team can do when everybody plays their best, and you're anxious to see how you'll do against a team that's bringing its best, too. We believed our A-game was better than Dallas's A-game, and we were dying to prove it.

Well, we came out in the first quarter like we were shot out of a cannon. The D-line did a tremendous job of harrassing Troy Aikman. We hit him constantly. The Cowboys could not stop us up front, and we grew bolder and more tenacious as the game wore on. I was up against Larry Allen, whom they moved from guard to tackle. He was about as good as you get at the position—All-NFL and Pro Bowl every year. But I was giving him fits. Allen didn't know what I was going to do next . . . except hit his quarterback. I was having my way with him, and this was benefiting us big time, because I forced Aikman to get rid of the ball faster than he liked. Aeneas Williams and Cory Chavous read this situation perfectly, and they both had big games. Williams had a couple of interceptions and I caused a fumble, which was three turnovers right there.

The Cowboys had the first opportunity to score, but their kicker, Richie Cunningham, missed. Jake Plummer went right at their defense, which was weakened due to Deion Sanders being injured. He connected with Frank Sanders on a 59-yard play, and Adrian Murrell finished the drive off when Jake gave him a shovel pass and he scored. We were up 10–0 at halftime, and the Cowboys had no answer for us. Even Emmitt Smith couldn't get the yards when he needed them.

The biggest play of that first half, in my opinion, came when Smith got a handoff on fourth and 1 at our 7-yard line, and Mark Maddox nailed him. Maddox was the "old man" of our linebacking crew, and I know it was a delicious moment for him. He had played with the Bills his whole career before we signed him, and was a member of the teams that Smith and Aikman had beaten in the Super Bowl back to back. That was one of four drives that we stopped for no points in the first half.

When a team is stymied like the Cowboys were in this game, their mind-set is that they have to come out and make a statement in the second half. Well, on like the second or third play of the third quarter, Murrell took the ball and ran it 74 yards. They were hoping that we had played our best football already, that we would revert to being the Cardinals they had humiliated twice already in 1998. But Adrian's run illustrated to them that this was a different team, and let them know we were going to be even better in the second half. Larry Centers finished off the drive with a touchdown catch, and we were ahead 17–0.

From that point on, our defense was unrelenting. There was no way the Cowboys were going to get back in the game, because we just got tougher and tougher on them until we broke their will. We never acted like we were beating them; we never gave each other high fives, we didn't celebrate, we didn't talk trash to them. We were very professional, very controlled, very businesslike. Tommy Bennett put the icing on the cake for us with an interception with under a minute to play. The final score was 20–7, but I'm always surprised at how close that makes the game seem. I forget that they got a touchdown late, but by then the game was under control. To me it felt like 40–0.

To Dallas Cowboys fans, our victory in the 1998 playoffs is like The Day The Earth Stood Still. It's as if aliens had landed on their field and rendered their weapons useless, then flew away. They still can't explain it, they don't want to remember it, and they don't want to talk about it. Maybe it signaled the end of an era or something. I don't know. But it ranks as a very dark day in their very bright history.

The mood was slightly different back home. When we returned from Dallas, the city of Phoenix was floating on air. For the first time in the history of the franchise, everyone was talking about the team in a positive way. The Cardinals who had broken everyone's hearts for years and years now had everyone ecstatic.

Unfortunately, our magic ended in Minnesota. The Vikings were the team everyone expected to sweep to the Super Bowl. They had more weapons than we had seen all year, and they hadn't lost a game in almost three months. They had three tremendous receivers in Randy Moss, Cris Carter, and Jake Reed. They had a powerful halfback in Robert Smith and also Leroy Hoard, a good short-yardage guy. They had a big-time tight end in Andrew Glover. They had a great line with Todd Steussie, Jeff Christy, Korey Stringer, and Randall McDaniel. And their quarterback, Randall Cunningham, was the story of the year.

The man had retired from football and had a successful business in Las Vegas when Minnesota asked him to serve as a backup to Brad Johnson in 1997. Brad was having a great year when he hurt his neck and Randall had to start the three games. In 1998 Randall took over again when Brad was injured and ended up as the league's top-ranked passer at the age of thirty-five.

I won't say the Vikings were unstoppable, because the Falcons beat them in the championship game, but this was a team that was just as prepared to play as we were, put more talent on the field, and made more plays. They had depth we didn't have, and experience we didn't have. Their defense wasn't quite what ours was, but it was damn good nonetheless.

We agreed that it was crucial to start strong and take that crowd of theirs out of the game. The Metrodome is a visiting team's nightmare—and in a playoff game I can't begin to describe how loud it is. The fans are bad enough, but the team pipes in music from behind the visiting team's bench, and it was so loud that you couldn't hear me if I were sitting a foot away and shouting at you. We actually were taken out of our rhythm by that music. There were several times, in fact, when our offensive sequences were messed up because the players couldn't hear over the music. I've never been in a situation like that. It was intolerable.

The Vikings were the team that started strong. They got the ball and wore a path through our defense, eating up half of the first quarter on one touchdown drive. I had a bad feeling at that point—like it might be a long day if we didn't do something fast. If it weren't for a great interception by Aeneas Williams, they would have put a second TD on the board. We saw this as a potential turning point, but Jake Plummer threw two bad interceptions and at halftime the score was 24–7.

We were being overwhelmed by our opponent, by the noise, and by the moment. We panicked, and that was the game. It was ugly—the most painful game for me to relive. We regained our composure and made it interesting in the second half for a while, but basically they slammed the lid 41–21.

I was really proud at the end of our season. We were two wins away from the Super Bowl, something no Arizona Cardinal had ever been able to say before. And for the first time I felt like a real football player, like the guys on the bubblegum cards I used to collect. I was convinced that next year we were going to come back and do it big. We had taken our licks, we had learned our lesson, and we would be stronger for it. The Vikings game was a rite of passage. Now it was time to pick up our shoulders, stick out our chests, and move forward. I felt that what we accomplished was a foreshadowing of great things to come.

Looking back, the 1998 Cardinals were a hot team that was not quite top shelf. You have to earn the right to play for the championship, and we didn't. We allowed another team to dismantle us, and we came back at them with nothing. The disappointing thing is that, had we found a way to beat the Vikings, we would have played Atlanta for the chance to advance to the Super Bowl. The Falcons had taken out the Green Bay Packers, who were regarded as the number two team in the postseason. I'm not saying we would have beaten Atlanta, because they had an excellent team. And when they played the Vikings the following week, they were the better club. But when I saw how the Falcons beat Minnesota in the championship game, I was like, *Oh shit! We could have done this!*

You can *what-if* yourself to death in football. I know fans do this all the time. If there's anyone out there who is still torn up about how our season ended, all I can say is that I understand. The truth is that the Super Bowl wasn't as close as it seemed . . . but it wasn't as distant, either.

6

When you come off a season like we had in 1998, you want to build on what you've already established. We had most of our key offensive guys back: Jake Plummer, Adrian Murrell, Rob Moore, and Frank Sanders. Our first draft choice, David Boston, was a big receiver out of Ohio State, so Jake had himself yet another weapon.

There were a couple of notable departures: Lomas Brown and Larry Centers. Lomas signed with the Browns. He had been the keystone of our O-line, and I can't recall him giving up a single sack while I was on the team. We all wondered what effect his leaving would have. Lester Holmes and Chris Dishman were very solid, and we drafted L. J. Shelton to fill Lomas's shoes. L. J. was a tackle out of Eastern Michigan. His dad was Lonnie Shelton, the old power forward with the Knicks. The line was now potentially an area of vulnerability, and we knew other teams would attack us there. It would be up to our quarterback, Jake Plummer, to keep his cool and use his weapons wisely. And quickly.

Centers signed with the Redskins. This was a worrisome development, because he accounted for damn near half our offense. We had Michael Pittman to fill his shoes, so the team must have figured Larry was a luxury. He was a special player, though.

The defensive line was still our principal strength. In our good games the previous year, the defense had been great, but in our bad games teams piled up a lot of yards on us. The goal for 1999 was to eliminate those bad games. Eric Swann hurt his knee toward the end of the 1998 season, so we didn't have him down the stretch. The team kind of questioned the injury, and I know they thought he should suck it up and play. But now he was back healthy, along with Mark Smith, Andre Wadsworth, and myself. The big loss on defense was Jamir Miller, who also went to the Browns via free agency. Jamir was good against the pass and good against the run—a rock back there at linebacker. We picked up Rob Fredrickson from the Lions to fill his spot.

We opened the season against the Eagles. After a tremendous college career at Syracuse University, Donovan McNabb was now wearing a Philadelphia uniform. We chatted briefly before the game, and I told Donovan to be prepared to take his throne at any time. I thought he might get in this game, but he didn't. He made his NFL debut the following week against Tampa Bay.

The Philly game was close all the way. I sacked their starter, Doug Pederson, twice, and Plummer engineered a fourth-quarter comeback for a 25–24 win. It was hard to say whether this was an encouraging start or not. A win is a win, don't get me wrong. But it would have been nice to trounce an opponent once in a while. In 1998 seven of our nine regular-season victories came after we were either tied or trailing in the fourth quarter. That's an amazing stat if you think about it, and it says a lot about the team we had that season. Keep taking games down to the wire, though, and eventually it's going to catch up with you. The level of play and the expertise of the coaching in the NFL tend to even things out over time. Sooner or later, the odds were going to go against us. The law of gravity would take hold.

The only way you can avoid this is by putting serious points on the scoreboard and then letting the defense do its job. We did do our job the following week, but the offense couldn't get much going against the Dolphins. The score was tied at halftime 13–13. Our lone touchdown came on an interception return by the new guy, Fredrickson. Both defenses clamped down in the second half. We got a field goal and they got two. Game over.

This was the second time I had played against Dan Marino in my career, so I knew what to expect. He never held the ball long. He read the play and threw very quickly. A pass rusher faces a difficult decision against a guy like Marino. You know you have less time to get to him, so you have to decide whether or not to alter your own game. Your first instinct is to try to do everything faster. But that means the quarterback has taken you out of the things that have made you successful, and chances are it will blow up on you. In the end the best you can do is play your game, and hope the coverage guys play theirs. You may not get a sack, but you can limit his options and possibly pressure him into making a mistake.

Our next game, against the 49ers, was a *Monday Night Football* game. They put 17 points on us fast, but we came back and scored 10 in the third quarter. San Francisco held that touchdown lead until late in the final period, when Lawrence Phillips broke off a 68-yard TD run to ice the game. This dude was kicked out of football for a year, and I swear half his rushing yards for the 1999 season came on this one play.

San Francisco's quarterback, Steve Young, presented an entirely different problem than Marino. Being left-handed, Young could see me coming when he dropped back to pass. Also, unlike Marino, Young could run very effectively. What this means to a right defensive end is that you have to play smarter. You can't take as many risks, because if Young spots an opening, he'll sprint right through it and then you get to watch your stupid ass on film all week. It's not exactly a containment strategy—you still bring it on every play—but you have to respect his ability to take what you give him. That said, I did sack him once that game.

Up next was Dallas. We were looking to even our record, and they were out to eviscerate us. Not exactly a recipe for success. They got their revenge with two defensive touchdowns and three offensive touchdowns and beat us 35–7. Plummer's first pass went right into defensive back George Teague's hands, and he ran it in from 32 yards. And it only got worse from there. Michael Irvin scored on Aeneas Williams—payback for the previous season, when Aeneas had shut him out after he'd caught passes in 117 straight games. The coup de grâce came in the fourth quarter, when Plummer coughed up the ball and Greg Ellis, their young defensive end, ran it 98 yards the other way for a score. This was a game to forget except for the fact that, no matter how bad they were beating us, the Cowboys weren't trash-talking or rubbing it in. I think they finally had some respect for us. Or at least they didn't want to give us fuel if we met again in the playoffs.

We were very concerned about our 1–3 record at this point. We had lost to two good clubs in Miami and Dallas, but we should have beaten the 49ers. They just didn't seem like they had their old magic. And the win over the Eagles wasn't very convincing. The loss of Larry and Lomas had clearly hampered our offense, and it wasn't the same without Jamir Miller running around making plays on defense.

You hate to say any game is a "must-win" this early in the schedule, but our Week 5 meeting with the Giants was big. Dallas and Washington were tough teams, and to have any hope in our division we would need to beat up on the Eagles and Giants, who were less than imposing. A loss to the Giants at this stage would have been extremely disheartening. No one was saying it, but we were beginning to feel like we might be fighting a losing battle in 1999. There had already been some critical plays where I know everyone was thinking, *Lomas would have made that block,* or *Larry would have broken that tackle,* or *Jamir would have nailed that guy.*

The Giants game was a war, but we prevailed. We scored twice in the second quarter and held them scoreless until they kicked a field goal in the fourth quarter. Our defense was as dominant as it had been at any time the previous season, so we came off the field feeling like things might be turning around. No disrespect to Kent Graham, but Kerry Collins, their new quarterback, made the Giants a very dangerous team. He was throwing the hell out of the ball, but we stopped him when we had to. I sacked him twice, and Pat Tillman made a nice interception.

Pat was starting to come into his own as an NFL defensive back. He had been an All-American linebacker in college, but was converted into a safety by the Cardinals. I was a linebacker converted to defensive end. When a college linebacker is moved to another position in the pros, that's a signal that you can expect something unusual from him. What you have is a player who was successful at a very athletic position in Division I, but who has some other attribute that is highly valued at some other NFL position. In my case quickness, footwork, and creativity made up for a lack of size at my position, and made me somewhat unique as a defensive end. In Pat's case coaches saw a player who could read the field and anticipate, and who exploded into his tackles. These are coveted traits in an NFL safety, and in Pat's case they made up for the fact that he was bigger and maybe half a step slower than other people at his position. When teams successfully convert a player, they look like geniuses. When they don't, they call the guy a 'tweener and discard him.

In 1998 Pat had split playing time with Kwamie Lassiter, and was an absolute terror on special teams. There's not much glamour for the special-teams guys, but ask anyone in the NFL and they'll tell you they can never find enough players like Pat. He was still kind of a no-frills football player in 1999, yet you could tell he was going to make it in the NFL. He was totally reliable, always had your back. What made Pat special, though, was how much he loved challenges. He loved the whole concept of challenges. He would visualize the situations that might arise in a game, and play them out in his head again and again. When the game actually started, every play was like a personal grudge match to him. Pat was a hard-nosed, throwback player whom you never questioned in terms of giving everything he had.

Off the field Pat was very serious and very studious. He was always reading a book when I saw him. The rest of us would be watching portable DVDs on the plane, but Pat would be lost in a book. When he first joined the Cardinals he was kind of a curiosity to me. There was one day in practice during his rookie season when he was just smacking everybody around. He was tenacious. I'm like, *Wow, this kid brings it.* He never had All-Pro talent, but he kept building layers on his game until he was a legitimate NFL starter.

The other interesting thing about Pat was that he would notice teammates who seemed to be drifting during games, and when they came back to the sideline he'd look at them and say, "You ready?" and kind of snap them out of it. It's unusual for someone on the bench to be talking that way to the first string, but that attention to detail made him an excellent role player and later an excellent starter. He never had the natural ability of other players, but I'll be damned if he wasn't always in the right place at the right time.

From Pat's perspective, I think fighting the Taliban in Afghanistan was being in the right place at the right time. He knew his own heart, and he felt that this was more important than playing football. I can tell you as someone who knew him that this was totally within his character. A lot of people know what they do, but not many do what they know, and Pat knew that his place was overseas doing his patriotic duty. This was as much an accomplishment and a challenge to him as any football game he was likely to play, and I doubt that giving up an NFL salary—which everyone was focused on when he enlisted—even entered his decision.

Some people believed that Pat enlisted to set an example for others, but I can tell you that's wrong. Pat did what was in his heart. If it inspired others to follow, that would be a bonus. But when he enlisted, you didn't see him hold a press conference. It was a private and personal decision.

Not to get ahead of myself, because there's a lot more on this later, but while I wasn't shocked when I heard Pat had joined the army, I was surprised that most people I talked to really believed he would come back and resume his NFL career. First of all, if football had been that important to him, he would have kept playing and found some other way to contribute to the war effort. Second, even if he wanted to return to the NFL, I don't believe he could have. I actually thought about this a lot when people started saying, "Oh, Pat will be back."

On one level, I recognize the fact that if there was one guy you could march into battle and be 100 percent sure was coming back, it would be Pat. But on a much deeper level, you're dealing with a lot of denial here. Listen, we tend to make life too much of a story. Life is reality. What happens *happens.* If people are shooting at you, there's a very real chance you're going to get shot. And if you get shot—especially on some remote mountainside—there's a very real chance you will die. And you almost certainly won't play football again.

Passion is a wonderful thing but it doesn't stop bullets. Pat going to war was not a movie script. You can't just write the ending you want. Everyone failed to understand what he was doing, why he was doing it, and what the possible consequences were. That's why every aspect of his story came as such a shock.

In terms of returning to the NFL, however, it wasn't going to happen. In combat, your diet changes radically, your body changes radically, your stress level skyrockets—there's no way you would be able to put on a football uniform and just pick up where you left off. And mentally, when you go off to war, you've given yourself to a greater cause. Sometimes you give your life. But you never believe you're coming home to continue life uninterrupted. Had Pat made it back from Afghanistan, I really doubt football would have been in his plans.

When it came to Arizona's plans for 1999, it was beginning to look like they wouldn't involve the postseason. Our next game was a 24–10 loss to the Redskins. They had played us tough twice the previous season, and now Washington was clearly the superior team. Jake Plummer was injured in this game, and although Dave Brown was not a bad backup, we knew our hopes were fading. When the news came that Jake would be out for more than a month, it was very disappointing.

After a bye week, we lost again, to the Patriots. I played well, and sacked Drew Bledsoe twice. But outside of that, the man played a near-perfect game. If I wasn't right in his face, he was completing damn near every pass he threw. I have to tip my hat to Bledsoe, but it made me wonder where all our playmakers were. I remember looking around the huddle and wishing I had more help.

It got worse a week later against the Jets, who were having a miserable year. They beat us on a fourth-quarter pass to Keyshawn Johnson. I couldn't believe it. I had been having one of my best games ever, against Jumbo Elliott, and was chasing Rick Mirer around the backfield all day long. I had two sacks in that game and almost had a few more. We pulled Aeneas Williams off Keyshawn for that one damn play, and they beat us 12–7.

At this point Dave Brown was getting crucified for not getting the job done at quarterback, which was completely unfair. The guys on the team felt bad, because we knew when he played under control, he was a good quarterback. If you were a member of the 1999 Cardinals, you knew that we couldn't score points because we didn't give Dave time to execute our plays, our runners didn't have the kind of years they had in 1998, and our receivers dropped balls they had caught the previous season. If we had blocked better and taken the stress off Brown—if the Cardinals had kept leaders like Lomas Brown, who made the whole line better—you would have seen a different offense.

The plain truth is that Dave Brown had just as much ability as Brad Johnson, who got us to the Super Bowl when I was with Tampa Bay a few years later. A couple of weeks later, before Plummer came back, we were actually believing in Dave. He played under control and made sound passes when the offense was functioning properly. Put Dave under duress, however, and he can't do what a Michael Vick does. He's not that guy. He just wasn't the type of player who could escape from the pocket, break tackles, and then rifle the ball 60 yards.

As for the team's mood, I would say that at this point we weren't giving up on the season, but we definitely recognized that the missing components from the previous season were hurting us. The people brought in to replace the key guys from the year before were not performing up to their capabilities. This was most noticeable on offense, but I had a real concern that our defense was about to implode, too. Our secondary didn't have the depth we needed, and I was playing with guys on the D-line whom no one had ever heard of. Eric Swann's knees were bothering him, Mark Smith was pissed about his contract, and Andre Wadsworth was injured, too. I was the only guy out there play after play, and we just didn't have the cohesiveness you need to mount an effective pass rush.

Still, there were flashes of hope. Our next game, against the Lions, was Michael Pittman's first NFL start. He was the man whom Vince Tobin hoped would replace Larry Centers as a pass-catching back. Michael had a nice game for us versus Detroit, but he fumbled with five minutes left and Terry Fair ran it in for a touchdown to cut our lead to 23–19. Instead of kicking the extra point, Bobby Ross, the Lions coach, went for 2 and they didn't make it, which meant we were up 4. An XP would have made it 23–20. Well, damned if they didn't get the ball back and, with a few seconds left, find themselves in field-goal range. Too bad, Bobby.

A shit storm came down on Ross for that decision, and he probably deserved it. I don't pretend to understand all the permutations that go into whether you go for 2 or not, but I can tell you that we were ecstatic when we saw Detroit's offense come on the field instead of their kicking unit. To the players, it seemed like a stupid move, and because we were able to stop the 2-point try it cost the Lions a ball game. It was a gift.

I found it interesting that, once Ross had taken his lumps in the press, the incident was more or less moved to the back burner. The Lions were leading the division when this happened and ended up with a .500 record. You could easily say that this one decision altered the course of their season—perhaps even cost them a postseason appearance. But when

you think about Bobby Ross today, do you think about that one moment, that one mental mistake? Now, if a player had committed an error
that cost his team the season, that would follow him around through his
career and into retirement. He would be crucified, whereas with a coach
it's put into perspective and everyone just moves on. I remember when
Dallas coach Barry Switzer went through airport security with a hand-
gun. It was no big deal. Let that be a player—especially one with a reputation—and they'd never let him forget it.

I'm not saying one is right and one is wrong, I'm just pointing out
how pro football takes care of its own. If you're a league guy or an organization guy, you don't want to go around bad-mouthing Bobby Ross
and calling him an imbecile, because who knows, one day you might be
sitting in front of him or one of his buddies looking for a job. It's an interesting double standard. I understand that they're the bosses and we're
the employees, but it still strikes me as being very lopsided.

Getting back to our "lost" season, suddenly things were looking up.
We beat Dallas 13–9 in Week 11 and now we were only two games off
the division lead at 4–6. The next week the Giants took a 10–6 lead into
the second half, and Coach Tobin put Jake Plummer in the game for
Dave Brown. He threw TD passes to Rob Moore and Johnny
McWilliams, and Eric Swann caught a tipped pass that he ran in for a
touchdown. I sacked Kerry Collins twice. It was a good win. We were
having fun again. At least, I was having fun.

I always enjoy it when I play well. I take great pride in playing at a
championship level, and it's unfortunate that we didn't have a team in
1999 that I could really help. This little winning streak, in fact, is when I
first began to think about what it might be like playing in a different situation. There were a few teams right on the verge of going to the Super
Bowl, and I felt that I could be the man who put them there. Tampa Bay
was the most obvious. They won with a very good defense, but it wasn't
enough against a high-octane team like the Rams, who ended up beating them in the NFC title game. I looked at the Bucs and really believed
I could give them a stone-cold, lockdown defense—and this was before
the postseason began.

The Eagles, whom we played the next week, were not a team I
could have helped. They were a mess. But that meant they had nothing

to lose by putting Donovan McNabb in the lineup, so I got to play against him for the first time as a pro. That was fun. I felt like a Jedi Master facing his former Padawan in battle. The night before the game we had dinner together at the Outback Steakhouse and talked for hours about how we'd grown up together, and how two kids from the same high school were facing each other in the NFL. We had lost touch a little bit when he was in college, but we reconnected immediately. I was so happy to see him out there, so proud to watch him play. Of course, I was also trying to run him down all day, which isn't easy. And he knew I'd be coming. Donovan was the fastest quarterback I'd ever played against at that point, but I knew him and I knew his game. It was a real cat-and-mouse battle within the battle.

In preparing for this game, I was wondering whether the coaching staff would come to me looking for information on Donovan. They didn't ask me specifically, because they had good tape on him already. It made me think of the first time Donovan's name had come up among the Cardinal coaches. Prior to the 1997 draft, Donovan was thinking about leaving Syracuse early. They asked me what I thought of him and I was emphatic with my answer. "We have to draft him," I said. "You do not want to miss drafting Donovan McNabb."

As it turned out, he stayed in school and we took Plummer, the hometown hero, instead. Jake was definitely the hero on this day, because Donovan had us down 17–7 with five minutes left. Jake put together one of the best drives of his career, 80 yards, and hit David Boston with a touchdown pass to make it 17–14. We got the ball back and Jake threw a long pass to Frank Sanders, who made a diving catch a few inches short of the end zone. Jake kept it himself and scored the go-ahead TD, and we won 24–17.

Meanwhile things were getting interesting in our division, because while we were on a four-game winning streak, everyone else was losing. You knew the Redskins were feeling the heat because after Detroit wiped them out, Michael Westbrook went a little crazy and claimed that the referees were "conspiring" against them. They had fourteen penalties called on them that day, and two questionable calls were made by the line judge, Byron Boston. Guess whose son played wide receiver for us? That's right, David.

Our whole season was on the line now. We were a game behind the Redskins, and we went into Washington with a chance to control our own destiny. Given what a train wreck our season had started out to be, this was more than we ever could have hoped for. The Redskins were nervous. They held a players-only, closed-door meeting prior to the game.

Maybe we should have, too, because they fucking destroyed us. Apparently my name came up in their little get-together, because I had two or three guys on me every play. I was still making tackles, but Stephen Davis went berserk on us and there was no way to stop the bleeding. He scored a 50-yard touchdown in the first quarter, then Brad Johnson threw TD passes to Irving Fryar and Westbrook in the second quarter. The game ended 28–3.

Let me go on record here as saying that Stephen Davis is a beast. He got that recognition years later, when he helped Carolina reach the Super Bowl, but he was at the height of his powers in 1999, and every time he got the ball it was like he was a dump truck rolling downhill. He was powerful and he had serious speed. If I had to make a list of running backs whom I don't like to hit when they've got a full head of steam, Stephen Davis would top that list. But I'm not going to make that list, so screw it—bring 'em on, I don't care who they are!

After the Washington game, Joe Greene talked to the defensive linemen. He singled me out for never giving up and said, "Hey, we have to help this kid out. This boy's been doing everything for us. Other people have to be accountable."

It felt good that he was recognizing my ability. It also showed that he knew I was playing my heart out when the other guys on the line seemed ready to pack it in. Coaches tend to have a blind eye when it comes to singling out a particular player for praise. Joe broke the rules by letting me know he thought I was the kind of player he had been in his own glory years.

I had been working with Joe for almost four years at this point, and although I didn't understand our relationship, I was beginning to see that, deep down, we were similar in that we both despised losing. I think his frustration was that I, as a player, could go out and redeem myself with a great game. As a coach he no longer had that option. A loss was a loss. You were either a winning coach or a losing coach, and he was a losing coach in the eyes of the football world. As far as I was concerned, he was a terrific coach for me. I can't remember a single instance when he had to physically instruct me on something. He'd tell me what to do and I'd go out and do it.

Prior to our next game, Joe took me aside and said, "Simeon, I know you've been doing everything this year, but for selfish reasons I'd like you to go out and win the game for us today."

I got a big smile on my face. Joe was asking me to forget about the team and challenging me to just go out and kick ass and win the game single-handedly. My relationship with Joe had been so complicated that I was never sure what he thought of me. The best thing about this talk was that I felt he had the kind of respect for me that would lead to a friendship after my football days. I wanted to be tight with Joe, I wanted to hang with him. I thought it would be beautiful if we ended up that way. He was a good man, and I was starting to see that he was one of the smartest guys I had ever been around. I know he went to college at North Texas, but he could have gone to an Ivy League school—that's how smart he was.

With two games left, our season was over. We played Atlanta and they wiped us out in the second half. That was the first time I could re-member looking around the locker room at halftime and seeing guys who didn't give a damn whether they played the last thirty minutes or not. It was embarrassing. If it looked that way on the field, then all I can say is that looks were not deceiving. The funny thing about the Falcons game is that, because I was trying so hard to respond to Joe's little speech, I was trying to do too much and ended up jumping offsides sev-eral times. It was one of the worst games of my career.

I didn't get a sack in that game, either. We were at the stage of the season where you begin to think about personal records, and I needed two sacks to break the franchise mark. We were headed up to Green Bay, the frozen tundra. I was worried about my chances of getting to Brett Favre because the undergarments the team supplied were not going to keep us warm. For me to get my sacks, I needed to be warm and loose and flexible.

I had been thinking about wearing an insulating bodysuit under my uniform for a while, and my friend Bennie Morrow had been scouting around for one without any luck. I decided we would sew one together ourselves. The material I chose was neoprene. I knew that divers wore it in cold water and that it held in their body heat, so we purchased a couple of extra-large diving suits and began piecing together something I could wear in Green Bay.

The night before this game, I couldn't sleep. I was playing video games in the hotel room until morning, thinking about the record, wondering whether my bodysuit would work. I was also trying to figure out how much passing the Packers would do. Obviously, the more times a quarterback drops back to pass, the more chances you have to tackle him. My fear was that Favre would put the ball in the end zone a few times and then run the ball the rest of the way. I felt better when I realized that Green Bay might potentially end up with the same 8–8 record as three other teams, in which case total points might be the tiebreaker. That meant Favre would be aggressive about throwing all day.

As I suspected, it was cold as shit on game day. But I was fine. I was all over the field against the Packers—so much so that people who saw me that off season said it looked like I was playing at a different speed than everyone else. I got to Favre twice to finish the year with 16.5 sacks, but we lost 49–24.

The bodysuit actually worked too well, because it wouldn't let any heat out except at the openings. It was hilarious. My teammates are shivering on the sidelines, looking like panhandlers, and I'm dying of heat, with clouds of steam shooting out from my uniform. This was actually the prototype for T3K, the performance apparel business I started officially in 2003. The game took place right after the millennium, when everyone was worried about Y2K, so T3K sounded like a cool shorthand for the brand.

Despite finishing 6–10, I was proud of the year I had for the Cardinals. There were times when I honestly believed that I was the only thing standing between us and a complete disaster. As it was, we ended up with a respectable record for the talent the franchise had assembled, and our defensive stats weren't horrible. We finished with 24 sacks—16.5 were mine, and I think the next guy had 2 or 3. Sacks can be a misleading statistic, but not when you have that kind of spread. I had an All-Pro-caliber season and I was coming into my own as an all-around defensive player. I was at the level, in terms of personal performance, where I had wanted to be since I was a kid. Now the trick was to put those skills to work for a winning team.

The sack record was a nice consolation for a season that fell short of our expectations. When you look back, you always want to say that you gave your all, that you did your best. For me it was a star-studded season in a hellhole, which counts for something. Having two great years in a row also counts for something, because it shows you aren't a flash in the pan. I had done well in my rookie year, had an off year in 1997, then was banging in 1998 and 1999.

Ironically, my rookie sack record fell that same season. Jevon Kearse, the defensive end for the Tennessee Titans, finished with 14.5. They say that records are made to be broken, and I experienced both sides of that in 1999. Honestly, I didn't mind losing the rookie record. Jevon was killing, so I have to tip my hat to him. He was my favorite player that year, no doubt. And it's still true to this day. I love to see that cat play. If he stays healthy, he can be one of the most dominant players ever to play this game.

Jevon reminds me of myself. And to be perfectly honest, I was pulling for him to break my record. I didn't even know him—I just liked the way he played. He plays balls to the wall on every down. He uses his body like I do, and he's got a seven-foot wingspan like I do. I love his energy. Where we differ—in fact, what separates me from almost everyone in the NFL, regardless of position—is body control. I can go from zero to sixty in a flash, whereas he requires a split second longer to get to full speed. That's why chip blocking works against him, but not against me. It all comes down to balance. In that respect, I have a slight advantage over Jevon, too. If you watch me when I'm double-teamed, they can stand me up, but I can still slip between the players trying to block me.

By the way, I think the success I had in the pros opened the minds of a lot of NFL people, and opened the door for players like Jevon. They played him everywhere in college, and he never got a chance to settle into any one spot. He didn't come into the draft with any kind of pass-rushing résumé, but because the Cardinals had success with me at that position, the Titans felt a similar athlete like Jevon would have success there, too. Not only did Jevon succeed, but he was also a big reason the Titans went to the Super Bowl his first year. And he almost won it for them. He made a potential game-turning play on Kurt Warner right near the end. He put a rush on Warner and caused him to underthrow a pass deep in his own territory. Isaac Bruce adjusted and Tennessee didn't, and Isaac went the length of the field for the winning touchdown. It could easily have been an interception and runback for a touchdown.

Sadly, the Super Bowl was something I could only dream about at this point in my career. Jevon was in the right place at the right time, coming out of college as an unknown quantity and surrounded by exceptional players. My rookie year, I had some great guys on my team, and the defensive coordinator, Dave McGinnis, was a great coach, but we didn't have great players.

Other than Jevon Kearse, there aren't a lot of players I enjoy watching on the defensive side. I'm still a football fan when I watch, so I like to see the offensive players do their thing. Funny, but after all these years, I still don't see the glamour of defense, and in truth you don't appreciate the speed and finesse of defensive players until you're right there on the field with them. I was actually happy when the Eagles signed Jevon after the 2003 season. To me, Jevon always belonged on the East Coast anyway. His game will really be highlighted. Tennessee was cool, but it wasn't as high profile. The Bears were always my favorite team, and they still are, but now that Philly has Donovan and Jevon, the Eagles are a close second.

7

knew my days in Arizona were numbered when the Cardinals made me a franchise player prior to the 2000 season. I was coming off a year in which I finished second in the NFL in sacks and was named to the Pro Bowl from an organization that wasn't exactly known for turning out Pro Bowl players. I had done all this for an unheralded team that was often behind in games. That meant our defense was playing against the run as our opponents nursed their leads by working time off the clock, so I didn't get the sack opportunities other defensive ends did. My reward for this performance was that Arizona ultimately decided to employ me for one more year at the market rate and then turn me loose. I sat out training camp and missed the first regular-season game until we got the deal done. It was not the way I wanted to begin the season.

I was pissed. I played my heart out for the Cardinals and they decided that their best move was to squeeze another year out of me instead of extending my contract and rebuilding the defense around me. Until this point, I never had a clear picture of how the Cardinals felt about me. But now I understood completely. This was about as subtle as getting kicked in the nuts.

Even so, I was being paid well and I still had the mentality that we could win it all, so I went into the season pumped up as always. The team could still offer me an extension, and I let them know what it would take to keep me in a Cardinal uniform. Football players are funny in that way. As hurt as I was, I still felt a sense of loyalty. All I wanted was something close to what I thought I should have been paid after 1999. Negotiations continued during the season, but I couldn't shake the feeling that year that Arizona no longer required my services.

The Cardinals in 2000 had a lot of holes, particularly on defense, which had long been our strength. Eric Swann, whose chronic injuries had kept him out of the regular lineup for two years, was cut during the summer and replaced by Tony McCoy. Eric was a big man who fought off double teams with his size. Tony was more of a finesse guy who used his quickness to make tackles. The two of us would have our work cut out for us, though, because Andre Wadsworth was going to miss time recovering from knee surgery, and there were big question marks on the D-line, at left linebacker and in the secondary.

On the bright side, six of our first nine games were at home, so the odds were decent that we wouldn't spend another year trying to recover from a slow start. On the dark side, by the time I suited up, we had already lost a game. The Giants beat us 21–17 in the opener. Tiki Barber ran roughshod over us, and New York was up 21–3 midway through the fourth quarter. Jake Plummer connected with David Boston on a pair of touchdowns late, but it just made the score look better.

Boston was a great talent, but he could be an impulsive guy. Sometimes this worked for him on the field, but sometimes his emotions would get away from him and he'd disappear. Nonetheless, David would be an important man for us in 2000. He was 100 percent healthy, which had not been true during his rookie campaign. David had injured his shoulder during camp a year earlier and was unable to do the upper-body work you need to excel at the receiver position. Now he was slated to replace Rob Moore as our go-to guy. Rob blew up his knee and was out for the season. But with Boston and Frank Sanders, Plummer would still have two good receivers to look for.

Our offensive line looked stronger than in 1999, so Plummer would have more time to find his receivers—provided the running game clicked. This provision was crucial and everyone knew it. Everyone was writing that Jake Plummer would be "under the microscope" in 2000, but the real pressure was on Michael Pittman to show he could be a full-time back, and on Thomas Jones, whom we drafted in the first round out of Virginia. Jones was an All-American. He actually showed enough in camp to open the year as our starter, but I didn't think that would last long.

In the end, neither guy could generate the kind of yards we needed to make the rest of the offense click. This set off a domino effect that put more pressure on the O-line, which gave Plummer less time to find his receivers, which forced him to improvise more. Jake's a great improviser, but you can't run an offense that way. My God, if it weren't for David Boston—who showed right away he had big-time skills—we would have gone 3 and out on half our possessions. This would have overwhelmed our already shaky defensive unit.

As it was, the defense often looked like Custer versus the Sioux. My first game—the Week 2 meeting with the Cowboys—was a perfect example. Dallas used a lot of motion before each snap, and it was very confusing at times. We gave up a lot of points, but made a fourth-quarter comeback and scored the go-ahead TD right after the two-minute warning. We failed on the 2-point conversion, but hung on for a 32–31 win. Dallas basically sucked that year (they had already lost 41–14 in the opener to the Eagles) but check it out, a win over the Cowboys is always precious.

I got a sack in this game, but already I could see this was not going to be a big statistical year for me. I was being doubled and even tripled on pass plays. On the one hand, this situation was detrimental for me, because I was going to hit the free-agent market without the gaudy sack numbers people looked for. On the other hand, I would be facing blocking schemes that would force me to get more creative, and that would theoretically enhance my value on the open market.

I would also be under pressure to demonstrate that I could handle myself against the run. My pass-rushing skills had always been my calling card, so naturally it had been said that the weakest part of my game was stopping the run. Technically, I suppose that would be true—but only in a relative sense. I am a more focused pass rusher than a run stopper, because that's what my teams pay me to do. Personally, I feel I play the run as well as anyone at my position. You can argue with that if you want, but my job is to get the man with the ball. If that happens to be the quarterback, then that's whose ass I'm chasing. If it's a runner trying to turn my corner or run through my part of the line, then he becomes my target. It's all a matter of perception.

The tricky thing about the 2000 season was that, while I was sitting out camp, Vince Tobin was telling everyone he was disappointed that I wouldn't be able to improve my play against the run. Taken at face value, that's a legitimate comment—you always work to improve during training camp. But within the context of the contract situation, it was unquestionably a slap at my skills. And probably a negotiating ploy. After all, it's easier to get a deal done with a guy who has a "hole" in his game. I thought this was pretty transparent, but the media picked up on it and threw down the gauntlet. What complicated things was that the Cardinals were looking for me to get to the quarterback. Over the years our defensive coordinator, Dave McGinnis, had even encouraged me to line up away from my normal position if I saw a mismatch I could exploit. If I continued to do this now, though, it would look as though I was avoiding run-stopping scenarios in favor of racking up sacks. It was a no-win situation.

The 2000 season began to look like a no-win (or, more correctly, a low-win) situation when we played Green Bay after a bye week. Brett Favre got the Packers an early lead, and they closed us out 29–3. Our D actually wasn't that bad in this game. They had two good runners in Dorsey Levens and Ahman Green, and obviously Favre knows how to manage a lead. But we kept them out of the end zone for the last forty-some minutes, limiting them to field goals. Unfortunately, our offense never got it going. Pittman and Jones were decent pass-catching backs, but neither were getting the tough yards we needed in crucial situations. We needed to get our shit together fast, because the 49ers were next on the schedule.

On paper, the San Francisco game wasn't too bad. We lost 27–20 to a superior team. But I felt we were stagnating. The defense—myself included—wasn't getting enough pressure on the quarterback, and we were still inconsistent against the run. Aeneas Williams was playing great, and I was doing my thing, but you need eleven guys working together, stepping up and making game-turning plays.

Meanwhile things weren't getting any better on offense. No one feared our ground attack, and Marc Trestman, the offensive coordinator, seemed reluctant to unleash Boston on long routes to stretch out opposing defenses. Some of the guys were beginning to question the coaching, which is a dangerous thing when you're a 1–3 team. Of course, nothing pulls you out of a funk like a victory. The Browns came into our building and we played a solid game for a change. We erased a 14–0 deficit to win 29–21, and limited Cleveland to a dozen first downs. Plummer was interception-free for the second game in a row, Pittman won back his starting job with a 100-yard performance, and we held together at the end when their QB, Tim Couch, tried to mount a comeback.

I can't say that we were at a turning point in our season, but our next test, against the Eagles, promised to tell us a lot about ourselves. They had an excellent pass rush and a dangerous offense, and I wasn't sure that we had answer for what they were going to throw at us. Well, we didn't. Donovan McNabb and friends beat us 33–14. We tried every kind of blitz package and junk defense, to no avail.

The nail in our coffin came early in 2000, perhaps even mercifully so. When the Cowboys demolished us 48–7, hope for a turnaround began to fade and the mood around the club became toxic. Troy Aikman had a bad back and was coming off a five-interception game, and the Dallas running attack was mediocre at best. This was winnable. So what happens? They run around us and through us, and throw over and underneath us almost at will. I played my heart out in this game, and Coach Tobin recognized me for my efforts, but there is no consolation when you get beat like that.

And it only looked like things were going to get worse. No disrespect to my linemates, but our front four was a shambles. Mark Smith, a holdout like me, hadn't bounced back to his previous form. Tony McCoy, was playing on a bad knee. Andre Wadsworth was just starting to practice again, but wasn't even close to 100 percent. I was playing next to guys like Jabari Issa and Russell Davis. Who? Exactly.

We blew a 10–7 lead to New Orleans the next week and lost 21–10. That was it for Vince Tobin. The Cardinals fired him and promoted Dave McGinnis. Dave is great, and the players, almost to a man, gave the change a thumbs-up. The cold fact, however, was that we would be facing a lot of good teams on the road in the second half, so the coaching change was unlikely to translate into more victories. We had blown our chance to get off to a fast start, and now we were reduced to playing for respect, and for next year.

As for me, it was looking more and more like next year I would not be wearing a Cardinals uniform. We weren't making any progress on a new contract. The team could have designated me a franchise player again, but I didn't see that happening. They didn't want to absorb the salary hit, and probably thought I'd be difficult to trade. They apparently had put feelers out the previous summer, but didn't receive the kind of offers they had hoped for. The lowballers had gotten lowballed in this case.

So I had to wrap my mind around the idea that I would be playing in a different city in 2001. It was a weird situation. As a player, you can't start looking at opposing teams and wondering how you would fit on their roster—certainly not if you expect to play effectively. And of course you aren't allowed to speak to another club until the season is over. So for the remainder of 2000, the main adjustment I had to make was just to keep up my enthusiasm for the remaining games. I had to dig deep and remember the things that make me love football, because I didn't want to pull on my uniform every Sunday and feel like I was punching a clock. Anyone who knows me knows I could never do that. Besides, that's the kind of mind-set that gets a player hurt. If I play my game at full speed, 100 percent, I don't worry about injuries—that's the other guy's problem. But if I play at three-quarters speed, I don't even want to think what could happen.

I understand why free-agents-to-be can't talk to other teams during the season. This would obviously compromise the integrity of the game. The hypocrisy of this situation, however, is that fans talk about it, the media talks about it, and every NFL club spends the whole year making personnel decisions based on whom they think will be available the following season. And everyone is always asking you, *Who would you like to play for next year? What would be your ideal situation? What kind of contract are you looking for?*

I dealt with this situation by blocking it out of my mind. That made it easier to sidestep the questions I was getting without feeling like I was lying to people. I was raised to tell the truth, yet in this case telling the truth might have created big problems. So I just shut it out. Even with my closest friends I found myself avoiding conversations about 2001. I knew it would only put them in a potentially difficult situation. If I told my boys that I was looking at one team over another, and they dropped that information on the wrong person, it would be all over the news, I'd be in hot water—and they would feel like crap.

We won our third and final game of the year against the Redskins 16–15. The defense played its best game of the season, sparked by Aeneas Williams, who scooped up a fumble in our end zone early in the game and returned it 104 yards for a score. The offense was stagnant, but we got 6 more points from MarTay Jenkins, our kick returner. This guy had game-breaking speed and great moves, but he was paranoid about fumbling and had been playing tentatively. McGinnis pulled him aside after he was made head coach and had a talk, and it worked wonders because Jenkins's 71-yard runback in the third quarter set up the winning TD.

That was about the last good moment for the Cardinals that season. We lost seven straight games, most by two touchdowns or more. We got creamed by the Eagles again, but I had a nice game with three sacks. Any pride I could take in that performance, however, was overshadowed by the fact that we missed so many damn tackles. I love Donovan, but I hate to lose to him in a sloppy game like that.

As the Cardinals played out the string in 2000, the media looked for positive angles on our season. They didn't focus much on me—I had one foot out the door and didn't have a lot of good things to say about the organization. I called Arizona an armpit at one point, which made me a pretty unpopular guy. (I was talking about the franchise, not the state.)

My final game in an Arizona Cardinals uniform was against the Washington Redskins on Christmas Eve. We gave the 'Skins an early present in the form of a 20–0 first-half lead, and watched them play with it for the rest of the afternoon. The final score was 20–3, I got one sack to give me 7.5 for the year, and I was a free man. An unrestricted free man. The Cardinals had cut me loose, and I could sell my services to the highest bidder.

The instant the season ended, I began to focus on where I would be playing the following year. I honestly felt that I was the type of player who could take a contending team and put them over the top. I had learned how to disrupt enemy offenses in ways that made my teammates more effective, so even if I didn't get X amount of tackles and X number of sacks, if we had good players at the other positions they would be able to do their thing. That's the kind of difference-making player every team is out there looking for, and I knew that others in the league viewed me that way. If a defensive coordinator or head coach couldn't see the impact I had on every down, all he had to do was ask his quarterback or offensive coordinator. So my strategy was to go meet with teams, put my chips on the table, and then talk dollars and years.

The clubs at the top my list were the Tampa Bay Buccaneers, New York Giants, Minnesota Vikings, and Chicago Bears. Just for the record, my order of preference was New York, Chicago, Tampa Bay and Minnesota.

The Bucs had impressed me a year earlier, during the 1999 playoffs. I was on a ski trip and watched them beat Washington to reach the NFC Championship game against the St. Louis Rams. They played with such confidence against the Redskins, and beat them 14–13. They played with such joy and really seemed to savor their triumph. I wasn't sure they had enough to beat the Rams the following week, they barely lost, 11–6. Of course, the Rams went on to win the Super Bowl in that great game against the Titans.

I watched the Tampa Bay–St. Louis game with my friend Bennie Morrow, and when it was over I turned to him and said, "Man, if I had been on that team, they would have won." I could tell from the way he answered, "You're right," that he was thinking the exact same thing. That moment stuck out in my mind when it came time to target certain clubs for 2001.

The Giants were appealing to me because I knew the coaches. Jim Fassel, the head coach, had been with Arizona for one season, my rookie year, in 1996. He was known for getting a lot out of quarterbacks, and I thought he did a good job with Kent Graham and Boomer Esiason. He took Kerry Collins, a castoff with a history of alcohol abuse, and resurrected his career. The Giants went all the way to the Super Bowl in 2000, and beat us twice that year. The Giants' defensive line coach was Denny Marcin, who coached me all those years at Illinois. He had been with the Giants since 1997, working under John Fox, who was a brilliant defensive coordinator. I had to wonder what it would have been like had the Cardinals skipped me in the draft and I'd been playing with the Giants. The player they took instead, Cedric Jones, never really got it going for New York. Who knows, we might have had a dynasty.

The Giants offered me that familiarity component. Football is a game where you are always proving yourself to someone. Even the top dogs feel like they have to prove themselves in new situations. The fact that the head coach and the line coach in New York knew me and knew my game meant I didn't have to prove anything to them.

The Vikings had been humiliated in the NFC Championship against the Giants, 41–0, but that didn't turn me off. Their coach, Dennis Green, always seemed to be dealing with some situation or another, and yet he always found a way to get the Vikings into the playoffs. I knew after the 2000 season they were going to lose John Randle and Dwayne Rudd, two outstanding defensive players, but I felt I could plug that hole. And they had a great young quarterback, Daunte Culpepper, along with talented guys like Randy Moss on offense. As it worked out, they ended up using some stopgap guys on defense and lost eleven games in 2001. I think Minnesota would have done better if I had been pass rushing, but we'll never know.

The attraction of the Bears was that I would be going home, and that weighed very heavily in their favor. They were coming off a 5–11 season, but that didn't mean a thing to me because they seemed to be another one of those teams that was just a player or two short of becoming a championship contender. They needed a pass rusher badly, so I had high hopes that we could come to an agreement. It would have been fun to play with Brian Urlacher. We seemed to have similar skills and a similar approach. He was a safety converted to linebacker, and I was a linebacker converted to end. We both cover a lot of territory. I definitely think I could have won a Super Bowl with that team. They finished with thirteen victories in 2001, ahead of the Bucs, but Donovan McNabb killed them in the playoffs.

After the season I began setting up meetings with the teams on my list. This was an eye-opening experience to say the least. Every conversation started with, "Here's what we've been hearing about you—that you're cancer in the clubhouse, that you take plays off, that you won't play the run, and that you aren't a leader." I was blown away. Instead of soaking up praise and discussing plans for 2001, I was on trial, expected to defend myself!

There I was, just about to turn 27, a player with fifty-plus sacks in his first five years—which was unprecedented—and not a team out there was willing to touch me. This was crazy. I couldn't believe that a player who had played as hard as I did—a banging player at the peak of his skills—would find free agency to be such a difficult ordeal. I felt like I had to *convince* people I could still play the game. Week in and week out, for five seasons all I'd done was dominate the guy on the other side of the line. I made the mistake of thinking that would speak for itself.

I didn't know where this was coming from, but I could guess. The Cardinals had been putting the word out that I was trouble, and with potentially thirty or forty million dollars on the table, other teams had no choice but to listen. Apparently the fact that Arizona was widely regarded as the league's most ass-backward franchise didn't raise anyone's suspicions.

I had always suspected that there was a game beyond the game in the NFL, but this was the first time I could see how it affected me directly and to my detriment. In this game the coaches talk to each other, the executives talk to each other, the big crank turns, and the players go into the grinder.

These are the people who'll be in the sport until they're old men, so while they are thinking about the performance of their team on the field, they are also trying to cement relationships with one another. It's an extension of the Bobby Ross situation. You never know when you might be out there looking for a job, so this is a form of networking. I don't begrudge the powers-that-be in football their right to do this. I've learned in my business ventures that every industry works this way to some degree. But still, when a piece of player information comes your way from the Arizona Cardinals, don't you investigate before basing a negotiation on it?

In retrospect, the stories the Cardinals were putting out probably kept the Cowboys and Eagles from pursuing me. They might have had salary-cap issues, or been planning to draft guys at my position, but they knew my game well enough to know how much I could have helped them. Yet they had no interest.

Philadelphia would have been a nice fit. They needed a guy like me to make plays in big situations. That's why they ended up giving Jevon Kearse all that money three years later. Yes, they had Hugh Douglas at one end, but together we would have made one hell of a tandem. The Eagles could have had one of the best defensive lines in football history. All they had to do was ask.

The fact is, I was on the open market and I couldn't find work. Even the teams I could have given some drama to were slow to pull the trigger, just in terms of setting up a sitdown. This was nuts. One of my friends said, "Sim, they just don't like you."

My response was, "Who are they? Who doesn't like me? Nobody even knows me!"

My first reaction to this strange turn of events was probably the wrong one. Privately I was like, *Fuck, wait a minute, I'm not a marginal player. I have been producing since my first day in the league. All I've done is play hard and break records.* So when I was confronted with all this bullshit my attitude at first was, *Okay, let's say I'm the bad guy the Cardinals claim. Why does this matter to you? I'm a young star hitting the market. My stats say I'm as good as any D-end ever in the first five years. This is a no-brainer—you should be knocking down my door!* Well, that didn't get me anywhere.

The truth is that I was confused. I am used to gathering all the facts in a situation, asking a lot of questions, and drawing a conclusion that helps me move forward. But in this case, the facts didn't make sense, no one had definitive answers to the questions I was asking, and therefore I didn't know what conclusion to draw, or how to proceed. Imagine what it's like to go into a phase of your life when you have achieved beyond everyone's wildest dreams only to find out everyone now thinks you're no good. How are you supposed to react to that?

I thought, *Damn, this makes no sense.* I literally couldn't conceptualize what was happening on the other side of the phone when we called.

The idea of me being a "cancer" in the locker room was particularly wounding. It's an offensive term, first of all, especially if you understand how insidious and painful cancer is. But people were throwing it around like the word meant nothing, like it was some sports term that didn't mean anything. Honestly, are there any players in the NFL who slowly gnaw away at their teammates and create a situation where the club is literally killing itself? Of course not. But that's what I think of when I hear the words *clubhouse cancer.*

I only had friends on that team. I was nothing but good to my teammates, and they were nothing but good to me. Now, I was never the kind of guy who tries to hang with everybody, but if you were a player on the Cardinals, you knew my door was always open. Where was this stuff coming from?

The only rift I had—if you could call it that—was with Jake Plummer. We were legit, we were cool. We were never great friends, but we never had any malice toward each other. Any feud or power struggle was a fabrication of the media, and he'll tell you so.

Here's how it went down. Toward the end of the 1999 season, I was asked what kind of a team leader Jake could be, and I answered that if he could play up to his potential and lead himself effectively, he could lead a team. I was acknowledged among my teammates as the leader of the Cardinals at that point, and I always felt it was because they saw how I prepared and performed. I had my own shit together and in that respect I led by example. That enabled me to be a vocal guy when need be, and also the kind of person who could pick you up when you were down. This was the idea I was trying to convey whenever anyone asked me about Jake.

This was a question people were asking around the Cardinal clubhouse for years, and after a while I felt like it was a slap in the face. It implied that I wasn't a good leader, or that I was just keeping a spot warm for Jake. I guess some of that came out in my answers, because the situation quickly became, *Simeon says Jake has to lead himself before he can lead anyone else*—and it made it seem like there was something wrong with Plummer. The real subtext was that we had enough leaders on the team, what we needed were performers. And Jake was a good player, so that wasn't even meant as a swipe against him.

Well, of course, the reporters go to Jake and tell him that Simeon said he couldn't lead. They tricked him into saying something negative about me. I could see what was developing and I stopped it right away. I confronted Jake, but in a cool way. I said, "C'mon Jake, don't play this game. You know me and you know I'm not a guy who shits on his teammates."

He said, "My fault, man."

I said, "Jake, you gotta know when people are setting you up like that. You know I'd never say anything to dis your game. Don't let these reporters play you—it's good between me and you."

I told him that even if he weren't one of the best players I'd ever played with—which he was—this was something between me and him. He acknowledged that, we talked it through, and we were fine. I was happy to see him get out of Arizona a couple of years later. He really flourished in the new environment with the Broncos.

The funny thing about that incident is that I knew Bennie Morrow would see Jake before I did, because I was in Hawaii for the Pro Bowl. I asked Bennie to tell him I wanted to talk. Apparently, Jake thought I was pissed, because he started ducking me. When I finally saw him we exchanged glances and he could see there wasn't a problem. We both started cracking up.

So it was my guess that's how the whole cancer thing must have started. Again, there was never a problem between me and my teammates in the Arizona locker room. It was a flat-out lie.

It was at this point in my career that I really came to understand—and, in a way, appreciate—just how well the machinery of football worked. It was extremely troubling, because you can't fight it. Yet at the same time, it's kind of awe inspiring. I was a Pro Bowl player, in the prime of my career, one of the most unique people to ever play my position, and here was this thing that was so much bigger than me. I'd never encountered anything like this in my life. I realized that no matter how big you get in football, there's always something bigger than you.

Even though evidence pointed to the contrary, the Cardinals were able to depict me however they wanted. All they needed to do was pull together a few shreds of evidence and the deal was done. They painted a certain picture of me that had nothing to do with reality, and there was literally nothing I could do about it.

The picture they chose was Simeon Rice as the NFL's version of Allen Iverson. No disrespect to Allen, but I was depicted as a player who had all sorts of off-the-field problems. When I'm away from football I spend my time with my close friends, people I've grown up with and have come to know along the way. This is not a gun-toting posse, these aren't wannabe gangsta rappers. They're cool. We watch each other's backs. We are all educated, intelligent, responsible individuals. In fact, we're damn boring most of the time. Yet just as I am about to embark on my free-agent journey, I find out that I'm this black sheep. I'm like, *Where do they come up with this stuff?* I don't drink, I don't smoke—if you're looking for a party animal, definitely don't look my way. You can't find a guy who is more focused on his craft than I am. I play football and I prepare to play football. If I think something's going to compromise these two goals, I don't do it.

Well, I was dealt this shitty hand and I had to play it. I didn't understand how to fight it. So I just tried to move forward. I figured I'd let my skills and my stats and my performance speak in my defense. My position was that anyone who looked at films of my final season in Arizona would know I'd played my ass off. Maybe this was naive. Maybe what they wanted was for me to approach teams hat in hand. Maybe I was supposed to admit my sins and cleanse my soul, so that I could play pure football again, or some bullshit like that. But that wasn't happening.

I sat down with Mark Hatley, the GM of the Bears, and got a taste of what was in store. He came right after me. "You're just a flash player," he said. "You can make the great plays, but you're all flash."

He compared me to Magic Johnson, saying I did things no one else could do, but that I didn't do all the right things. So when he got through telling me everything I ever wanted to know about myself, he said, "What do you think?"

I wasn't born yesterday. I knew there were a couple of things going on here. First, he wanted to see if I was a hothead. And of course, he wanted me to sell myself. Well, since he'd come at me sideways, I went back at him the same way. "I guess you just summed me up," I replied. "You didn't leave me much *to* say. If that's how you really feel, there's nothing I can do to refute that."

I was sitting there thinking, *Why should I go to a team where I would have to fight that perception?* After that meeting, I decided I would *only* go to a team that demonstrated from the start that they appreciated me. They didn't have to love *me,* but they had to love the way I played and what I could do for them. In Arizona, Dave McGinnis and Joe Greene felt that way about me and they told me so. As for the Vikings, it's safe to say that there wasn't much love to be found there. They called my agent and told him they didn't even want to meet with me based on what they'd heard around the league.

When I met with the Bucs, they appreciated me big time. They knew I could do all the things they needed a lineman to do to make their entire defense better. They didn't care what the rumors were, and didn't even understand where they came from. They were actually happy that they didn't have to outbid a dozen teams. I talked to everyone on the staff and got the same good feeling—Tony Dungy, the coach; Monte Kiffin, the defensive coordinator; and Rod Marinelli, the D-line coach. They did everything they could to show me they wanted my services. Their main focus was on trying to talk me out of going to the Giants.

The only time they brought up what I would call a negative—where they questioned my approach to defending against the run—it was done in a highly professional and intelligent manner. The Tampa coaches would give me an example and ask me why I'd played it the way I had. In most cases I responded that the coach had instructed me to play it that way. They were fine with that. They knew certain schemes require you to do certain things that may be construed as you not doing your best. The Buc coaches said, "Well, we'll want you to handle this situation in a different way."

I was so happy. That told me they got it. They got me. I was like, "Not a problem!"

The problem came when we began to talk about a contract. I don't know much about the history of contracts in the NFL, but I would venture to say that the deal I made with Tampa Bay was the most unconventional one ever signed by a star player in his prime.

Originally my goal was to find the right team, then negotiate a long-term contract that gave me a fair salary and at least five years. Ideally I was shooting for a ten-million-dollar signing bonus and fifty million over six years. The Bucs weren't offering that. Maybe it was the stuff they were hearing about me, or maybe it was just the way they had decided to shop the free-agent market, but the GM, Rich McKay, wanted something that protected the franchise no matter how I played. I know that's his job, but at this point I had convinced myself that I would have an immediate, transforming effect on this team. I just needed to convince them.

Rich was tough. He said, "Simeon, we don't have the money to pay what you want."

I told him I would take thirty-seven million over five years. "C'mon man," I said, "you've got to pay me something. Doesn't my performance count for anything? No one has done what I've done over the past five years in this league, and I'm still getting better."

There was silence at the other end of the phone.

I went on, "You know what? Forget the money. Just fuck it. Let's do a one-year deal. One year, one million dollars, and see what I do for you. "

My strategy was to play one year for nothing, have my best season ever, and then let the Bucs bid against twenty other teams. That's how badly I wanted to play for Tampa Bay.

I thought the Bucs would jump at this offer, but Rich wanted no part of it.

I said, "One year, five hundred grand. Hell, pay me the bare minimum for one year. I don't give a damn. I know who I am and what I can do. I'll come there for one year and bang out, then we can sit down."

"I'm not doing that," he said. "You could come down here and get twenty or thirty sacks. Then what?"

"Then I want to get paid!" I said.

"You'd be like a hired gun coming down here to collect your money and then leave to go somewhere else."

"Yeah," I told him. "I'm telling you *now* I'd do that. That's business. If you're not willing to pay me what I should get, what's the problem? Besides, I can't play the run, remember?"

"Well, where would that leave us?"

"That would leave you with one hell of a year, and then you'd have to take care of me. I would definitely want the whammy then."

Finally I asked Rich how many players of my caliber he'd dealt with who had said they'd take less than what they're worth. I knew the answer: None. The negotiations went back and forth for a while, and no one was moving. So I called and said, "Listen, Rich, if you bring me down there you're going to win the Super Bowl. Man, why are we playing around with this? You could have one of the greatest defenses of all time. We would have a huge impact on the game."

I told him to face reality. They needed a D-end who could chase quarterbacks, and there was no one better than me in the league. I was revolutionizing my position and I wanted to play for someone who saw the possibilities that would create. It was nitty-gritty time and he had to make a choice. "Let me come down there and show you what I'm about. We're hung up on the money, and I don't care about the money. Take what you think I'd be worth if I win you the Super Bowl and put it in the bank. I'll come get it when we win."

Rich told me they wouldn't do a one-year deal. I suggested they structure it to look like a five-year deal if that made him feel better. I couldn't believe what a fight this was.

I was putting the Bucs in an interesting position. They knew I had a deal on the table with the Giants at this point, so I definitely wasn't blowing smoke up their ass. It wasn't a great deal, either—the Bucs could have beaten it easily. New York had offered me twenty-four million over six years, which was far less than I was worth. What the Bucs may not have known was that I was not willing to consider this offer. It was one thing to take less than I was worth in order to showcase my talents on a team that was one step away from reaching the Super Bowl. But the Giants situation was that they were coming off a Super Bowl, and I would be playing on the other side from Michael Strahan.

I couldn't do that. I believed I was a better player than Strahan, and I knew myself well enough to know that would have gnawed away at me. This may sound silly given my peculiar circumstances, but in the NFL there is a pecking order in terms of talent and a pecking order in terms of salary. The money part of the equation is affected by salary cap and bonuses, but once you figure that into the equation, the elite players prefer the talent and money to be fairly consistent. In this case Michael, who is an excellent player, would have been making almost three times what I was, and that would have been a problem.

All along, I assumed I'd be in Tampa Bay. I didn't see a way that they *wouldn't* sign me. Eventually they took me up on my offer. I got a million dollars for one season, with a club option for a second year. I left a truckload of money on the table with the Giants, but it was respect I was looking for, not dollars. The Giants didn't respect me, my numbers, or the less-than-ideal situation I was coming from. And I knew Tampa Bay did.

When I came into camp and began doing my thing within the Bucs' defensive system, they realized what an asset I could be. They told me that they'd known I was a special player, but I was even more special than they had anticipated. Coach Dungy asked me if I could handle more responsibilities—make harder, more athletic plays. He told me that if they could redesign their D and count on me to make plays no one else could make, that would increase the effectiveness of the other people on the defense. We had Warren Sapp and Anthony McFarland at tackle, and they did a great job of clogging up the middle. Dungy believed that an athletic pass rusher like myself was the missing puzzle piece.

Man, I was so happy to do these things. I seriously felt I embodied what it meant to be a Tampa Bay Buccaneer, and I wanted to contribute whatever I could to take our defense to the next level. I thought we could be heralded as one of the greatest defenses of all time. That, in turn, would put me on the map, which was becoming increasingly important to me as I entered the prime phase of my career. I had played in anonymity in Arizona, but I knew if I could be seen as the ingredient that elevated Tampa to the Super Bowl, I would get the attention that was rightfully mine. So my goal in coming to Tampa was selfish in some respects. Everyone was saying the Bucs were one great player away from fulfilling their destiny; I wanted to assume that role. I desperately wanted to be that one great player.

In terms of putting pressure on myself, that pressure already existed when I arrived at camp. The Bucs had signed me and they had signed Brad Johnson, and Warren Sapp had been saying that if we didn't win a Super Bowl the team should be disbanded. That may have crystallized for me what the team's goal was, but in terms of pressure, I'd basically put my whole career and financial future on the line to get Tampa to the Super Bowl. Warren may have been "guaranteeing" a Super Bowl in his way, but I was literally putting my money where his mouth was.

My confidence level was sky high. I felt like I was a winning lotto ticket waiting to be cashed in. Nothing anyone wrote about me or the Bucs was going to change how excited I was about this opportunity. I was joining a team that supposedly had bad chemistry (by the way, it *didn't*), and that's why they hadn't reached their potential. I knew some people said I'd only make things worse, but those were people who didn't know me.

In truth, the chemistry issue was more about Warren than about me. There was always someone on the team he wasn't getting along with, and the assumption around the league was that the two of us would inevitably clash. Well, of course we were going to clash—our personalities are completely different. You don't have to understand the mentality of players like us to know that would happen. You do, however, have to understand our mentality to know that there wasn't going to be any kind of a long-term problem. My goal was to bridge into this new phase of my career smoothly and painlessly, and play a role that would help the Bucs win it all. Warren's goal was to win it all, too, and grab a few headlines in the process. Those goals were, to my mind, absolutely compatible.

The moment Warren and I came to face-to-face he started feeling me out. He wanted to know if I was the type of guy the press had made me out to be. And incidentally, he had every right to do so. I can tell you that if I *was* that guy, we definitely wouldn't have gotten along. But once we got to know each other, we hit it off like brothers, and we're really tight to this day. We had a natural chemistry, which doesn't surprise me. I grew up in a city where you had to deal with a lot of different personalities. Warren has a big personality, but he reminded me of guys off the block I grew up with. So we got along great.

Warren said, "Sim, you're one of the best I've ever seen play this game of football. You're special." For him to say that—especially knowing how he views his own skills—was one of the best moments in my career. That's better than any award I've ever received. Warren also told me that the defense was designed around players who had great skills. He said if I was as great as I was supposed to be, it would show—but if I wasn't, if it was all hype, that I would be exposed. I was cool with that.

Looking back, I think this was a key moment in the evolution of the team. We both were aware that people in the locker room thought the two of us might collide, like a couple of lions fighting for control of the pride. We were two alpha males competing on the same turf and I think the other players were afraid of what might happen. Once they saw that we had a very high level of respect for each other's skills and personalities, everything was cool and we could focus on playing football.

That was important, because I needed time to digest Dungy's defensive system. He played a lot of zones, and my responsibilities were different on a play-to-play basis than they had been in Arizona. I'll be honest, I was expecting it to click right away, but that wasn't happening. I wasn't getting it. It was taking me time to learn how to take advantage of the opportunities that were created by this new scheme. This was the first time I'd ever felt I was being challenged mentally by football and not responding. The frustrating thing was that, at its core, the Tampa Bay defense was actually a simpler one than we played with the Cardinals. I had always based my game on a combination of speed, strength, and creativity, but to be creative you had to have a complete knowledge of the system in which you are operating.

My position coach, Rod Marinelli, decided he would keep me in a three-man rotation until I'd mastered the system. That pissed me off. We got into it a couple of times, because I was used to being the man, and here I was reduced to being platooned with Marcus Jones and Steve White. Also, when we lost, the coaching staff would focus on me and ask me in front of the other players what I could have done better. It pained me to play the fool, because deep down I knew I was doing special things out there. I was coming from a team where I was praised and admired, and now I was rotating.

That's probably the only time I felt pressure in Tampa Bay. We were expected to win every game, but in the first half of the season we failed to win two games in a row. We started well enough, holding off a late charge by Quincy Carter and the Cowboys in the opener for a 10–6 win. We didn't play again until we met the Vikings in Week 4, because of a postponed game in Philadelphia (this was when the September 11 attacks occurred), followed by a bye week.

The time off slowed my transition into the system, and probably didn't do our offense much good, either. Brad Johnson moved the ball okay, but we couldn't score when we got close. We managed only 16 points against the Vikings in that game. Still, we had them pinned at their own 4 needing a touchdown to win late in the fourth quarter. This is where a great defense doesn't give the other team a chance to breathe, but they took it all the way, with Daunte Culpepper hitting tight end Byron Chamberlain with a short pass that he took another 30 yards down to our 3. Minnesota scored to win 20–16. It was embarrassing.

The next week we held the fort on the final drive and beat Green Bay 14–10. Shelton Quarles, our linebacker, ran an interception back for a 98-yard TD in the first quarter, and our offense put together a great drive to win it late. On the final play of the game we chased Brett Favre all over the place and John Lynch batted away his pass to Donald Driver. A good, hard-fought victory. I was looking forward to many more of these as a Buccaneer.

We lost the following week to Tennessee when my old teammate Joe Nedney kicked a field goal in overtime. The Steelers beat us a week later to run our record down to 2–3. The Bucs had a reputation for starting slow and finishing strong, but you still hate to lose close games early. We rebounded with a 41–14 blowout of the Vikings to even our record, but to be honest I was still lost at times in Dungy's defense. The low point of the year followed when we lost to the Packers 21–20. We did a nice job against Favre again, but Ahman Green ran for 169 yards against us. Dexter Jackson, our safety, blitzed Favre and caused a fumble in Green Bay territory, but we couldn't come up with the ball. That was the game right there.

After what I'd been through in the off season, to come to a sub-.500 team and then not get the new defense, I was ready to say *The hell with it, I guess I don't understand a damn thing about football after all*. Well, that's not how I was raised, and that's not the kind of attitude that had helped me succeed in the past. I was searching for a way to motivate myself to reach the next level when I decided, *You know what? My goal is to make these coaches regret the day they decided to rotate me. I'm going to shine so bright they can't ignore me*. Here I was, an impact performer in my prime, stuck in a rotation—what other top player has to put up with this? I realized I could either brood about this or excel. I chose to excel.

Then, suddenly, it all clicked. I remember telling my friends, "It's snapping off—I understand this defense now, and it's going to be big." Up to that point, it seemed like I'd always get to the quarterbacks a half beat too late. Now I began nailing them while they still had the ball. Over the final ten weeks I got nine sacks, and I was in their faces constantly. The funny thing is that they kept the rotation going for a while even after I clearly was comfortable in the system. It got to the point where after a play when it was my turn to go out, my teammates would say, "Sim, just stay in the game." I'll never forget, we were playing Detroit and I was just bringing hell to the Lions on every play. They started moving the ball and Tony looked over at me and gave me a look like *What're you doing here on the sideline?* I smiled at him and shrugged. "It's my rotation."

We won that game to go 4–4. The following week I played the game of my life against Chicago and they kept taking me out. It was getting ridiculous. So as I was coming back to the sideline after a series, Rob Marinelli said, "Sim, just stay in the game." They never substituted again for me that year.

In the second half of the 2001 season we showed what kind of team we could be. We had so many talented players with the Bucs. My job as an incoming free agent was to make them better, and they made my job easy. I was playing with a group of guys who could consistently hold their own. Knowing there was not a weak link behind me was something new, something special, and it amplified my performance. It eventually enabled me to reach a plateau in my own career that I might not have reached in a different situation.

The impact of a good, consistent defense is that it messes up the timing of your opponent's offense. If they need 2.5 seconds to get a play off and you are on top of them in 2.2, it forces them to divert from their game plan and move away from their strengths. The beauty of great defense like we had in Tampa Bay was that we not only stopped the other team, but also took the ball away and actually scored points against them. A great defense can also "manage" a game, which a lot of fans don't appreciate. By not allowing the other team to make first downs and put up points, you give the ball back to your offense and let it find its rhythm. This is crucial late in games, because it enables your offense to play to its strengths and keep it out of situations where it might be forced to throw interceptions.

Let me tell you, every person on that defense was rock solid. The standout guys besides Warren Sapp and myself were Derrick Brooks, John Lynch, and Ronde Barber. Derrick is very sound and very smart. He is like most of the great players in football—very cerebral, with a high IQ. The thing that blew me away about Derrick when I joined the Bucs was how in tune he was with what was going on in a game. This was true of Warren, too. Every second they were on the field, nothing got by them. They understood the little things about football to the point that even if a certain player was inserted in a certain situation, they knew exactly what the play would be. When other teams tried some bullshit trick 'em dick 'em play, they picked it up instantly. It was like having two brilliant coaches on the field at all times.

Derrick studies films religiously and knows tendencies as well as anyone in the league. He is as knowledgeable about football as anyone I've met. Is he the best linebacker I've ever played with? If I can divide linebackers into inside and outside guys, I would say yes. Derrick, along with Kevin Hardy, my teammate at Illinois, play their respective positions at an extremely high level—a Hall of Fame level. The interesting thing is that they approach the game differently. Derrick plays inside, and he plays it like an anaconda. You're lured into thinking you're safe and then *Bam!* he's eating you alive. Kevin is more overt and more aggressive in the way he plays, which is what you look for in an outside guy.

John Lynch is a really sound player as well. He had been with the team for years, and had seen a lot of bad times before the good times came, but he had plenty left in the tank when I got there. From his safety position, John reads and reacts extremely quickly, and he works off an amazing store of football knowledge. To a certain extent, he was also like an extra coach on the field. He was a very vocal leader, a rally-the-troops kind of guy. On some teams, you want to smack a guy like that, but on the Bucs we developed a chemistry where he knew his type of leadership could be effective.

Stat-wise, the breakout player during my first season with the Bucs was Ronde, who intercepted ten passes. He is an exceptional talent, and we made each other's jobs easier. People don't appreciate the way an end and a cornerback work together, because it's not obvious from what you see on the field. But rest assured, it's a hand-in-glove relationship. The better cornerbacks you have, the better your ends look, and the better ends you have, the better your cornerbacks look.

Think of it this way: The instant the ball is snapped, an imaginary clock starts ticking. An end only has a certain amount of time to close in on the quarterback before he selects his receiver and throws. A good cornerback can extend that time by covering his man well, which results in a forced pass, an intentional incompletion, or a sack. A good end can get to the quarterback quickly, forcing him to make a decision earlier than he would like. This can result in a hurried pass, which might be intercepted by the cornerback. If the end puts consistent pressure on the quarterback, he has to resort to short passes, which brings the linebackers into the picture. This not only limits the possibility of a long gain, but also sets up the LBs for interceptions they can run back for touchdowns. Derrick Brooks specialized in this play, and we were very conscious of creating opportunities for him. Suffice it to say, the end–cornerback relationship—when working well—has a very positive effect on the entire defense.

By the same token, a cornerback who loses his man early makes it impossible for a pass rusher to get to the quarterback. Likewise, if an end can't generate a consistent pass rush, the cornerback has to stay close to his receiver longer, which is difficult to do. The receiver knows where he wants to go and the defender can only guess, so eventually he will shake loose and find a way to get open. That had been a problem for the Bucs before I got to Tampa Bay, which is why they were desperate to get a pass-rushing end. So like I said, I made Ronde's job much easier. And Ronde—being a special cover guy—forced the quarterback to hang on to the ball longer, which gave me the extra time I needed to do my thing. Brian Kelly, who really blossomed the next year when he led the league in interceptions, is one of the best defensive backs I've ever played with. He has really been overlooked by the league, despite the fact that he and Ronde rank among the best of their generation. Props to you, Brian!

The main man in the Tampa Bay defense for years, of course, was Warren. Fans think of him as a great player with a big mouth, and they are correct on both counts. What they don't realize is that he may be a genius, too. No bullshit.

Warren also has a little bully in him. What makes him a great player is that he can spot a weakness that others don't see, then exploit it over and over again. Unfortunately, he can be the same way with people, especially with a guy who's just coming into the league. It was unbearable to watch sometimes. The man pulls no punches.

Yet he'll then turn around and do something totally above and be-yond for the same person he's been torturing. I've seen him shit on someone mercilessly, then extend himself beyond all reason and under-standing. We had a rookie on the Bucs in 2002 whom Warren rode the hell out of for months. He was relentless. Finally this guy was cut before we went to the Super Bowl, and the team wasn't going to make him a ring. We all thought that sucked, but it was Warren who fought for the guy and got him his ring. When I found out, I asked Warren if he had called the guy to let him know. He said, "I ain't calling that fuckin' white boy." That's Warren Sapp in a nutshell.

I'd have to say Warren is the most unique person I've met in my life. You know how in cartoons, a guy's got a little angel on one shoulder telling him the right thing to do, and a devil on his other shoulder, whis-pering all kinds of bad ideas? Well, that's Warren. And you never know which side he's listening to. I'll never forget my reaction when I first met the man. I thought, *Wow, this is the first person I've ever met who is definitely going to hell!*

As a player, Warren is as talented as they come. He's like a grizzly bear. He is a big, big guy who is extremely athletic. He has all the moves—he is quick and strong, he can overpower you or make you miss him completely. He has a signature game, a game that's his alone. I don't think I've seen a better pass rusher from the defensive tackle position. If he were any better, I don't see how anyone could possibly stop him.

Warren and I played on the same line for three seasons before he went to the Raiders, and the perception was that when we lined up to-gether, we were unstoppable. I'd like to go on record as saying that this was a misperception. We actually played better when we were away from each other. The two of us attracted too much traffic. When Warren and I lined up together, half the blockers slid our way after the ball was snapped.

The Buccaneers turned it up a notch against the St. Louis Rams in late November, on a *Monday Night Football* game. We put together three classic touchdown drives, forced five turnovers against a superb offense, and saved Tony Dungy's job (or so we thought) with a 24–17 win. Our lack of consistency had had the fans and the press calling for Tony's head. But on this night it was all good. Mike Alstott scored twice and Warrick

Dunn made a beautiful run for a TD that gave us the winning margin at the beginning of the fourth quarter. From there the defense and special teams just kicked ass.

The following week I had a big game against the Bengals in a 16–13 win, then we beat the Lions in another close contest, 15–12, for our third straight victory. Keyshawn Johnson, who was leading the league in catches, got his first touchdown of the year to win it. Had we lost to the Lions, the fans would have run us out of Tampa. They were 0–11. Unfortunately, any hope we had of winning the division disappeared the following week, when we lost badly at Chicago, 27–3. Anthony Thomas killed us, and we managed only a field goal against their defense.

To reach the playoffs at this point, we needed a minimum of nine wins, and we had seven with three games to play. The good news was that we played at home the rest of the way. The bad news was that we were scheduled to play the Saints, Ravens, and Eagles, who were all quality teams with an eye on the postseason. With our mission clear, we were really focused in practice and meetings the week before the New Orleans game, and it showed. We destroyed them 48–21. Everything was clicking. That team on that day could have won the Super Bowl. It was easily our best game of the season.

We followed that up with a 22–10 win in a Saturday game against Baltimore, the defending Super Bowl champions. They had beaten the Giants right in this stadium less than a year earlier, so they were pretty confident coming into Tampa. They were certain they could win the mini battles that take place on a football field, but on this day we won them all. We were in the playoffs and genuinely psyched about our chances. We kept saying that the road to the Super Bowl must go through the Super Bowl champs, so this felt like a very significant win.

A lot of that goodwill evaporated in our home finale, however, when the Eagles put in a couple of no-names and stole a win from us in front of our own fans. Philly was already a lock for the playoffs at 10–5, so Donovan McNabb only played the first series. He was replaced by Ty Detmer, who eventually gave way to AJ Feeley, a rookie out of Oregon who'd never set foot on an NFL football field. He threw two touchdown passes to Dameane Douglas, literally the last guy on their bench, and they won 17–13. We were playing our second string, too, but that's no way to go into the playoffs—especially since we were going to play them up in Philly in the first round.

The Bucs had enough talent on defense to beat anyone, but our offense never really got in gear in 2001. Brad Johnson provided the expected improvement over the young guy, Shaun King, but the running game could not repeat its success of past seasons. Traditionally, Warrick Dunn had gotten most of the carries, while Mike Alstott got the ball when we needed tough yards. In 2001 Warrick played a lot of games hurt, so the carries were more evenly divided. The result was that both runners were less effective.

Still, the finger-pointing was mostly in Brad's direction. At this level of sports, you ultimately prove yourself by doing one thing: winning. Brad had a nice résumé, but just like in my case, in order to achieve greatness you actually have to play great. You have to be as good or better than advertised. Brad was expected to be the front half of the "Johnson & Johnson" connection, with Keyshawn on the receiving end. When the offense failed to raise hell in 2001, the skeptics came out and Brad—who played with a lot of injuries—found himself in the hot seat. People were looking at his 2001 numbers and saying that they were similar to Shaun's. So the question was: What had the Bucs gained by making this move?

Early in the season, when the offense wasn't moving the ball and I was stuck in that rotation, Brad and I both felt like we were getting slapped in the face. We were the newcomers who had been brought in to boost the team's fortunes, and we were being told that we weren't getting the job done. The jury was definitely out on us during the first half, which is an uncomfortable feeling. But we both had great second halves, which was a big reason the Bucs pulled together and made the playoffs. Now we had to take this team forward. Brad, who was pretty banged up, had the bigger challenge. Keyshawn and Warrick were too hurt to play against the Eagles, so he was missing a couple of key weapons.

In preparing for the Philly game, there was a lot of talk about exorcising demons. The Eagles had humiliated the Bucs in the wild-card game a year earlier, 21–3. I wasn't a part of that team, so I didn't really use that as a motivating factor. Maybe my teammates shouldn't have, either, because this was an ugly, ugly game.

We got inside their 20 twice in the first half, but the best we could do was a pair of field goals. The Eagles were running the ball well against us, but we had contained them to 10 points as the first half was drawing to a close. Then after the two-minute warning, all kinds of shit happened. First, Philly was forced to punt, and they pinned us back on our 3-yard line. After we failed to get a first down, our guy, Mark Royals, punted short, and Donovan got the ball back just 31 yards from our end zone. He threw a little screen to Duce Staley, who ran right through us for a touchdown. There was enough time on the clock for us to put together a mini drive, and Martin Gramatica kicked a third field goal to cut the deficit to 17–9.

That was it for highlights. Our running game stalled in the second half, and we were forced to go to the air after Correll Buckhalter scored for Philly in the third quarter. All week Tony Dungy had told the offense that we could run on these guys, but it wasn't happening. And the Eagles had too disciplined a defense to let us come back through the air. They already had 24 points, and they hadn't allowed anyone to score 21 all season. The final score was 31–9; we never even got close to scoring again.

The guys were pretty depressed about this loss. To me, the saddest thing about the game was watching Tony on the sidelines. He had been Tampa Bay's greatest coach, and we all knew this would probably be his last game. We wanted to use that as motivation, but it didn't happen. That made the loss all the more disappointing. Rich McKay, who was also on the way out, had been right: This team was more than a year away from the Super Bowl. He'd been smart to tie me up for two seasons.

After the postseason I was kind of disappointed that I hadn't been invited to play in the Pro Bowl. I had eleven sacks in my first go-round with the Bucs, which put me among the league leaders. You only play a few years in this game, and when you have a good season and don't get recognized for it, it's almost like it didn't exist. I was talking to some of the people in the Tampa Bay PR office about this, and they had a very interesting take on the situation. They thought I needed to be more like Warren: more vocal, more brash. I asked them why I couldn't get recognized for my work on the field. *I have to create some antics just to get some love? I'm not doing that.*

Ask anyone about me. I don't have a superstar's mentality. I don't elevate myself to that level. It's a burden I'm unwilling to bear. It's hard enough playing the game, much less keeping up that kind of an image. I see guys like that and wonder how they do it. It's got to be exhausting. How does a player like me get some attention in this world? The right kind, I mean. I told myself if we won the Super Bowl, maybe I'd write a book.

One of the traps athletes fall into is thinking that if they believe in something badly enough, then it's got to be true. This can lead to some catastrophic decisions, personally, professionally, and financially. One of the challenges for someone like me is to separate the good shit from the bullshit, especially when you're surrounded by people who, in trying to be supportive, sometimes agree with something you say for no better reason than you just said it. The older you get, the better you become at telling the difference.

But what happens when the bullshit in your *own* head keeps you from experiencing the good shit? A case in point is a relationship I had with a woman during my final days with the Arizona Cardinals. Her name was Courtney. And she was white.

I never really understood interracial relationships. In fact, I was against them. My brother, Diallo, married a white woman, and I refused to meet her. I refused to acknowledge this relationship because it was so alien to me. Eventually they were divorced, and to this day I have never laid eyes on her. And I didn't just ignore their marriage, I gave Diallo hell about it.

Call me a racist, a bigot, whatever, but for years that was just how I felt. Having white friends, white teammates, white business partners, white fans—even having sex with white girls—was never a problem for me. I got along with people regardless of their race or nationality, and I was used to white people, having gone to predominantly white schools my entire life. But crossing that emotional point of no return with a white woman, I simply could not wrap my mind around that.

I don't recall my parents ever saying stuff like, *Stick to your own kind,* but everyone is a product of their environment, so I'll go ahead and blame it on them anyway. Actually, I'm a big believer in keeping life simple and stress-free, and to me nothing seemed more complicated and stressful than an interracial relationship. I first remember feeling this way in third grade, after I sent a letter to a white girl named Rebecca saying that I liked her. This was not the 1950s, mind you; this was the 1980s. But I got into all kinds of trouble. I was told that black boys didn't send letters to white girls. And I wasn't told nicely. This was burned into my consciousness, and that's all I care to say about the episode.

When I came to Phoenix in 1996, I started to encounter a different way of thinking. All the brothers were talking to white girls. I'm like, *What the fuck?* The truth was, there simply weren't that many black people out there; Phoenix was wall-to-wall white people. Still, I figured if you looked hard enough you could probably find what you were looking for. After a while, however, I realized it wasn't that my black teammates weren't looking hard enough—believe me, there were some fine sisters available—it was actually a preference. I was in a state of complete culture shock that lasted for a good four years. When I was in Phoenix, I felt like I was a space traveler spending time on a strange and distant planet, and this was a big reason why.

One night, I went out to a club with a friend, a white woman, who introduced me to Courtney. My eyes lit up when I saw her. *Wow,* I thought, *that girl is fine! She's banging!* And as I talked to her I realized, *Damn, she's good people.* This was the first time I had been smitten by a white woman, and I was both curious about my reaction and incredibly attracted to her.

As I got to know Courtney, I tried to compare her to other people I'd encountered. She kind of reminded me of the black girls I'd known who were from the suburbs. She was into the same music, and the way she acted reminded me of people I'd grown up with. Only she didn't talk like a black girl. Or a white girl, for that matter. All the stereotypes of white girls I'd grown up with—the freaks, the hos, the girls gone wild—were shattered just like that. She was sweet, compassionate, very classy, very independent. The best way I can describe Courtney is that she was always herself. And in the end, is there anything more attractive than that?

Courtney and I were kindred spirits. She was comfortable with who she was, and not afraid to do anything, go anywhere, or take on any challenge. She was skilled and she was dependable. She could go into an all-black club and feel right at home. It was like there was nothing she couldn't do. The other thing about Courtney is that she always had a great job. One company was always hiring her away from another company because she was so charming and capable, and within a couple of months it seemed like she was practically running the new company.

Another thing I liked about her was that she wasn't into black men because they were black. When I was at her place I'd sneak a look at her pictures, and the guys she'd been with—white or black—were really smooth looking. Not to sound gay, but I would think, *Hey that's a handsome cat.* She had high standards for herself, and high standards for the men in her life. This I found especially intriguing.

Anyway, we started messing around, and the more time I spent with her the more I liked her, despite my being kind of intimidated at first. Usually I like to do my share of the talking, but the fact that I couldn't predict what she was going to say next made me hesitant to speak sometimes. It took me a good month before I could really engage her in a long conversation. With other girls I could just say whatever popped into my head, because I was Simeon Rice and I was in control, but with Courtney I had to think stuff through before I said it.

In time I discovered that we were on exactly the same wavelength. That's the thing that caught me completely off guard. We read people the same way. We listened to the same music. We were intrigued by the same topics. We disliked the same things. Her culture was my culture, but because she was white it took me a long, long time to trust my own judgment enough to move the relationship along.

I saw Courtney for almost two years, and this spanned the time I went from Arizona to Tampa Bay, so we always had a lot to talk about. Eventually, however, the distance became an issue, which meant we were nearing that point where you've got to make a decision. We could have gotten closer, I suppose, and done something more permanent, but instead, with that added pressure, we drifted apart. I stopped calling her, and it broke her heart. I think she was in love with me. But the next move would have been marriage, and the idea of marrying a white girl was still frightening to me. This was not a surprise to Courtney, but I think she believed I would get past it. When she asked me why I felt this way, I'd always say, "It's not my fault, the world raised me like this."

I learned a lot about myself during and after Courtney. I felt dumb for ending a relationship for that reason. I wanted to be a more enlightened person, and I was ashamed that I hadn't evolved in my views. I thought I was so cultured, so sophisticated, so open to new ideas, but when the time came to take the next step I'd chickened out. I still feel bad about that relationship, but I grew from there. Thanks to her, I doubt the black–white obstacle will affect my future relationships. Consequently, I have more love and respect for Courtney today than ever. And I told her so recently—when she called to say she was getting married. People are just people, and if you bring stereotypes into a relationship you may be creating problems where none exist.

I've taken that philosophy into my current relationship, and it has helped me see advantages where I used to see pitfalls. There is mutual respect and admiration as we grow and learn from each other, a case of two people becoming better individuals because they are together. There are still growing pains, and my profession puts unique demands on us, but I feel like I'm mature enough now to handle anything.

I learned this lesson too late to reconcile with Courtney, but I did end up with something to show for the experience. I began writing a screenplay for a story based on our relationship, but this one ends happily ever after. Where I fucked up the real one, I fix the one in the movie. I finished the script in 2004 and through some connections in LA got it looked at by a few studios. Who knows where it will go, but writing it was very therapeutic. In Hollywood pitchspeak, it's *Guess Who's Coming to Dinner* meets *Good Will Hunting*. And no, I will not be playing the lead.

There was some *football* to be played in 2002. Some great football, as it turned out. The big news heading into the season was that Tony

Dungy was out and Jon Gruden was in. We were sad to see Tony go, but we understood that things like this happen in this game, and unfortunately it was simply his time. As a player, you just focus on playing your game and trust that the new guy's plan works out for the team. Besides, we felt we were so close to taking that next step, and we were anxious to see if we could become what we were supposed to become. The only difference was that now we had a new leader.

The Bucs traded draft picks for Gruden, who had been the head coach of the Oakland Raiders for the past four years. He was the youngest coach in the league, but already he had a reputation for getting a lot out of his offensive personnel. Obviously, this was important to our team, because we'd never really gotten it in gear during the previous season.

As a defensive player you don't really get involved in the inner workings of the offense, even though you practice against it and watch it from the sidelines during games. Still, you think about it to a fair degree, because the more time they spend on the field, the less time the defense has to. What I found most encouraging about having a guy like Gruden running the show was that he had been the offensive coordinator for the Eagles and receivers coach for the Green Bay Packers. If we hoped to reach the Super Bowl, the chances were good that we would have to go through at least one of those teams—and both were on our schedule for 2002. I never even thought far enough ahead to see an advantage we would have in the Super Bowl, but of course that's exactly how it shook out.

There were a couple of other changes Gruden was likely to bring about. Whereas Tony was a pretty laid-back coach where the press was concerned, Jon was a fiery type, a lightning rod. That's his personality, but I think there was a calculated aspect to it, too. A coach like that can step in front of the microphones and divert attention from the team if he feels that it will be beneficial. Some people were speculating that Jon's strong personality might generate lightning itself, but the truth is that most NFL coaches have strong personalities. It's just that the fans and the press don't always see it. The second thing about Gruden was that he was the first offensive-oriented head coach I'd ever played for, so I was curious to see how that would work out. I wasn't sure what kind of relationship we would have, if any. I thought maybe he would give Monte Kiffin and Rob Marinelli more autonomy.

All that being said, I didn't spend a lot of time analyzing the coaching change. You can only deal with so much before you get distracted, and players just don't get caught up in all that. You might think about it as a response to a reporter's question or when your friends ask you about it. In my mind, if the players did what we were supposed to do—and basically, that's how all players think heading into a new season—then these scenarios wouldn't really come into play. If the issue was how the coach would affect team continuity and chemistry, then yes, I was concerned. But that's something the players really take care of themselves. We knew a new boss might bring some changes, and some of us might have to do things in a way we weren't used to or didn't like, but that's life, whether you work for the transit authority or the Tampa Bay Buccaneers. You roll with the punches, you move forward, you be a man about things.

When we gathered for camp that summer, however, something did feel a little different. I'd gone into every season of my career believing that if everyone played up to their ability, my team had a chance to reach the playoffs. But this time the expectation was higher than that. It wasn't *if,* and it wasn't *when.* It was going to happen that year or it wasn't going to happen at all.

The Bucs had a really good team. Our defense was so strong and so sound and so confident, it was as if at that point in our collective careers we owed ourselves a championship. We needed to win a championship to crystallize the caliber of play that veterans like Warren Sapp, Derrick Brooks, John Lynch, Brad Johnson, and I had produced over the years. It was time to do something special, to finish as a group what we had started as individuals. And I won't lie—we knew the clock was ticking on us. After 2002 the odds were that some key people would be leaving, and we would all be a year older, too.

For me, winning it all took on a more personal urgency. I had developed a sense of history, of how a player is measured and where he fits into the pro football time line. I recognized how ideal this situation was. Warren and John and Derrick had begun to turn things around for the Tampa Bay franchise before I got there, and together our group had gotten the job done and brought the team's performance up a notch. If we made it to the Super Bowl—if we *won* the Super Bowl—it would be a highlight that would define each of our careers.

We stayed healthy throughout camp and the exhibition games, beating the Dolphins, Jaguars, and Texans. The Redskins blew us out, but the only people who care about that are the fans. As we prepared for the first regular-season game against the New Orleans Saints, we were very pleased about the kind of playmakers we had in our lineup. Warrick Dunn was gone, replaced by my old Arizona teammate Michael Pittman, who had developed into a nice runner. The fullback was still Mike Alstott; the idea was that we'd go back to the formula where he was not asked to carry the load, except on short-yardage plays and around the goal line. Keyshawn Johnson and Keenan McCardell were back, along with Joe Jurevicius—all three of those guys could make big-time catches. The O-line was anchored by the center, Jeff Christy, and we had two very good tackles in Roman Oben and Kenyatta Walker.

The defense, I have to say, was magnificent. Greg Spires was coming into his own as a defensive end, and Warren Sapp and Chartric Darby brought hell in the middle. Anthony McFarland, Ellis Wyms, and Buck Gurley also had outstanding seasons. Derrick Brooks was the man at linebacker, at the absolute peak of his skills, both physically and mentally. The same could be said of our entire defensive backfield, which included Ronde Barber, Brian Kelly, Dexter Jackson, and John Lynch. Every time I looked around that huddle I saw a defense that wasn't just capable of shutting down an opponent; we had the kind of talent that could actually be counted on to put points on the board. The master-mind of this unit was Rob Marinelli, who I swear is the best defensive coach that ever lived.

There literally wasn't a weak link in our defense in 2002. Fans probably don't realize how rare that is, and they certainly can't feel what the players do on the field. If you know that the other ten guys are going to get the job done, you can really concentrate on beating your man, controlling your part of the field, and you have a better sense of when to gamble on a big play. You can still get beat, mind you—it's the NFL, after all, and there's a lot of talent on the other side of the ball. But you feed off the success of your teammates, and once you find a good rhythm it's almost impossible for the other team to move the ball with any kind of consistency.

Unfortunately, we didn't quite find that rhythm in our opening game. We were playing the Saints, a team that historically you expect to put in your pocket. Little did we know that they had some serious talent, and in fact they dogged us in the standings for most of the season. In this game their quarterback, Aaron Brooks, made some big-time throws, including a TD pass to their first-round pick, Donté Stallworth. Their other wideout, Joe Horn, burned our secondary for eight catches, and Deuce McAllister went over 100 yards on the ground. We weren't playing badly, we just weren't playing together as a defense, and we were down 20–10 with time running out. Brad Johnson got us into the end zone with less than three minutes left, and the defense went out and got him the ball back for one last try. He drove us within field-goal range, and Martin Gramatica put it through to force overtime.

Normally this is the kind of game a team like ours wins—and definitely the kind of game the Saints specialized in losing. But both defenses stepped up in OT. With about three minutes left, the Saints pinned us back against our goal line, and the punting team came on. Tom Tupa received the snap, but almost immediately Fred McAfee—a little running back who played special teams—was in his face. There was no time to kick, so Tom made the right play and tried to throw a pass. A safety meant the game, remember, so he had nothing to lose, even if it had fallen incomplete. But Tom's pass went right to James Allen, a linebacker seeing action in his first NFL game, and he ran it in for a touchdown.

As ugly a loss as that was, you don't put your season on one game. The fans may have been stunned by that defeat and taken it as a bad omen, but the players didn't see it like that. There had been a lot of talk in the locker room about how a team that wins the Super Bowl has to take a long journey. We knew we would be tested and surprised and disappointed along the way, as a rite of passage in a sense. So our attitude was, *This is just part of the journey.*

What we took from that game was that we couldn't take any team lightly, especially a team like the Saints, which was always up for the Tampa Bay Buccaneers, whom they saw as a rival. We didn't recognize how deeply they disliked us. We didn't play the game we were supposed to play. And we paid the price. That New Orleans loss helped us lock in, and it gave our coaches plenty to talk about during the week. We wanted a great bounce-back game, and we had the perfect situation for it—a road game against the Baltimore Ravens, the 2001 Super Bowl champions.

The Ravens game was a special moment for us. Our defense and special teams went crazy on them. We played strong from the opening kickoff to the final gun, and even though they were an outstanding team, we went out and dominated. That's a word that's used a lot in football, and I'm not sure we all still appreciate its meaning. But that game was a textbook example of a truly dominant NFL defense. That's the day I became convinced the Bucs could have a historic season.

In that game, which we won 25–0, Derrick Brooks picked off a pass from Chris Redman right in front of our goal line and ran it back 97 yards. Over the course of the season he was able to turn this type of play into our trademark. This is what I mean when I talk about what a defense without weaknesses can do. The combination of our pass rush and coverage forced opposing quarterbacks to make decisions before they wanted to, which enabled us to disguise our schemes and lure them into throwing passes underneath. In these situations Derrick, who reads quarterbacks as well as anyone who's ever played the game, was like a spider waiting for the fly. All year long, in fact, we were able to decoy teams into throwing blindly into coverages they didn't see. That's the game within the game in the NFL, but so few teams are able to do it consistently, and I'm not sure anyone ever did it as well as the Bucs did in 2002.

The Week 2 victory over the Ravens typified our season. Nine of our 25 points came on field goals by Martin Gramatica, who added two more PATs. The touchdowns came from Brooks's TD and a score by Karl Williams, who returned a punt 56 yards. The defense put 2 more points on the board when we bottled Redman up in his own end and he fumbled the ball out of the end zone for a safety. Offense 11, defense 14.

We had another chance to assert ourselves the following week on *Monday Night Football,* when we played the St. Louis Rams, the reigning NFC champs. This was Kurt Warner's debacle. We picked him off four times, including another interception by Derrick, who ran for another touchdown to seal the deal 26–14. That was a win where the coaching staff deserved a lot of credit. St. Louis has a multitude of offensive weapons, and simply playing well doesn't guarantee that a defense will stop them. We went into that game against the Rams totally prepared for everything they showed us, and at the end of the evening they were 0–3 on the season and basically a nonfactor from that point on.

I felt Warner was a little shell-shocked after that game. He suffered a lot of hard blows. When you're under that type of fire you start to lose confidence in your offensive line, which is another way of saying you have a lot of confidence that you're going to get hit. It's human nature to want to get the ball out of your hands as quickly as possible, which forces a lot of bad throws. Warner, who already has a very quick release, was rushing his passes, and in the end it killed the Rams.

This was the second straight year we had beaten St. Louis on *Monday Night Football.* It's extra special to play well in front of a nation-wide audience in prime time, but it doesn't actually affect the way a team prepares or plays. Winners play to win, regardless of the circumstances. For instance, our next game was in Cincinnati against the Bengals, a horrible team with basically one offensive weapon: running back Corey Dillon. We were just as relentless in that game (which had no TV audience) as we had been six days earlier in prime time.

In fact, a good team tends to be even more aggressive against someone like the Bengals. In that type of game, where you know your opponents simply aren't prepared to deal with what you're bringing, you get excited because there's a chance to show off, pile up some stats, and get some recognition. A team like that is just looking for the exits—deep down they don't want to play.

Of course, that doesn't guarantee a win in the NFL. The danger is that sometimes you look past a bad team when you've got a difficult game ahead, and they drag you down to their level. We didn't fall into that trap against the Bengals, whom we beat 35–7. But we did have a test coming up against the Atlanta Falcons, and the moment the Cincinnati game was over we began to prepare for Michael Vick.

Michael changes the geometry of the football field with his mobility and throwing arm, and renders X's and O's obsolete with his explosive speed. When you have to contend with a guy who's physically better than anyone on your side of the ball, you're going to experience problems, and often those problems are unfixable. As a left-handed quarterback, Vick poses an additional challenge for me because I can't sneak up on him—he sees me coming, just like Steve Young did when I played the 49ers. On the other hand, I pose a problem for Michael because, try as he might, he can't turn the corner on me. I may be the only end in the NFL who can say that. In that respect, I am to the defensive end position what Michael is to the quarterback position.

Pro football often comes down to a game of matchups. If one team can exploit the matchups in which it enjoys an advantage—and avoid the ones it doesn't—it will usually win. So even though my side of the field is basically shut down to Michael Vick, he can hurt us elsewhere. He can beat defenders to a hole, he can shed pass rushers, he can deliver passes other quarterbacks can't, he's got body control like you wouldn't believe—basically, he just "out-athletics" you. The matchup he wins is speed-on-speed, and that translates into first downs and touchdowns instead of incompletions and sacks. Yet as hard as he is to plan for, you've still got to formulate a plan against Michael, and do your best to accomplish it.

When Michael gets another season or two under his belt, he's going to be a phenomenal player. He's already changing the game, and I think he will have a profound impact on the future of football. Imagine a league of quarterbacks you can't defend against in a traditional way. As more players with skill levels like Vick's gravitate to the quarterback position, it will force the other positions on the field to evolve in response, to turn to nontraditional athletes. Just look at the history of this game—whenever the offense speeds up, whether it's new plays or new players, the defense speeds up, too, in order to neutralize it.

In this game, however, we were having success against Michael. But our offense wasn't putting points on the board. We were only up 10–6 in the third quarter, which is almost like an invitation for this man to beat you. So what's a team to do? In the third quarter I knocked his ass out of the game! I'm not saying I intentionally try to injure anyone, but the only way to play this dude is to get him before he gets you. During that game Rob Marinelli sat us down and said, "We've got to go get him, we've got to shut down their big gun or he'll pick us apart." He was talking to the entire defensive line, but he was looking right at me.

As you might expect, removing Vick from the equation was the turning point. Doug Johnson came in for the Falcons and threw three interceptions, including a ball Warren Sapp caught after I buried Johnson. It went in the books as an INT, but in my mind the stat should be a caused fumble for me and a fumble recovery for Warren. Anyway, he lateraled it to Derrick Brooks, who ran it in for the game-ending touchdown in a 20–6 victory. We were now 4–1 with Cleveland next and a showdown with the Eagles two weeks out.

The game against the Browns went as expected. We opened up a 17–0 lead on the first play of the fourth quarter, and won 17–3. This marked the third time in a row we hadn't allowed the other team a touchdown. We felt good going into Philly, and even though there was some concern over the offense, our defense was the strength of our team, and we honestly believed that if the offense didn't put points on the board, the defense would. Part of that confidence comes from the fact that the minute you start creating excuses for losing, you increase the chances of losing. That's one thing I learned on the Cardinals. You take what you've got and you go into battle with it. Our defense was our strength, and we expected to make the plays we needed to in order to beat our opponents.

This is how all good teams think. The Eagles, for instance, came into the game with the Bucs confident that Donovan McNabb and their main running back, Duce Staley, would make the plays on offense they needed to overcome our defense. And on this particular Sunday, they did, and they beat us. Donovan threw a beautiful touchdown pass to Todd Pinkston right before the half, and Duce ran it down our throats all day to win 20–10. When our defense was called upon to make those big plays, it was the Eagles who made them instead. The same held true the other way: Their defense stifled our offense in key situations. I suppose a simpler way of looking at that game is that we just didn't play well.

The loss to the Eagles was unquestionably a missed opportunity. They came out of that game believing they could handle us, and we failed to exact revenge for our loss in the playoffs. To make matters worse, the Saints continued to win, and now they were a game up in the division. But that's football. Each week, someone's got to win, and some-one's got lose.

The Carolina Panthers were next on the schedule, and although they had lost a bunch of times, they were a rapidly improving defensive team. It was a battle. They started a rookie at quarterback, Randy Fasani, which I have to say was like dangling a piñata in front of our defense. We held Carolina to nine first downs the whole game, but they still managed three field goals in the second and third quarters, and we found ourselves down 9–3.

Fortunately Martin Gramatica was money in the fourth quarter. He kicked a 52-yarder to make it 9–6, then booted the tying field goal from 53 yards right after the two-minute warning. The defense went out and smothered the Panthers, and we got the ball back on a punt. We got into their territory quickly, then Gramatica hit one from 47 to win it. Obviously, this was a key victory for us. You don't like to lose two in a row, and you don't like to lose to the Panthers, who had no offense at that time.

We got a lot of questions from the media after this game about where we stood in the division race with the Saints, and what lay ahead for the rest of the year. I know the public thinks this way, always looking at the standings and the schedule, always figuring out the different permutations. What they don't understand—and this seems crazy—is that the players rarely think about those things. If the coaches want to think that way, fine, but the players have other things on their mind between the kickoff and the final gun. Players by and large are mostly focused on playing up to their ability—sometimes more so than "playing to win." Except for a handful of situations, where winning or losing literally hangs in the balance, how can you put your finger on what is a "winning" play and what isn't? You can't. So you just focus on execution, and try to do your job to perfection each time the ball is snapped.

In the bigger scheme of things, where standings and schedules are concerned, players are content to hang their hat on the team's performance and have faith in the fact that good performances will translate into wins, and wins will translate into a shot at the playoffs. Even guys on bad teams think this way, especially at the beginning or in the middle of a season. The only "permutation" we know is that we need to win every game—that's how we prepare ourselves mentally, and hopefully that's the way it plays out on the field.

That said, after a close victory like this one you tend to think, *Man, I'm glad we didn't cough that one up!* That would have been an ugly loss. I mean, the Panthers were fortunate to get three field-goal attempts against us that day. We dominated them. I went to town on their offensive line, and got to Fasani twice for sacks. This was the beginning of a wild run for me. I went five straight games with two or more sacks, which set a new NFL record.

Can a defensive end get hot the way a Reggie Miller or an A-Rod can? *I* can. The way I'm wired allows me to. My speed and balance and explosiveness enable me to dictate the initial action after every snap. This allows me to play mind games with the blockers and quarterbacks. I can concentrate on just stifling anything that comes my way, or I can break through to create problems in the pocket. The offensive lineman knows this, so he's trying to guess what I'll do next. Sometimes I'll let him think he's guessing right, then on a key down I'll cross him up so badly that he literally doesn't even touch me, even though we're lining up only a foot or two apart. If there's no one around to pick me up, I'm on the quarterback or the ball carrier in about one second and it's lights-out.

Once I've done this a couple of times (letting someone think he's close to controlling me, then yanking the rug out), the lineman is completely demoralized. I then build on this and pretty much have my way with him after that. There are some good offensive linemen in the NFL, but I've never taken the field feeling that my man was better than me. And when I get into a zone where I'm outguessing the guy and outplaying him, the sacks come in bunches.

At this point in my career, I also had some history with the guys trying to block me. I knew what they could and couldn't do, and I had a pretty good idea of how their minds worked. They had some history with me, too, so sometimes they were quick to recognize what I was doing. But if I saw this was the case, I'd throw something new at them and our little game would begin all over again. This is when football is at its most fun.

This mental edge, this creativity I bring to the defensive end position, is what distinguishes me from the other players out there. I've been told as much by my coaches. It not only leads to nice streaks like the one I was on in 2002, but also enables me to be a "closer." That's what Dave

McGinnis called me in Arizona. He loved it when everything was coming together for me in a game. He could see me getting excited, and he knew I was going to be unstoppable.

Multiple-sack games are very rare in the NFL, and I guess you could say they are my specialty. I'm not sure I receive enough credit for this accomplishment. Think about what kind of a player it takes to string together five straight multiple-sack games. Think about how many defensive lineman have been chasing quarterbacks over the last couple of generations, how many All-Pros and Hall of Famers have been ringing up sacks since they started keeping track of them officially. I expect someone, someday, to break this record, but by the same token I wouldn't be surprised if it held up for a long, long time.

A sack requires skill, intelligence, determination, and a little bit of luck. You have to rain hell down on the quarterback play after play after play. Then if everything else falls into place you'll get a clear shot at him maybe twice, three times a game. Some people think of a sack as a team statistic, because it requires ten other guys doing their jobs well enough so that you can do yours. To an extent, that's true. But there are times when it's just you blowing through everyone and wrapping up the quarterback before he knows what hit him. That's the case more than half the time. In Arizona I was putting up huge sack numbers when often it was me and three guys no one even knew. Also, don't forget that without a great individual effort, it doesn't matter what your teammates are doing—if you don't have the complete package, you're not going to get to the quarterback in the first place.

In Tampa I was playing on a line with a superstar, Warren Sapp. Were some of my sacks aided by what he was doing at the defensive tackle position? Yeah. But the reverse was also true. He got sacks sometimes because I was tying up three guys. Still, most of our sacks were the result of supreme and consistent individual efforts. When I heard that Warren had gone to Oakland for the 2004 season, it never even occurred to me that this would affect my performance or my sack total. With what I bring to every play, I have no doubt I will continue to shine.

Our offense didn't just shine in Week 9 against the Vikings. It was blinding. Brad Johnson threw five touchdown passes, and then it was just a matter of containing Minnesota's quarterback, Daunte Culpepper.

Culpepper presents problems with his mobility, like Michael Vick, but the problems are different. Daunte is really big, about my size, which is unusual for a quarterback. Where Michael just takes off on you, Daunte will blow through a tackle. He can also see the field really well when he runs, and with Randy Moss darting around trying to get open, this is a major concern. You know Moss is going to make big plays if given the chance, so there's real urgency in getting to Culpepper. We were up 31–10, and he put together a couple of nice drives to make the final score 38–24. We intercepted him twice and I sacked him twice, so we did a good job against a very dangerous player.

That victory made us 7–2, and with New Orleans in their bye week, technically we assumed the division lead. The following Sunday was our off day, and the Saints beat Carolina to pull even again. As I've stated, I never pay much attention to the standings in the middle of the season. I lock in on the next challenge, concentrate on the moment, and build off that. There are times you can ask me who we just played and I can't remember.

Obviously, the team and our fans watch the standings, so it was good when the race began to loosen up in Week 11. Atlanta beat the Saints, and we defeated the Panthers again. Brad Johnson played a nice game for us. He capitalized on an interception Dwight Smith made with the score tied 10–10, following that up with a 22-yard touchdown pass to Keenan McCardell that put us up for good. Martin Gramatica finished them off with two late field goals, 23–10. I had two more sacks, this time against Rodney Peete, whose game I knew very well. I prefer to go after mobile guys like Peete rather than pocket passers. Quarterbacks who feel they can run around back there tend to hold the ball a lot longer, giving me a better opportunity to get to them. They also think they can dodge a pass rusher with a little shimmy, or by stepping up as you go by. That doesn't work against me.

We were firing on all cylinders at this point. Our quarterback was on a roll, making clutch plays when we needed them and managing the offense nicely. The defense was killing, too. Green Bay came into town and played us very tough in the first half. But in the second half we just shut them down. Normally Brett Favre pulls those games out. He thrives in situations where the clock is winding down and the score is close. But I sacked him twice and we picked off four of his passes, and the final score was 21–7.

Favre is a great player, but like many talented guys he sometimes tries to do a little too much. We knew how frustrating our defense could be, and we also knew that he is ultracompetitive and would try to force some plays. That's probably the one bad thing you can say about Brett as a player—if you can create the right set of circumstances with your defense, he'll make piss-poor decisions and give you the game. On this day, he did, and we were waiting.

Does that keep him from being an all-time great quarterback? Hey, in my mind, you can't question greatness. It's not something you can measure in degrees. Great is great. It's not about a few bad outings, it's about how far you take your team. Favre will go to Canton because he has a Super Bowl ring, because he won a lot of memorable battles, and because he played a legendary game in a legendary city. When you've got juice like that and credentials to boot, losses like this one tend to be forgotten.

This was a satisfying victory, but we still had to make the playoffs, and it looked like we'd have a fight on our hands. Atlanta was surging in our division, and the Saints beat us again the following week to tighten things up even more. This was a weird game. Aaron Brooks could barely complete a pass and I sacked him a bunch of times, but he made some good plays when they counted, their special teams outplayed ours, and the final score was 23–20. That shows you how misleading stats can be. If you saw Brooks's stat line (four sacks, a fumble out of the end zone, nine completions, and sixteen incompletions) and mine (three sacks, a few more tackles), you would guess that we had killed the Saints. The bottom line is that they were really up for us, and once again we weren't up for them.

We knew it was time to send a message, this time to the Falcons, who hadn't lost a game since we'd beaten them in the fifth week. Vick was now the toast of football, a red-hot quarterback putting his team on his shoulders, writing the kind of story line the NFL just loves. We were all business against Atlanta, and played a near-perfect defensive game to win 34–10. Our defense was probably the only one in the league that year he had no chance to exploit. We were incredibly fast at almost every position, which nullified the advantage he had when plays break down.

So we broke down as many plays as possible, then bottled him up when he tried to use his speed. If you want to see the perfect anti-Vick defense, get a hold of that tape and go to school with it.

The Lions had a hot young quarterback, too, in Joey Harrington. We played them next and knocked him out in the first half. It was a fight from there, but Gramatica kicked the go-ahead field goal in the fourth quarter and we ran out the clock to win 23–20. That victory clinched a playoff spot for the Bucs, and allowed us to rest Brad Johnson for the final two games. He had a bad back, and we wanted him fresh for the playoffs.

Shaun King started our *Monday Night Football* game against the Steelers. Pittsburgh scored right out of the gate, then ran back one of Shaun's passes for a touchdown. When the first quarter ended we were down 17–0. We clamped down on the Steelers the rest of the way, but Shaun couldn't get us going and we lost 17–7. We knew this loss would probably be costly, and it was.

We shut out the Bears in the final game, which assured us of a bye. But because we had the same 12–4 record as the Eagles, all the tie-breaking formulas went into effect, and they got home field throughout the playoffs on the strength of their conference record being better than ours. Had we beaten the Steelers—or for that matter the Eagles back in October—we would have had the home field.

The Bears game is noteworthy because it was also the first game I wore the new T3K prototype. The garment had come a long way since Bennie and I had sewed the first one together. This was a Sunday night contest, in Chicago, so you can image how cold it was. I felt fantastic.

I don't expect anyone to believe me, but the prospect of playing the Eagles for the championship in Philadelphia was actually very appealing to the players. If we were going to beat this team, we wanted to do it on their turf. A win is a win, no matter where the game is played, and we liked the idea of closing down that horrible building of theirs by denying them a trip to the Super Bowl. Our philosophy was, *What better way to go all the way than to go through Philly?*

First, though, we had to get past the San Francisco 49ers. We used the bye week as recovery time. The main concern was having Brad back at 100 percent, which he was. The bye week is a double-edged sword, however. By going almost two weeks without playing, you run the risk of being stale. But if you play the extra game, you run the risk of guys getting hurt, too. Personally, I just chilled. I thought a lot about our chances to reach the Super Bowl and realized how much closer this team was to achieving that goal than the 1998 Cardinals. I was really excited.

That weekend I watched the playoffs, less as a player than as a fan. The Giants–49ers game was off the hook—New York ran up a big score and then San Francisco erased a 38–14 deficit to win 39–38 on a botched field goal by the Giants. I'd like to say that I was analyzing their offensive sets and all, but the truth is I was yelling at the TV like a maniac. I loved it. Given a choice, I would have preferred to play the Giants, but just because I like them better. The Atlanta–Green Bay game was also fun to watch. Michael Vick went into Green Bay—which probably hadn't lost a home postseason game since they outlawed leather helmets—and won 27–7. Michael played really well, and the defense and special teams came up big.

I felt bad for Brett Favre after that game. The league had set him up as the grizzled old gunslinger matching up against the young sharpshooter, and it almost felt like the end of an era—like he was supposed to ride off into the sunset. I was totally buying into this. The NFL is great at storytelling. Vick really opened my eyes in that game, though. He was getting better and better, and the thought suddenly crossed my mind that we might have to play him instead of Donovan McNabb.

But the Eagles took care of business the next Saturday and beat Atlanta 20–6. The outcome was clear from the way the two quarterbacks played. Donovan was making better decisions under pressure. Michael played gallantly, though. He scrambled 20 yards to tie the game in the third quarter, but the touchdown was called back for holding. Then they missed the field goal, and that was the game, because the Philly defense stepped up and just pounded Atlanta. I was happy the Eagles won. It almost seemed like destiny that Tampa Bay would play Philadelphia, and that I would face Donovan, with the Super Bowl on the line.

Of course we still had to win our game against the 49ers, who had a lot of injuries on defense. Brad Johnson was excellent on our first two possessions. He went right after them and converted every third-down play to put us up 14–3 at the beginning of the second quarter. We added a third TD after San Francisco was penalized for interference on a long pass, and Johnson hit our tight end Rickey Dudley for a score.

After that we just teed off on Jeff Garcia, who was forced to go to the air and get points back against us in a hurry. This is when our defense was at its most dangerous. It was like a feeding frenzy. Garcia is a good player, but he was in over his head and he knew it. We sacked him four times and intercepted him three. I got to him and stripped the ball out of his hands—my signature Mount Carmel play! The final score was 31–6, but I'm telling you it wasn't even that close.

Finally we had our shot at the Eagles. As an added bonus, Donovan McNabb wasn't 100 percent, so we planned to exploit that. We'd need to, because we spotted them 7 points in the first minute. Brian Mitchell, who had been mouthing off about us—and about me—on a local radio show, returned the opening kickoff 70 yards, then Duce Staley ran it in from 20 yards to make it 7–0. Mitchell was playing a word-association game with the DJs, and when they said "Simeon Rice," he said "soft." Gruden made sure to play that for me and the guys before the game, but nothing a punt returner says is going to motivate me to play any harder than I already do.

We got 3 points back on a field goal, and then Joe Jurevicius caught a short pass and ran 71 yards down the sideline to set up a touchdown by Mike Alstott. They got another field goal to tie the score 10–10, but that was basically it for the Eagles. For the rest of the game, whenever they got close we pinched off the drive. Brad Johnson hit Keyshawn Johnson with a pass to make it 17–10, and then right before the half I ran down Donovan, made him fumble, and recovered the ball. That saved us at least 3 points and sent Philly into the locker room with their backs against the wall.

The Eagles didn't know what hit them. They'd really expected to win this game, and we were beating them up on every play. In the first half they played with confidence, but in the second half they played with hope. We sensed this change and exploited it, making a point of knocking the hope out of them. We were ferocious and tenacious. We played with a lot of malice in our hearts. The Eagles had knocked the Buccaneers out of the playoffs before, and we knew this was the way we had to approach the game to get past them.

The difference in this game, in my opinion, came down to attitude. It was personal for us: We didn't like them. They were hitting to tackle and we were hitting to run through their hearts. They were trying to win and we were trying to annihilate them. This approach is not always the best. A young team or an inexperienced team playing like this might have too much adrenaline, and run the risk of becoming undisciplined. But we were a veteran team, a cerebral team, and our coaches barely had to tell us what we needed to do.

Something else that may have made a difference was that I brought a bag full of T3K insulating garments to the stadium that day, and handed them out to a bunch of the guys. Now, no one is saying they made the difference between winning and losing, but I've always found it interesting that not one player bothered to give his bodysuit back.

The one time the Eagles penetrated into our territory, Ronde Barber stepped in front of an out pattern and intercepted the ball. He ran 92 yards for a touchdown that iced the game 27--10. People have asked me if Ronde gambled and got lucky on that play, or whether he knew what was coming. The answer is that he knew what was coming. He not only knew that play, but actually baited Donovan to throw that pass. That's the only way you get to look like the intended receiver on an interception, which he did in this instance. Ronde was having another phenomenal season, and it was great that he made the ultimate highlight play in the NFC Championship game.

We were excited that we had taken this game and put it in our pocket, that we had taken this stage and made it ours. That marquee matchup between the Eagles and Buccaneers never materialized because every starter, every substitute, every special-teams unit played hard, focusing their talent and energy in a way that carried us right through to the end of the game. We never allowed that game to become competitive. It's hard to explain what happens in a game like this—how it takes on a life of its own. Very early on, everyone on that field knew that, on some level, it was not about them. It was about us. That had been our slogan all year, and finally we understood what a powerful thought this was.

When you get to the championship game, you've done a lot of things right. You're on a roll. In Philly our momentum continued—we did almost nothing wrong. We hadn't just beaten the Eagles for the NFC

Championship. We'd imposed our will on them. And in doing so, we'd exorcised demons that had haunted the Tampa Bay Buccaneers for many, many years.

Our opponent in the Super Bowl would be the Oakland Raiders, who'd outlasted the Tennessee Titans in the AFC Championship 41–24. The Titans had seemed to have the game under control as the first half drew to a close, but they fumbled twice right at the end of the second quarter and let the Raiders back in with 10 easy points. Rich Gannon, the Oakland quarterback, was passing on almost every play during the game, but in the fourth quarter the Raiders ran the ball on two long drives that ate up the clock and put things out of reach. They had a good club. A dangerous club.

After the initial jubilation that came with defeating the Eagles, our focus turned to the final step in our season-long quest. You'd think we would have celebrated more after winning the NFC Championship but, almost to a man, we didn't want to pop the champagne or let the confetti fly until we reached our ultimate goal. We acknowledged what we'd done and then turned our attention to what we were about to encounter. In truth, there really wasn't time to celebrate. The Super Bowl was on the West Coast, and it was only a week away—not the usual two-week lay-off. We left Philly on a charter flight almost immediately after the game, and we were given the next morning in Tampa to gather our things. Then we were off on Monday afternoon to San Diego. It was rough. Everyone was tired and sore, and there was no time to flake out and heal.

The good thing was that my brother, Diallo, lives in San Diego, so at least I was heading toward familiar territory. I ended up spending some time with him. Meanwhile I flew in my family and friends, as well as Frank Lenti, my old coach from Mount Carmel—basically anyone who wanted to come.

The schedule that week in San Diego was morning practice, meetings, and then afternoon practice. You also had the option of meeting with the media in the morning, so they could write their stories and make their deadlines. After practice everyone went their separate ways. Some of the players hung out together; others spent time with friends and family. I saw my brother one day, but the rest of the time I just chilled by myself.

Well, not exactly by myself. I had agreed to let a film crew follow me around to show what it was like to be me, I guess. I didn't mind, but it kind of bugged out my brother. We didn't have the quality time we wanted at that moment. We're pretty uninhibited when we're together, so we couldn't be how we usually are. The concept was very *EdTV.* The idea was to show how I prepared and how I relaxed—to make the Super Bowl experience more understandable to the average fan. It aired during the pregame show on ABC. I didn't see it until almost a year later. It wasn't bad.

I figured it was worth doing, mainly to make myself more marketable. A lot of people don't have a sense of my personality. I'm always turning things over in my head, looking at situations from different angles, poking and prodding people, figuring out where they're coming from, what kind of sense of humor they have. I'm serious, I'm cool, I'm playful, I'm curious, I'm self-indulgent, I'm a lot things all at once—I basically enjoy myself the way I think most people would in my situation. How do you get that across? You've got to let the people see you.

Now, if you're going to let millions of people into your world, the best time to do it is right before the Super Bowl. It's like no other week in your life. The culture of football is turned upside down, and no matter how you try to follow your routine, every time you turn a corner something unexpected is going to happen. So ABC had a chance to see how I think and react to stuff off the field, during a life-altering experience.

Looking back, I think maybe I was a little boring. Everyone knows I like to enjoy myself; I'm a night person, not a morning person. One night I went to a party hosted by Rodney Peete and Holly Robinson Peete, but that was about it. Curfew was eleven o'clock, but mostly I would go back to my room at nine or ten and do nothing—just think about the game and the opportunity. I couldn't wait for the moment. I know some of my teammates didn't sleep well that week for the same reason. Me, I'm an insomniac, so it was just the normal routine.

That week on TV they were running a lot of programs about past Super Bowls. I stayed up and watched some of the legendary teams. I felt like I was putting myself in the proximity of greatness, and I even tried to picture myself on the field in those games. People often ask me if there is a player from the past who reminds me of myself. Well, in these

Super Bowls, I didn't see a single Simeon Rice–like player. I come off the line like a pass receiver, not a defensive end, and I didn't see anyone on TV who played like that.

As for the Super Bowl changing your life, I can tell you that's not a cliché. I'd been hearing since the day I came into the league that once you go to the Super Bowl, you are never the same. Your fame, your prestige, your marketability, your lifestyle—everything is different. I was very curious as the week went on whether I would sense any of these changes, or whether that would happen afterward.

From the standpoint of my teammates who did not have big years, or who weren't well known to the fans, being a member of a Super Bowl team definitely did for them what everyone said it would. People became interested in who they are, where they're from, and how they got here. The press hung on their every word. As for players like Warren Sapp and Keyshawn Johnson, who were media stars already, they were in their element, so they knew how to work all the extra attention to their favor.

Personally, I hoped the exposure I received during the game would benefit me. At that time I felt that I had never gotten the credit I should have for the type of player I was, at least from a business standpoint. I was already going to be an All-Pro for that season, and adding to that a Super Bowl appearance figured to greatly enhance the Simeon Rice "brand" from a marketability and promotion standpoint.

I should have known better, and the tip-off was Media Day. This is when all the reporters get access to all the players, who sit at podiums and field question after question. For me, this experience was extremely disappointing. In fact, the whole media situation that week, at least from my perspective, was very strange. But I'll get to that later.

Like everything else about the Super Bowl when you have one week instead of two to prepare, practice was extremely intense. And in contrast to most things in San Diego, it was a very positive experience. The team was really focused. Some of the guys were nervous, but I would say what I was feeling was more like excitement. I was only days away from an opportunity to put the uniqueness and brilliance of my game on a national stage. I wouldn't say I was relaxed, but I was definitely confident.

The people who really get tight are the individual coaches. They have so much to gain when things go right, and so much to lose when they don't. For instance, if a linebacker misses an assignment and it costs us the game, then the linebacker coach takes the hit for that. It's not something the fans understand—they either forget about the play in a week, or maybe they don't notice it at all. In the coaching fraternity, however, it sticks to your record. And down the road, it could make the difference between getting the job you want and being passed over without ever being told why. On the positive side, each coach has a chance for his unit to do something football people will remember forever. Just as there are permanent black marks on your record, there are heroic stories that get told again and again.

Here's an example. The Oakland line coach, Aaron Kromer, had an opportunity to make a name for himself if he devised a way to stop Warren Sapp, Greg Spires, Chartric Darby, and me. Kromer had been an offensive lineman at Miami of Ohio in the 1980s, then coached there in the 1990s. He was hired as an assistant by Northwestern and helped transform a 3–8 team in 1999 to a bowl-game participant in 2000. That got Kromer a job on the Raiders, so he was definitely a man on the rise. Now here he was in the Super Bowl, up against impossible odds—but with a chance to make history if things broke his way. Imagine being in his shoes, having a week to figure out the secret of stopping the Tampa Bay D-line. He couldn't have been much fun to be around.

Even for a coach who is holding all the cards, like our guy, Rob Marinelli, Super Bowl week is not an enjoyable environment. He knows that the coach on the other team is picking apart his unit and trying to find a way to make him look bad—taking food off his table, in a sense. His players are expected to dominate, and if they don't, it could be a career-killer. Long after the four of us were retired, his fellow coaches would still be saying, *Marinelli had a great line and he fucked up in the Super Bowl.*

Needless to say, the coaches don't exactly make it fun for us. They approach Super Bowl week like it's a business trip. As a result, the practices are more serious, and there is more severity to the hitting. Also, there was a grave undertone to everything having to do with the game, which kind of took me by surprise. You don't expect the atmosphere to be loose like the Pro Bowl, but still, you'd like to feel like you could take some pride in the accomplishment of getting to the Super Bowl.

There wasn't much smiling during our practices. Just intense focus, a real no-nonsense atmosphere. And the closer we got to the game, the more on edge the coaches were. I appreciated that they weren't ripping the players, though. We were their prize horses, and they treated us right. Besides, at that point it doesn't make sense to cut guys up. What they tried to do was bring us more into the moment.

Coach Marinelli has a rare talent for putting your game into proper context, and in some respects he's changed the way I look at football. I have always found it interesting, for example, how players are constantly asked to put their faith in things they cannot see. I'm not referring to X's and O's and game plans and such. I'm talking about a much bigger picture. Before the start of the season, each team makes a plan that the coaches believe will get them to within striking distance of the Super Bowl. Players get cut, players get kept, players get hurt. Roles change and expectations shift. And that's just in training camp. When the regular schedule begins, you look at yourself and your teammates and convince yourself that if everything goes right and everyone plays up to his potential, you'll earn a playoff spot. And of course, when you look ahead to the postseason, you know anything can happen. To get through the year, you have to trust that everyone in the organization will do whatever has to be done to execute that plan. If you waver even slightly from that belief, bad things happen. That is why so much in the NFL revolves around the concepts of perseverance, discipline, and execution. You have to see every moment as a building block, and do every little thing as perfectly as you can. And part of that is believing that, if you don't, it will tear everything apart. So once we got the vibe from the coaches that practice had to be better than perfect, it wasn't difficult to get serious.

The one coach who tried to loosen up practice was Gruden. He had basically designed the Raider offense when he was coaching there. He had plucked Rich Gannon off the scrap heap and designed a system in which he could flourish, and Gannon put up MVP numbers. No one knew more about what we would be facing as a defense than Jon. So when it came time to run the plays the Raiders would be running, he actually stepped in and played quarterback. That was cool. He had to make the pool reporters swear not to write about it, because he thought the Raiders would start changing their offense.

Gruden had been a quarterback in college, and at the time he wasn't even forty, so he did all right. He did a good job of mimicking Gannon, particularly when it came to the timing of their pass plays. If a play took 2.5 seconds to get off, he took 2.5 seconds. That gave us a sense of how much time we had to shave off on the D-line in terms of getting into the backfield. If it took Jerry Rice and Tim Brown 2.5 seconds to run their routes, and we could flush Gannon out of the pocket in 2.1 or 2.2, then it would disrupt the timing of their offense and let us do what we needed to do to get a sack or an interception. Also, if we consistently penetrated the backfield, it would diminish the effectiveness of a receiver like Jerry Porter, their number three wideout, who killed teams all year. We considered him their most dangerous receiver, so if we could keep him from being a third option for Gannon, that would be big.

The most important thing Gruden did was show us how Gannon was going to audible. This was an offense Gruden had designed, so he knew what the quarterback's options were when he changed the play at the line. As soon as we recognized an offensive set and heard him audible, we knew there were only a couple of ways for him to go at that point, and we could adjust accordingly. We became increasingly confident as the game approached that we could get inside Gannon's head. And in a Super Bowl, that's an amazing advantage.

Gruden understood the Raider game plan so completely that it seemed like a joke at times. He was the fox in the henhouse, because he knew exactly how to combat it, too. The only laughing you heard in our practice, in fact, was when we realized the kind of trouble Oakland was heading for.

I can't imagine being more confident going into a game than our defense was. Yet we also knew that the Raiders were a very fine team. You don't really allow the thought of losing to creep into your mind at this point, but you do have to acknowledge where an opponent might be able to gain an edge. In Oakland's case, there is no question that the guy who concerned us the most was their running back Charlie Garner. He is quick, he is fast, he knows how to make you miss, he catches the ball well—he's a big-play guy, a home-run hitter. He was their Marshall Faulk, a player who can create something out of nothing. Rich Gannon, Jerry Rice, and Tim Brown may have gotten all the media attention, but down on the field, between the white lines, you know who the players are. Down there it doesn't matter who's the most marketable; you have to know which players are capable of changing the game. For us, that was Charlie, because no matter how well we dealt with the Raider passing game, we still had to bring him down when they put the ball in his hands. It's funny, but I think we as players were more worried about Charlie than our coach was. Jon Gruden had Charlie as a reserve when he was offensive coordinator for the Eagles in the mid-1990s. Back then Charlie had a reputation for being unfocused, forgetting his assignments, or just messing up plays. Even so, he led the league in yards per carry one year, so the ability was always there.

One guy I wasn't worried about was the man I would be facing, Oakland's left tackle, Barry Sims. He and Lincoln Kennedy, the right tackle (who would be going against Greg Spires), were their two best offensive linemen. The Raiders had a group of massive guys, power blockers, but Sims was the exception. He's my height, weighs about three hundred, has decent balance, and is pretty quick—a Pro Bowl player. But he had no answer for the kind of game I was bringing. I knew I could take him upfield and turn the corner, or get inside him. And he wasn't big enough to push me over, so he was going to be doing a lot of backpedaling that Sunday.

As I've said before, I never think too much about who's in front of me. Coach Marinelli will review the tendencies of the tackles I face each week, and I watch the films, but I really don't care. If I'm faster and quicker than the man blocking me, what does it matter what he'd like to do? I already know what he'd like to do: keep up with me. Mostly, before a game, I'm concentrating on the plays the other team runs.

Meanwhile, I heard that Frank Middleton, one of Oakland's guards, was telling reporters, *We don't worry about Simeon Rice—he's not that good, he's just fast.* I always like to take a step back when something like that goes down, because it's almost never what it seems to be. I can only put myself in Frank's shoes (by the way, he used to play in Tampa Bay) and assume that he was just tired of answering questions about me, and some reporter made more of his comment than it was. More to the point, when a player hears these types of remarks, he should take it as a sign of respect. Out of all the members of our great defense, Middleton chose to single *me* out. I was having the best year of any defensive end in the NFL, so he wasn't going to motivate me to play any better. In this instance, I took it as a compliment. Besides, he was going against Warren Sapp, not me.

I knew no one on Oakland could block me. And we felt we could control the rest of the line of scrimmage. Then right before the game, their center, Barret Robbins, went AWOL. We didn't know what was up with that—we assumed they were having some internal issues, until we found out it was a personal thing, some emotional problems. Your first thought is, *What if someone on my team did that? Would I be pissed?* I don't think so, not even in a Super Bowl situation. My first reaction would be concern, because a man's got to be hurting bad to do what he did, when he did it. I would try to find out, *Is he okay, is he getting the help he needs?* I would be worried about his well-being as an individual.

Of course, Robbins was a Raider, and I didn't know him, so I didn't really care. What we looked at was Robbins's replacement, Adam Treu, who was mostly a long snapper and not much of a pass protection guy. At this point, we knew they couldn't beat us, because they couldn't block us. We were going to be in their backfield all game long, which meant they were going to struggle to find their rhythm. The key to defeating Oakland, therefore, would be for our offense to put points up early. If we could force the Raiders to play from behind, where they abandon the run and become more of a one-dimensional offense, then they were dead.

Even with all this going for us, regardless of how confident we were, until the game starts you can't help being curious about how everything will play out. You are operating in such rarefied air that it's impossible to get a grasp on what is going to happen when you put all these variables into play. You're not thinking, *Man I wonder what could go wrong.* We were playing too well for that. Besides, we had gotten the "can't win the big one" monkey off our back in the Philly game, so there was virtually no self-doubt in the locker room. The closer we got to kickoff, the more we believed that this was our game to win.

The weirdest aspect of Super Bowl week was the extent to which the media was involved in absolutely everything. It was an alien situation for me, not having been a part of it before, and it really took me by surprise. The event is so celebrated by the media, and the fact that the media is everywhere is also celebrated. It's a big party, where everyone involved in the game of football gives himself a big pat on the back.

There are also a lot of media people around who don't know shit about football. I was amazed at how many people came up and congratulated me on a breakthrough season, telling me how much better I was playing, asking me what I was doing differently. What do you say to that? How do you tell them that you played as well in 2001 as in 2002? Or that you've been doing the same thing—game in, game out—since your rookie year?

Then it dawned on me. This was the same crank turning on that same meat grinder, only this time when I was being fed into it, filet mignon was coming out the other end, not hamburger. All those people who thought I couldn't play the run, or that I was a bad influence, or that I couldn't win the big one, or that I was greedy or whatever—now they had a new story to write. I was Sim the model citizen, the man who came back from oblivion, the missing ingredient, the man with the plan. It was a different spin on the same bullshit, but at least it was a *good* spin. And yo, I may be a lot of things but I'm no fool. When anyone in San Diego congratulated me on "turning my career around," I smiled and said *Thanks.* They could write that story all day.

Apparently, these journalists didn't need any background information or quotes to write that story, because when Media Day came, I was the only football player in San Diego who didn't have a hundred reporters waiting to ask me stupid questions. I was the last player out there, and by the time I took my seat, there were like ten or fifteen people waiting. When I saw that, I didn't even want to do it. What a horrible thing to face.

I'd been overlooked all season, and I was okay with that. But at the Super Bowl? Come on! Here I am, helping to take my team to the highest level, and now I'm sitting at the podium and there's barely anyone talking to me. My game warrants more attention than that. If those people had asked me about the Super Bowl, I would have told them things that would have made them look like NFL experts. I knew what was going to happen in the trenches, and I could have laid it out for anyone willing to listen. But I guess that's not what Media Day is about.

9

Among the handful of moments I regret in my life is one that went almost unnoticed by the vast majority of football fans on Super Sunday. During the pregame introductions, each player had to say which school he came from. I said, "School of hard knocks." I was just being playful, of course. I never imagined it would offend so many people at the University of Illinois. For the record, I am Simeon Rice, from the University of Illinois. That's who I am. And I have nothing but love for the school and the Champaign community.

Actually, as the game neared, my mind was focused on the last thing I anticipated: the Arizona Cardinals. Of all the thoughts to be rattling around my head! I was standing on the sideline while the national anthem was playing and all I could think about was how great it would have been to do this with that group of guys. Then I started to think about all the people who had helped me get to where I was, all the people I had played with and against, all my friends, my coaches and teachers. It made me realize that you never really do anything for yourself as a professional athlete; there is always a long line of people who feel connected to you, win or lose, good or bad.

As we got ready for kickoff, I began to focus on the task at hand. *This is it. This is what everyone who straps on a helmet from Pee Wee on up plays for. You've made it to the grandest stage in your sport, and it's time to perform. Play your game, do your thing, make the world see what kind of man you are.*

The Raiders kicked off and we started on our 26-yard line. We wanted to establish our passing attack, so Brad Johnson opened with a short strike to Mike Alstott. Two plays later, on third down, Brad dropped back and Regan Upshaw, who played my position for Oakland, broke through and hit Brad just as he released the ball. Charles Woodson picked off the pass, and the Raiders were in business.

Rich Gannon opened up with an empty backfield and four receivers to spread out our defense, and completed some short passes, but I got past Barry Sims and sacked him. That forced them to go for a field goal, which Sebastian Janikowski hit from 40 yards. They had 3 points and had proved absolutely nothing. Meanwhile I had given Sims something to think about. On the other side of the line, Greg Spires was having his way early with Lincoln Kennedy, so the defense came off the field down 3–0, but feeling like we had the advantage.

On the ensuing kickoff, Aaron Stecker fumbled for us, but Coach Gruden challenged and the refs reversed their call. Then we went right back to passing. Brad hit Joe Jurevicius on third and 10 on a nice crossing pattern, then Michael Pittman took a handoff and gained 23 yards on our first running play. This put us within field-goal range, and Martin Gramatica booted it through to knot the score.

The Raiders went nowhere on their next possession after Spires sacked Gannon on second down. We were getting into their backfield almost at will, and you could see the panic in their eyes after each play. Their pass rush was working, too, because we went three and out on our next possession, and had to punt. The Raiders started their next drive on our 49, but again they went nowhere. Spires was in Gannon's face mask again, deflecting his pass on third down. We moved the sticks just once on our next possession, and the quarter ended 3–3.

The guy we all feared, Charlie Garner, made a nice catch and run for Oakland early in the second quarter, and they had third and short on our 43. Gannon rolled right with me hot on his tail, and Dexter Jackson picked off his pass. Gannon moved pretty well for a guy his age, and usually wasn't flustered when he left the pocket. But we were abusing their offensive linemen, and he was definitely rattled. We took the ball the other way, with Keyshawn Johnson catching two passes, but our drive stalled on the 26. Gramatica came on and gave us a 6–3 lead with his second field goal.

Gannon continued his attempt to establish the Oakland passing game, and on the one play when we couldn't pressure him, he pump-faked and then tried to hit Jerry Porter downfield. Jackson recognized this ploy instantly and ran over to make his second interception of the half. Meanwhile, Barry Sims and I knew something the rest of the world would soon find out: This was just the beginning of the longest day of his professional life. I was beating him on almost every play, and beating him badly. There were times when I came off the line and he never laid a hand on me.

We went three and out again and punted, and the Raiders began their next series on their own 11. This time they tried a bunch formation, but Gannon's screen pass was bad and fell incomplete. They had already gone through half the stuff in their passing repertoire and nothing was working. On the next play he dropped back again, and I buried him for my second sack. The rest of the day he basically ran away from me, but he didn't find the going much better on the other side of the field. Oakland punted and Karl Williams made a clutch return to the 27. The Raiders bit on a fake reverse and Pittman ran to their 2-yard line, then Alstott scored two plays later for a 13–6 lead.

Give Oakland credit. They kept trying different things. This time they almost caught us napping twice, but Garner and Tim Brown each dropped a catchable pass on a potentially big play. We got the ball back on our 23 and Brad Johnson marched us right down the field. The Raiders helped us with three penalties, and we pretty much ate up the rest of the quarter handing the ball off to Pittman and Alstott. We capped it off with a short TD pass to Keenan McCardell. Despite his earlier interception, Charles Woodson was injured and not at his best. McCardell burned him on this one, and we would go back his way again in the second half. As for the first half, we went into the locker room up 20–3, and the Raiders had done nothing against us. Only two of their drives had lasted more than three plays. For an offense as highly touted as theirs, this was astonishing.

Brian Kelly, our cornerback, set the tone for us in the second half when he stymied Oakland's first drive with terrific coverage and we forced them to punt again. This time we took the ball 89 yards for a score. The drive used up more than half the clock in the third quarter and ended with another short strike to McCardell. The Raider defense was exhausted, and there were still over twenty minutes to play. You knew they were tired when Brad Johnson scrambled for 10 yards. I love the guy, but he's not exactly a burner.

Our defense had been on the field a little over ten minutes since the game started, and we were practically popping out of our uniforms when we took the field. On the second play of Oakland's next drive, Gannon tried to hit Jerry Rice going down the sideline. Dwight Smith, our third corner, timed his move perfectly and snagged the ball. He ran unmolested 44 yards for a touchdown to make the score 34–3.

As I've mentioned earlier, whenever you see DBs making a lot of interceptions, watch what's happening in the trenches on the replay. Our front line was overwhelming them on every snap. At least one or two Bucs were shedding their blockers almost instantly, and I was having the best game of my career in terms of putting pressure on the offense.

Oakland finally saw some daylight on their next possession, when Dwight Smith fell down and Jerry Porter was standing all alone with no one between him and the goal line. This is how badly we were in Gannon's head—he almost missed Porter with his pass! He had to go to the ground to get it, and initially the catch was ruled incomplete. The play was reversed on a challenge, and they got the touchdown. They failed on the 2-point conversion, to make the score 34–9 with a quarter left to play.

We had the game in the bag, but as I've said before, you never want to think that way. The Raiders immediately proved me correct when Tim Johnson blocked Tom Tupa's punt on our next possession. Eric Johnson recovered the ball and ran it in for a touchdown. When we got the ball back, we took it down to the 11, and Tupa fumbled the snap on Gramatica's field-goal attempt. Fortunately, we had shaved another five minutes off the clock.

At this point we were giving Rich Gannon all the short passes he wanted, and he got the Raiders across midfield. Then he finally burned us, connecting with Jerry Rice on a long touchdown. But for the third straight time we stuffed them on their 2-point try. It was 34–21 with six minutes left. Had they converted all three times, it would have been 34–27.

Had we fallen into that trap of thinking we were "winning"? Maybe a few of us. But 13 points against the Raiders was nothing, so we knew it was time to assert ourselves once and for all. Our offense gobbled up another three-plus minutes before punting back to Oakland, and then we waited for a chance to slam the lid. Warren Sapp blasted through the line on second down and crushed Gannon for a 9-yard loss, then Derrick Brooks picked off his next pass and ran it in to make the score 41–21. That was the fifth time Brooks ran an interception back for a TD that year. The coup de grâce was applied by Dwight Smith, who picked off a tipped pass and also ran it in for a touchdown with two seconds left. That made the final score 48–21.

The game statistics illustrate how well we played. Time of possession was 37–23. Rushing yards 150–19. First downs 24–11. Interceptions 5–1. Sacks 5–0. My stats on the day were impressive, but only hint at the kind of game I produced. I had two sacks, brought down Gannon on a 2-point try, and was credited with five solo tackles. But this was one of those days when I can honestly say I had a positive impact on virtually every play. If I wasn't wrapping my arms around the man with the ball, I was driving him into my teammates' arms or forcing the quarterback to get rid of the ball faster than he wanted to. This was true of all four guys on the defensive line. We played a near-perfect game, and the guys behind us did their thing to near perfection, too.

Dexter Jackson was named Super Bowl MVP, but it could have been any of us—me, Warren, Dwight, Derrick, Greg. Each of us played the game of his life. Michael Pittman, who'd gone through all those down years with me in Arizona, played the game of his life, too. He gained 124 yards. Keyshawn Johnson caught six balls, Mike Alstott caught five, Keenan McCardell beat Charles Woodson for two TDs—the list goes on and on. And Brad Johnson, who had come in with me to lift these Bucs up to super status, looked like the happiest man on the planet.

When the final gun made our victory over the Raiders official, I was proud and pleased, but it wasn't as big a deal as I'd thought it would be. I felt strangely empty. Or maybe a better word is *unfulfilled*. Ever since that day in January 1982 when I'd seen Ken Anderson scrambling for a first down against the 49ers, I had assumed that this was where my life was headed. When you come into the league, all anyone ever talks about is *How are you going to get to the Super Bowl; your career's not complete until you get to the Super Bowl; your life will change forever when you win a Super Bowl.* But honestly, I felt like I had merely turned a page in my football life. I hadn't closed the book.

This was a sobering realization for me. Intellectually, you know this is likely to be the pinnacle of your career. And you half expect yourself to be out-of-your-mind happy, whether that's your personality or not. But in my heart, the quest continued. There was something bigger I was after as a person and as a football player, but if you had stopped me and asked at that moment what it was, I'm not sure I could have explained what could be bigger than what I had just accomplished. That's kind of sobering.

Not many athletes can say they played the best game of their lives in the biggest game of their lives, but I've sat through a tape of that Super Bowl and I don't think I could have improved on my performance. I did what every little kid dreams of when he watches a Super Bowl, and yet it was no big thing. I was surrounded by teammates who were scream-ing like mental patients, guys who were weeping, guys hugging each other like they never wanted to let go. That was some confusing shit, be-cause I couldn't get caught up in it.

After the locker room ceremony, I just dressed and went back to my hotel room. I sat in bed and tried to put the game, and my reaction to the game, into perspective. Tears came to my eyes. Finally I arrived at the conclusion that in my mind winning the Super Bowl was like a rite of passage for me, and in that regard I had reacted in an understandable and entirely reasonable way. We had been saying all year long that "it's the journey that matters, not the destination," but I'm not sure anyone ever stopped to think about what that meant. Now we had reached the desti-nation, and what I was reflecting on was the journey. I was really proud of what the team had done, but more proud about how we had done it. The joy was in the hunt, not in the kill. For nineteen games, week in and week out, we had maybe the best defense ever. That's the memory that will last forever for me.

I dropped in on the team party for a few minutes, but I quickly real-ized I wasn't in the mood for that scene. I'm not a party guy to begin with. I left with Sean Green, Jonathan Miller, and his wife, Penny, and we went looking for some dinner. It was close to midnight at this point, and the only place open that late on a Sunday was a non-descript coffee shop. The four of us sat down, ordered, and then realized everyone in the place was staring at me. Was this the guy they had just watched kick ass in the big game? Eating chicken at midnight in a coffee shop? You bet. Welcome to the glamorous life of a Super Bowl champion!

From a purely personal standpoint, the Super Bowl had a negligible effect on my career. Within the football community, people recognized the impact I had on the game, and I received a lot of respect and compliments. But that was the extent of it. I had this fantasy that my Super Bowl performance would elevate me to household-name status, that I would assume my place among the pantheon of the best to ever play the game. I'm not ashamed to admit that's how I'd like to be remembered, and I figured a stellar performance in the Super Bowl might do that for me. But there were no postseason accolades, no endorsement deals, nothing. The guys who cashed in were the guys who already had the media wrapped around their fingers.

I'm not saying it doesn't look impressive on the résumé. And years from now I'll be able to say I won a Super Bowl, which a lot of great players can't. But it didn't spark anything. When I looked in the mirror a month later, I saw the same Simeon Rice. And apparently the rest of the world did, too. In a game of illusions, the brass ring of winning the Super Bowl turned out to be the biggest one of all.

While I'm on the topic of smoke and mirrors, I'd like to offer a brief word on talk shows. I'm like the moth heading for the flame when I get an opportunity to talk sports. I should hire someone just to talk me out of doing talk shows. For a long time I subscribed to the idea that actions speak louder than words, so how much trouble could my words get me into?

I have since reassessed that position.

Right after the Super Bowl in 2003, I was invited on Jim Rome's talk show. It's one of the few places in sports where an athlete has a chance to be honest and show his true personality, because it's such a bizarre show to begin with, and you figure, *What the fuck, why not?* You never know where's he's coming from, and sometimes you're not sure what he's talking about. When Jim gets on a roll, the adrenaline takes over and it's anyone's guess what will happen next, but that's the cool thing about the show.

A couple of minutes into the show, the conversation turned to my former Arizona teammate, Pat Tillman. Rome asked the question that had been on the lips of most football fans, which is basically *How can someone turn down millions to play a game, then go risk his life for chump change?* The mood of the show when he posed this question was pretty silly, so I gave a silly answer, like maybe Pat had seen one too many Rambo movies.

You could almost see the lightbulb flicker on over Rome's head, which should have been a warning sign. He pressed me to answer the question again, but more seriously and from a fellow player's perspective, in order to gain some new insight. I understood the tone of the question and decided to answer it as honestly and accurately as I could—to give the audience a better understanding of how a football player would evaluate the variables Pat faced as he arrived at this decision, just as I have done earlier in this book.

I always feel an honest, intelligent question should be met with an honest, thoughtful answer. In my profession that often lands you in hot water, but at the end of the day it's just so much easier to say what you think than it is to make shit up.

My response to Jim's question was that Pat Tillman, as a football player, was not a star-caliber performer looking at a potential Hall of Fame career, and this probably made his decision easier. I tried to put myself in Pat's shoes, and the choice I suspected he was weighing was a few more years as a decent player on a crap team versus doing his patriotic duty, which obviously he felt more strongly about than football. He saw a chance to do something great, and he took that opportunity.

I told Jim that 9/11 had affected Pat very deeply, which I knew it had, and that Pat should be commended for what he was doing. He was a teammate and a friend of mine—a straight-up guy who always let you know where you stood. Pat and I were a lot alike in that we did what we wanted to do, and didn't feel like we owed anyone an explanation or a reason. The last thing I intended to do was slight him as an individual. Like all Americans he was personally offended by the terror attacks in

2001, but he chose to respond by doing something 99.999 percent of Americans—myself included—did not do. He enlisted. My brother was in the military for six years, so I understood Pat's choice not only from a football perspective, but from a personal one, too.

Something that Rome was not quick enough to have realized is that I could bring an additional layer of perspective to this situation. Everyone was coming at Pat Tillman asking why he would give up an NFL career, and his reaction was that it was a personal decision and please respect that. Well, remember, I was supposedly guaranteed millions as a first-round pick in the 1995 NFL draft after my junior season at Illinois, and I put the league on hold for personal reasons, too.

Pat was looking for a way to give his life greater purpose (which I told Jim in the interview), while I was looking for a way to live one more year *without* purpose. In terms of people asking you the same damn question every five minutes, however, I knew exactly how Pat felt. You want the world to leave you alone, shut the hell up, and get out of your face.

Anyway, I believe my answer gave fans a glimpse into the mind of a professional athlete. It truly did put Pat's actions into perspective. If you go back and look at the full conversation on that show, it's clear that what I'm trying to convey to Jim Rome and his audience was that Pat Tillman's choice to become a U.S. Army Ranger showed that, to some NFL players, football is not that important. A simple concept, right?

Wrong.

How it turned out was that everyone focused on the first part of my answer—that Pat was a "marginal" talent—and conveniently separated it from the rest of my explanation. The NFL had already painted me as kind of a bad guy, and now I had applied the finishing brushstrokes. Pat was the poster boy for patriotism, and I was the guy looking to tear that poster down. Needless to say, the endorsement offers didn't come rolling in after that.

The irony of this whole episode is that Jim Rome knew where I was coming from; he recognized that there was not even a hint of disrespect in my statements. That's crystal clear on the tape, too. He got so many calls after the interview aired, however, that he ended up switching sides. At first he was deflecting criticism of what I had said, but later he came out against it. He went from telling people Simeon Rice had brought valuable perspective to his question to saying he couldn't believe what Simeon Rice had said!

Jim smelled a better story, so he rolled with it. That included some editing magic, too, which made what I said seem even worse when the clips were replayed. This was an opportunity for Rome to do something that would boost his profile, and further his career, if only for a couple of days. But that's how his game is played. My publicist called me in a panic to tell me that Rome had done this flip-flop and was now hanging me out to dry. Was I surprised? Yeah, to a point. But I'm a realist. I know a man of true conviction can't do what Jim Rome does for a living and be successful at it—in a sense he's a product of the format he created. If he was worried about looking like a hypocrite, he'd have to burn his tapes after every show.

Unfortunately, that one appearance basically wiped out my single greatest accomplishment. And needless to say, I've had to defend my comments and explain the context in which they were delivered again and again and again. The morning the news came that Pat had been killed in a firefight with the Taliban in the mountains of Afghanistan, I was still getting my bearings in my apartment in Phoenix. I was already reeling from two other pieces of incredibly bad news—my aunt died the same day, and a kid named Marcus Ford, who was a great friend to my sisters and almost like a family member, had been gunned down at a rap concert in Michigan because he wouldn't give up some jewelry. There are a lot of sunny days in my life, and then there are some rainy ones. You learn to enjoy the nice days and to weather the bad ones. Still, this day was like a monsoon. I was already numb from dealing with the family tragedies, and now the entire city of Phoenix, myself included, was in mourning over a fallen friend.

Somewhere in the craziness I realized, *Damn, now my words are really going to come back to haunt me.* And yes, they were replayed on television and radio all over the country, along with some pretty colorful commentary. The bright side of this situation was that I was given another opportunity to put my comments into perspective and honor Pat in a number of television appearances I made that day. I knew why I was being asked to appear—I was the person who'd supposedly ridiculed him after he made his decision, and it was a chance to make me eat my words.

But to my mind the comments I'd made on Jim Rome's show a year earlier carried even more weight now. Pat's decision to fight for the flag had nothing to do with football, and that's what Jim and everyone else failed to see. Pat made the same decision, for the same reasons, that thousands of people do every day, and they have nothing to do with football. Everyone who joins the military gives up a career at something. It may not be a glamorous career, but they put their lives on hold to do something important. You have young people who delay college in order to join, at a time when the world is full of possibilities for them. That's not *a* career—it's *any* career. And I'm sure there are people who come from posh backgrounds who give up all the advantages money can buy to join the military, and their families don't understand why. You never see *those* stories on the news.

Every young man and woman who says good-bye to their family and puts on the uniform has a story about what could have been, just like Pat Tillman. There may not be millions of dollars on the table, but they are putting themselves in harm's way for a great cause. In this respect, Pat's death in Afghanistan served as a poignant reminder about the sacrifices all soldiers make. He put doing his duty above everything, including his own life.

As far as the Jim Rome controversy is concerned, I felt at the time that I could look at myself in the mirror and be satisfied I had done the stand-up thing regardless of the shit storm that followed. How Jim could look himself in the mirror was beyond me. Now, with what happened to Pat, I feel even more strongly about my words on that talk show.

10

In a perfect world, every career ends with a Super Bowl victory. The hero—or, in my case, the villain—walks off into the sunset, à la John Elway. The reality of football is that the instant one season ends, a new one begins, and by the time you've caught your breath and savored your victory, everyone else has started thinking about what it will take to defend your championship. The advantage a Super Bowl–winning team has over the competition is that each player now knows what it takes to win. As I would discover, what each player does with that information varies wildly.

When we arrived in training camp to prepare for the 2003 season, I got the uncomfortable feeling that we weren't all on the same page. It's a hard thing to earn a crown, and an easy thing to wear it. So easy that you don't fully appreciate the effort it will take to keep it on your head another year. Yes, you now recognize all the little things it takes to win it all, but that only gives you a minimal advantage. This can be outweighed by the fact that every team that faces you is now, in its mind, playing its own little version of the Super Bowl. Teams that let you roll over them the previous year have a little extra fight in them. This is what really caught us by surprise in 2003, because on several occasions we lost games we could have and should have won, and in each case it came down to one or two plays that, for whatever reason, didn't go our way.

Winning back-to-back Super Bowls has got to be the hardest achievement in sports, because you almost have to double your effort—and stay healthy—that second year. I hate to say it, but there wasn't much effort-doubling that I could see in 2003. We played hard at times and we played well, but there was a feeling on the team—and I was as guilty of this as anyone—that we could shift into a higher gear whenever we had to. The fallacy of this reasoning is obvious when you are looking at the team from the outside. But when you are a member of the team, you look around and see the same talent that got you to the big game the year before and naturally you assume you can do it again. You tend to ignore the fact that some guys are hurt, some guys are older, some guys are gone, and some guys are complacent. Also, personal conflicts that were subdued by winning boil over when the L's start piling up.

When a season blows up on you—like when I played with the Cardinals—you face the reality and try to fix things. But when it comes apart like a bad shirt, a few threads at a time, you keep thinking the losing will stop. You keep doing the same thing game after game, you have faith that talent and experience will win out, but all you're doing is pulling that thread until one day the sleeve drops off and you're out of the playoffs.

I don't like to think about the 2003 season. To me, it was a missed opportunity. I had my best statistical year and, on the whole, played as well as I ever had in all facets of the game. I also got the big contract I deserved. But the satisfaction I took from this season was like what I experienced with the Cardinals. Once you've tasted that Super Bowl champagne, nothing less will ever do again. In that respect, the Super Bowl does change your life forever, because it sucks when you don't win it.

The year began on a high note, against the Eagles. It was a Monday-night game, the city was inaugurating its new football stadium, and the atmosphere was fantastic. Philly wanted revenge, and the fans were tailgating and getting drunk seven hours before kickoff. The place was rocking, with F-16s buzzing the field, a fireworks show—even Sylvester Stallone was there doing his Rocky thing. It was nuts.

Prior to the game, we talked about continuing exactly where we'd left off the previous year. We could all remember the passion we took into the Super Bowl against Oakland, and we vowed to play with that kind of focus and intensity all season long. And against the Eagles that Monday night we did. We beat their asses. Joe Jurevicius made some unbelievable catches, our defense suffocated Donovan McNabb, and I had one series in the first half where I stuffed every play and pretty much ruined their game plan for the whole evening. We won 17–0, and were certain we were on course for another Super Bowl.

Then the weird shit started happening. Our next game was against the Carolina Panthers. We knew their defense was improving, but if you had asked me which teams had a chance of making the Super Bowl that year, I never would have listed the Panthers. They came together well at the end of the season and did make it to the Super Bowl, and I think a lot of what they accomplished in 2003 came off their September game against us.

In this game Martin Gramatica had two kicks blocked, including an extra point that would have been the game winner, which sent us into overtime. Carolina won it 12–9. Having one kick blocked is bad. It means someone's not doing his job. Having two blocked is unheard of. That takes a mental breakdown that is hard for me to describe. As a team, you feel stupid. You almost don't want to face up to your mistakes, because you feel a loss like this is so far beneath you. After the game I tried to be philosophical. I told the sportswriters, "Hey, it's one loss. You accept it and move on."

When you look back on a comment like that, given that the losing continued, it has the appearance of being nonchalant. Buccaneers fans pointed to remarks of that nature in December and said, "See, you weren't taking things seriously three months ago, and that's why you're out of the playoffs now." My view on this is that it's a free country, and people can express whatever opinion they like. But in sports, you can't always look at what someone says in response to one set of circumstances, then later apply to a totally different set of circumstances.

And here was a case in point. At that moment the Buccaneers were 1–1, coming off two great defensive efforts. The Panthers hadn't run the ball particularly well; they hadn't scored five touchdowns. Basically, they'd made five very good defensive plays over the course of seventy minutes, and if they had only made four we probably would have put that game away. What else can you say at that point, when you are asked to characterize the mood of the team? It was the truth. Could that have been a window into the soul of the Bucs at that point? No. I may have been speaking for the team, but I certainly wasn't the caretaker of their collective consciousness. We lost a tough game, and from the perspective of a 1–1 team coming off a Super Bowl, my words reflected very accurately how we felt.

So if you're going to analyze what someone says in the moment, that's fine. Like I said, everyone's entitled to their own opinions. But don't cut and paste something a player says into another context just to support some theory—especially if you're a sportswriter, because someone might actually believe you. And sportswriters would never want their readers believing something that's not true, right?

Now that I've said my piece about time travel in sports journalism, I will admit that when you take our 2003 season as a whole, that first Carolina game *was* legitimately troubling, my remarks notwithstanding. Attending to the details was a big reason we won games in 2002. We lost this game because we didn't take care of the details, and it wouldn't be the last time this happened. That bad feeling I had during training camp was getting stronger by the week.

Still, our next game was a fun one. We beat the Atlanta Falcons 31–10 and I had a sack. I was banging, in the backfield constantly, for the third game in a row. This was the game when I tipped a pass and Warren Sapp intercepted the ball, ran it in for a touchdown, then did his Beyoncé impression in the end zone. Warren is something else, man. And no, that wasn't another symptom of a season going wrong. Warren is Warren, you just have to understand that.

We went into our next game, a *Monday Night Football* contest, feeling very confident. Our defense had allowed one touchdown all year, and now our offense was rolling. The Colts were known for their offense, with Peyton Manning, Edgerrin James, and Marvin Harrison, but they had a good defense going, too, so it sized up as a good battle. Well, we went out and just destroyed them. We ran up a big score and then, with five minutes left, they made the biggest comeback in NFL history and tied the game. Then they beat us in overtime. It was truly shocking.

The lowlight of this game for me was getting whistled for a bizarre penalty when Mike Vanderjagt missed his first attempt at the game-winning field goal. I started a few steps in back of the line and rose up as he kicked it to see if I could deflect the ball. It was a long shot, but if a kick is on a low trajectory, it passes over the line of scrimmage at about ten feet. I can get up over eleven feet, so it was worth a try. I didn't get the ball, which went wide, but the referee threw a flag on me for "leaping." This is a rule that, first of all, is never enforced. It's only in there to protect a defensive player's teammates if he jumps on the pile cleats-first. Instead of the Bucs taking possession of the ball, the Colts got another shot, and Vanderjagt won the game 38–35.

Everyone asks me if I am now well versed on the NFL's leaping rule, but the truth is I know the rulebook backward and forward, and I knew it already. It specifically states you can't come down on another player, and I didn't. I came down behind the guy, and someone got backed up into me. But I definitely did not land on anyone. From the official's perspective it may have looked that way, but if you watch the replay my feet both touched the ground. We got shafted, plain and simple.

Washington was up next, and we were really up for that game. It was probably the best we played all year. It was definitely *my* best game. I went up against Chris Samuels, who's my height but outweighs me by about forty or fifty pounds. He won the Outland Trophy with Alabama and was the third pick in the 1999 draft. He's started every game of his career for the Redskins and had made the Pro Bowl the last two years. This was a good challenge, and I rose to the occasion. I knew what Chris was going to do before he knew himself, and I just abused him. I was in quarterback Patrick Ramsey's face all day long. I got four sacks, our offense scored over 30 again, and we looked like the Super Bowl champions we were.

Now, you would think that after a game like this, I would be all over TV. I had produced four highlight-reel-quality plays, and I hit Ramsey I don't know how many times. And four sacks against anyone, let alone Samuels, is a very hard thing to achieve in the NFL. But this was the game when Warren Sapp went out during pregame while the Redskins were stretching and skipped through their warm-ups. You gotta love the guy. I mean, how can you get angry about that? Afterward my friends all said, *Simeon, you would be the league's most famous defensive player if you didn't have such a distraction on your team*. Well, this was three years of my stellar performances being overshadowed by a Warren Sapp moment, so I was pretty well used to it. And if you can't see the humor in it after a while, then you're simply not human.

Unfortunately, there was nothing funny about what happened next. We lost five of our next seven games to go from 3–2 to 5–7. With the exception of a blowout at the hands of the 49ers, we were in each of the other four defeats right to the final whistle. It was one thing to lose games like this in Arizona, where you'd look around and say, *Well, they exploited our weaknesses* or *They were just better than us.* But on paper the Bucs were every bit as good as the teams that beat us in 2003, and probably better.

I was never a big believer in bad chemistry, but when I look back at all the little things that went wrong, all the miscommunication, and all of failures to put out 100 percent on key downs, I have to think that chemistry had something to do with it. I can't think of another explanation. We weren't getting blown out, we were just losing. How else do you explain a historic defense that suddenly can't stop the run? The irony is that I was doing a good job tackling ball carriers, and was finally getting recognition for it.

We were beating ourselves on defense. Our strength became our weakness, and that just threw the whole team out of whack. Our offense, which was very good at the beginning of the year, found itself in situations where it had to win games, not just manage leads, and that took its toll. John Lynch got injured, which removed a vocal leader and a playmaker from the lineup. And then there was the whole Keyshawn thing.

Keyshawn Johnson and Jon Gruden were like oil and water from the moment they came together. The idea that they got along great one year and then turned on each the next is a fantasy. There was never a moment when they saw eye to eye; they had a bad working relationship from the start. The only difference between 2002 and 2003 was that we were losing, and I think Keyshawn saw that as his chance to become vocal and possibly force a trade. Had we won all year I think he would have kept quiet, like he did during our Super Bowl season.

They didn't like each other, and they had opposing philosophies on when, where, and how often Keyshawn should get the ball. What more can you say? Coach had it in his mind to use Keyshawn one way, and Keyshawn didn't understand why he wasn't the focal point of the offense.

It was a big distraction, but when he got put off the team it was the residual of a bad season, not the cause of it, or even the last straw. Besides, the problem wasn't a Keyshawn problem, it was a Keyshawn–Jon problem. Neither man was willing to put his pride aside. I know people watching at home thought, *Shit, if I were the coach I'd stick my foot where the sun don't shine.* That just shows how people lose their ability for rational thought when they're watching a football game. Coaches and players don't kick each other's asses. You have to have some semblance of a working environment.

I wasn't in such a good mood, either. The worse we played, the angrier and more frustrated I became. All I could think was, *What a wasted year.* I knew this would be the last time this group of guys would be together, and we blew it. I channeled a lot of those feelings into my play, which gave me an outlet, and it also made me perform better. In my little corner of the world, I was having a great year. A wasted year from a team perspective, but a great year nonetheless. I achieved a personal high in terms of sacks, and I was voted All-Pro at defensive end. But I'll admit, by the season's final three games I couldn't think of any reason to play other than pride.

I suppose the one memorable moment from the 2003 season was when I guaranteed a Tampa Bay victory prior to the second Carolina game. We were 4–4 at that point, and it was a must-win game. Gruden reminded us that the team we had faced in the Super Bowl, the Oakland Raiders, were 4–4 at the same point in 2002, so all we had to do was start winning. I went out a bit farther on a limb and told the media that the game was as good as won. I knew this to be the great taboo in sports, but I was hoping to jump-start the team. I figured if we won it might help get our energy level back. And hell, if we lost there was almost no way we were going to win the division. So there was less to lose than you'd think.

Why me? Because, as I explained, I was having a great season and sensed that the guys felt like they were letting me down a little. I put the pressure back on me, hoping that it might help them reach down and find a little extra. Everyone on the team knows me, and they knew why I said what I said.

Anyway, I was looking like the black Joe Namath with less than three minutes left. I was shutting down my side to the running game, and I had already sacked Jake Delhomme twice. The Panthers had blown a 13-point fourth-quarter lead to give us a 24–20 advantage. They had the ball on their own 22 with no time-outs. We never lost games like this.

Well, I'll be damned if Delhomme didn't hit on five of six passes, including a short strike to Steve Smith in the end zone. That game epitomized our season. Everything went the way we had planned all week, but we had a breakdown and gave up two bad passes. And that was the game—another example of us falling short on the details. We knew those plays were coming and we failed to stop them.

Our defensive coordinator, Monte Kiffin, was great after the game. He accepted full responsibility for the failure of our two-minute defense. But the players knew we were to blame. And of course I now had to defend my guarantee. What could I say? I took a shot and it didn't work. The Panthers didn't win because of what I said. They weren't thinking about Simeon Rice's guarantee when they picked us apart at the end of the game. They won and we didn't.

Will I be guaranteeing a victory again? Hell yeah. When the reporters came to my locker looking for me to eat crow, I told them I'd guarantee a win the next week if they wanted me to. I'd do it every game if I thought it would help us win. They laughed, but these are words I play by and live by. I was just expressing them publicly.

Rasheed Wallace did the same thing during the 2004 NBA playoffs. After the Pistons lost the opening game of the Eastern Conference Finals, he guaranteed Detroit would beat the Indiana Pacers in Game 2. As you might expect, there was a lot of discussion about this after the Pistons won. There's always a lot of discussion in sports after the outcome has been determined, but that's all it is. Discussion.

Dan Patrick, who does a radio show for ESPN, talked about the guarantee *before* the Pacers–Pistons game. You know what he said? He wished every player on every team would guarantee a victory before a big game. He cut through the crap and got right to the essence of the issue. The fact is, every player on a talented, winning team believes he will win every time he pulls on his uniform. You have to believe that or you'll find yourself out of the league, or on a losing team, very quickly.

Every Sunday I wake up and the first thing I do is basically guarantee to myself that I will play a winning football game. I assume that's the way it is in any competitive job. If a salesperson goes to work thinking of reasons he can't sell the company's product, he'd better find himself a new career. If you can't guarantee yourself that you will be at your best when it matters most, you'll find out fast what it's like to be at your absolute worst. If I give my all and lose, that's okay, because I'm in a job where half the people end up losing. But to lose and not give your all is a disgusting thought to me. I will not accept a piss-poor effort from me or my teammates.

My football year ended on—what else?—a bizarre note. After the season, I began to focus my efforts on T3K. We had generated a lot of interest prior to our launch, with some major articles about me and the company in different consumer and trade publications. When we finally started shipping product in November, people loved it. Originally, we figured we would sell a lot to cold-weather athletes, like football teams and hockey teams, and maybe skiers, and a lot of team sports dealers. Those sales take a while to develop, and require some appearances and handshaking—which I was able to do once the season was over.

The idea was always for the quality and performance of T3K to sell on its own merits, but at least initially, I needed to get out there and meet with the key accounts. The company set up an exhibit at The Super Show, a big sporting goods trade show in Orlando, and we were overwhelmed with people. I showed up one morning just to check out the booth and it was jammed with people, even though no one knew I was coming. A few feet away, the guys from Under Armour were watching from their exhibit, and they didn't like what they were seeing. That was cool.

We set up at another trade show in Salt Lake City, Outdoor Retailer, which caters to all the camping and hiking and outdoor stores. I didn't make it to that one, but the T3K team—including my old friends Lamon Caldwell and Kevin Wilson—were there. They ran a picture of Lamon in the booth in the paper, and the next day everyone was pissed that they had missed Simeon Rice. That cracked me up. Utah is about the whitest place on earth so I'm not surprised they mistook Lamon for me. We're both big guys, but I'm the charming, good-looking one.

I was running all over the country making sales calls for T3K, and I contacted the NFL and let them know I'd be a couple of days late for the Pro Bowl in Hawaii. I honestly did have a prior engagement. Most of the players came in over the weekend, and practice started on Monday. I wasn't going to get there until early Wednesday. The league bucked a little bit, but in the end they said, *No problem.*

Then, right before I left, Kevin called and told me, "The NFL is bugging. I don't think they want you to go."

I told him not to worry, and I flew out to Honolulu. I practiced on Thursday, then early Friday morning I started getting calls from friends who know people in the NFL. They wanted to see if I was okay. Some had heard a rumor that I had been in a skiing accident. Others had heard it was a snorkeling accident. Someone else said they'd heard I'd gotten into it with the coach, Andy Reid. Someone was making shit up, and the league was spreading the story through back channels for some reason.

I practiced on Friday and posed for the team picture, but there was nothing that raised my suspicion, so I went back to the hotel, had dinner, and kicked back in the room. The next morning, before practice, I got a call from a friend who said he'd heard I'd been sent home from the Pro Bowl, that I was off the official roster. I told him I had no idea what he was talking about. He said, "Turn on ESPN."

What I saw was surreal. ESPN had this whole piece on me getting booted off the team, and they had never even *attempted* to get in touch with me. I had arrived when I'd said I was going to arrive, I hadn't missed practice, and none of the coaches had said anything to me. What the story was saying was that I showed up to Hawaii late and that I didn't go to practice—both lies. Talk about the power of the media, though. The story was so well done and so convincing that if it had been about anyone but me, I'd have believed it myself. I started laughing, because I realized there was no way to deal with this. Then I remembered that I had seen a defensive end around practice who wasn't even on the roster. *Oh shit,* I'm thinking, *this is like one of those conspiracies you see in the movies!*

They got comments from a number of people, only one of whom did the right thing in that situation. Jim Brown was interviewed, and he said he wouldn't comment until he had spoken with me personally. I thought that was commendable.

The icing on the cake was Sean Salisbury's commentary on the story. Sean and I had gone out together a couple of times in New York and were pretty friendly. He was talking about me like we had never met, saying a player has to show he is worthy of the right to play in the Pro Bowl, or something like that. I was *selected* to play! I think I had more votes than any defensive player in the NFC! *Wow, so this is how it goes now. Thanks, Sean. You dick.*

I had a message on my hotel phone from a call that had come in at like one o'clock in the morning. I had been in the room, but there was no way I was going to answer it. The message was from hotel security, and said I should check under the door. Sure enough, there was an envelope on the floor. I opened it up and there was a letter from the NFL informing me that I was off the team, that I had to check out immediately, and that my per diem was canceled. The reason given was that I had arrived "almost late" for practice and that my shoes were untied, and therefore I was not ready to play. I kept the letter because no one believes this story. But there it is: "almost late." I've shown it to everyone I know and they laugh their asses off.

At first, I didn't really digest it. I called my agent, who had me read it to a lawyer. When I read the words "almost late" again, he wanted to know what that meant. I said, "How the hell should I know?"

He said, "So you missed practice?"

"No."

"So you were late to practice?"

"No."

He couldn't figure out what it meant, either. So what does "almost late" mean? How about I put that up for official review: Is that like almost dead? Almost pregnant? Almost stupid? Almost guilty? Almost good? An interesting footnote is that the morning I was "almost late" for practice happened to be the same morning we took the team picture *prior* to the practice I was "almost late" for. Look closely at that picture. Was I "almost" in it? No, I *was* in it.

I do have to come clean on the other charge, though. I plead guilty to having my shoes untied when I showed up. You see, in every deceit there is always a kernel of truth!

I think Andy Reid was party to this whole charade. I'm not sure why he would involve himself in this type of thing, but I know he was still angry about being humiliated by the Bucs when they'd opened their stadium earlier that season. And he was probably still pissed that I'd checked out of the Pro Bowl after a quarter the year before. My shoulder was killing me. I went out for a couple of series, and then I just didn't feel it was worth risking further injury. Man, they were hot about that. They couldn't believe I wasn't going back in. So maybe this was payback.

Anyway, Reid said he handled this like he would have between himself and any other player. "It was between me and Simeon," he said. I'm like, *Wait, I didn't even talk to you! What the fuck!* The most he said to me that week was, "Simeon Rice!" like he was glad I made it. I'm like, *Wow, this dude lied!*

In the middle of this fiasco I talked to a guy I know at the NFL and asked him, *What's to prevent me from doing something that makes this look like a haywire league? What's to prevent me from holding a press conference and saying some bullshit myself? What if I go extreme and say, "Andy Reid made some sexually suggestive comments to me"?*

"What do you mean?" he asked.

I explained that I could announce that Andy Reid had said some inappropriate shit to me, I could let the whole thing build up, force people to take sides, and turn the Pro Bowl into a big soap opera. It's no more of a concoction than what was said about me. Why not concoct some bullshit and watch the league squirm a little? I was putting this to him rhetorically, of course, but I hope it got back to the commissioner because something like that's going to happen someday. I guarantee it. They're going to push the wrong button on the wrong guy and all hell is going to break loose. It won't be me, but it'll be someone. When it happens—and it will happen eventually—I'm just going to sit back and enjoy it. You know what they say: What goes around comes around.

In the meantime I decided to get out of there and go to Maui. Ah, there's no place like Maui to help you put things into perspective. Life is simple, nature is exploding all around you, and the distractions are few. I had time to catch my breath, regain my sanity, and actually think about where I was as a human being and as a football player. As you may have already guessed, I felt pretty good about both.

I have always placed high standards on my personal life, and I have to say when I look in the mirror, I am satisfied with the man who's looking back at me. Away from the game, my family relationships are tight and my friendships are evolving in some very interesting directions. I have love and respect from the people who matter to me, and I love and respect them in return. I have sunny days and rainy days, and I think I deal with both pretty well, never getting too high, never getting too low.

People have described me as being paradoxical, but you can be that in a good way, I think. For instance, I spend a fair amount of time alone, but I'm not a lonely man. I have matured as an individual, but there's still a lot of kid in me. I am unpredictable, but also reliable. I am impulsive, but also analytical. I have a healthy ego, but I find other people a lot more fascinating than I find myself. I understand ten times more about life than I did five years ago, which means I understand I have a lot more to learn.

On the football field, my standards are even higher. At this point in my career, I feel like I should be the guy whom the offense can't plan for and can't stop. I shouldn't have to memorize offensive tendencies or watch film of the man I'm going to face, because my job is to get past that man and disrupt the opponent's game plan. If I get beat on a play, then I've got thirty seconds to figure out what happened and make sure it doesn't happen again. I have enough moves and techniques and strategies at this point in my career that I can literally give my man a different look on every play. You have to be an offensive lineman to appreciate what a nightmare that is, but trust me, I am a nightmare to contend with.

If I do my job the way I expect to, the rest of the defense can feed off that. I create opportunities for my teammates, and it becomes their job to take advantage of the havoc I cause on the right corner of the line. I do not fear age or injury, I never think about my team's record or position in the standings during a game, and I have yet to begin a season believing anything less than that my team can go to the Super Bowl. Between games, I do nothing that will adversely affect my play on Sunday. And between seasons I defy you to find someone in this league who dedicates more time and effort to getting ready for the coming year.

In the aftermath of the 2004 Pro Bowl, it actually felt good to do a life review. I don't believe there's anything wrong with giving yourself a pat on the back from time to time. It's good for the soul if you do it right. It also helped me put the events of that crazy week into perspective. My life may be together and my football may be together, but the irony of Simeon Rice is that where they intersect is completely screwed up.

By this I mean that in the illusion that is NFL football, Simeon Rice wears a black hat.

I've been in denial about this for almost my entire career, but the Pro Bowl incident finally forced me to address it. When you have so much firepower lined up against you, there comes a time when you have to acknowledge the situation. After that, you can begin to analyze it. And once you understand it, you can move forward in an intelligent manner. I've always been confused about the right way to react when this type of shit comes down on me. I've tried everything from launching a vocal defense to not commenting to just laughing it off. But it never seems to get better and it never seems to end.

Putting this book together introduced me to a new process of organizing information. It also helped me draw connections I hadn't seen before. And it forced me to confront some things that I would have just as soon left alone. It was on this issue of my image, however, that I gained considerable clarity. I finally began to understand why I was a so-called bad guy in the NFL. For this reason alone, it was worth every moment of time and effort that went into the process.

The NFL loves to create its own mythology. As a student of football and its history, I understand this better than most people in my profession. The league is successful because the more layers you peel away, the more texture you see. It's never just two teams on the field hammering each other for sixty minutes. It's good versus evil, right versus wrong, the future versus the past, fate versus destiny—something that gets fans to invest their emotions in the game. In the bigger picture there are dynasties, there are epic battles, there are pioneers, and, most of all—most important—there are heroes. The NFL's version of the classic storybook hero keeps people tuning in, it puts fans in the seats, and it gets them to spend their money on any piece of memorabilia that makes them feel more connected to the game.

Without heroes, I think pro football would still be a fringe sport, like it was back in the 1950s. Back then, college football had all these components and it was far more successful than pro ball, from both a popularity standpoint and a financial standpoint. Johnny Unitas was probably the first guy who awakened this idea of a pro football hero, and Pete Rozelle, the old commissioner, knew that he could sell it on television.

By the time I was a kid, the model was already well established. Growing up in Chicago, I could rattle off names like *Gale Sayers* and *Dick Butkus* before I knew who they really were. They were great players on shitty teams, but to a Bears fan in the 1970s and 1980s they were as relevant as Walter Payton and Mike Singletary, who were great players on one of the greatest teams ever. Butkus, by the way, was a bad dude. I hear he did shit on the field that was practically criminal. But somehow he ended up being a hero. Let a player like me pull that stuff today and I'd be suspended for life.

The NFL likes to have a hand in developing its heroes. When a player rises above the anonymous struggle and begins to acquire a public face, the image-making process begins. The first decision the league has to make is, *Do we steer this guy toward hero status or not?* If the answer is yes, the first thing you notice is that the television announcers and pregame shows start talking him up and running clips of him. The next thing you notice is a lot more reporters around the guy's locker. Then you'll see newspaper profiles and magazine features. And he'll start popping up in highlights more often. His charity appearances will get a lot more coverage, too. Then everyone keeps their fingers crossed that the guy doesn't screw up, on the field or off the field.

If this individual breaks a record, makes a game-winning or game-saving play, wins an award, or does something else to justify his buildup, then the NFL may have a bona fide hero on its hands. It will guard that image and build it up, and then plug it right into the pro football time line. This player could be a rookie, a veteran, or a washout who finds redemption at the end of his career. Heroes come in all shapes and sizes, in all colors, and at all positions. Hero status is bestowed upon big guys, little guys, fast guys, slow guys, guys who do great things with their bodies, and guys who do great things with their minds. This is one of the aspects about football I've loved since I was a kid, and I admit it makes me a huge football fan today. I love rooting for the good guys, even though I'm one of the bad guys.

That leads me to the flip side to this process. If the NFL is shrewd enough to create and promote its heroes, then surely it must see the benefit of having villains. Lots of them, in fact. And indeed it does. Everyone trying to tackle a good guy is, almost by definition, a bad guy.

Anyone scoring a touchdown on a good guy is a bad guy, too. A good guy versus another good guy? Are you kidding? The NFL loves that shit. It's Grant versus Lee—pure mythology.

Now go back to when a player hits the fan radar in the NFL. The instant he crosses the line between just a hometown guy and someone who's gaining leaguewide recognition, the wheels start to turn in New York. Maybe, just maybe, this player would make a better villain than he would a hero. People like villains, too, so it's not like they're ruining his career. Jeremy Shockey on the Giants is a perfect example of this. As soon as he started making an impact for that team, all you heard about was the negative stuff. He makes a great bad guy.

The other thing about casting someone as a villain is that, in the upside-down world of pro football, he can find redemption and undergo a transformation into a hero. I can definitely see this happening to Shockey. On the other hand, heroes make lousy villains, so from the NFL's perspective, they are right in choosing their heroes carefully. That's why, sometimes, the league doesn't jump on a guy's bandwagon as soon as they could. They take a wait-and-see approach until they get a better gauge of what kind of person he is.

So when Simeon Rice emerged from the primordial ooze of the 1996 Arizona Cardinals and served notice that he was an impact player in this league, the NFL had a decision on its hands. Given that I had held out after the draft, they probably decided to wait and see on me. When I was plagued by injuries in my second season, I went off the radar again. But during the next three years in Arizona, when I put up big numbers and became an elite player, someone somewhere decided the black hat suited me better than the white one.

Who knows? From a marketing standpoint, maybe they were right. Do I take it personally? Yes, I do. It's one thing to make someone into a cartoon-character bad guy, but it's not right to then go ahead and treat him that way. And to tell you the truth, sometimes that's how I have felt over the years—especially when teams didn't sign me as a free agent and no one ever knocked on my door for an endorsement deal. That's money and respect I deserved and didn't get. The league often loses sight of the fact that they are dealing with human beings, and this taking the whole hero–villain thing to extremes is just another example of that.

Am I bitter about it? A little, though much less than I used to be. When you understand what's happening it's easier to work through it. Will I be one of those villains who is transformed into a hero? That would be a trip! Hey, I know football history. So I know that, if I continue to perform at this level for a few more seasons, the NFL may have no choice but to reinvent me.

Imagine that. Simeon Rice. Football hero.

Epilogue

When a football career ends, what do you have? The answer to that question depends on whom you ask. Money? Fame? Family? Religion? Chronic pain? Depression? Rage issues? None of the above? All of the above?

My answer to that question is that, if you're lucky, you have your friends.

Professional athletes tend to trace the course of their lives by their games and teams and seasons and statistics, and I've done that in this book because it is a convenient framework with which to tell my story. However, in personal moments, when I look back on my life, I view it through the prism of my friendships. It's not crucial that people know everything about my friends, and I've only mentioned a few of them, but it's helpful to understand some of the basics in order to understand where I'm coming from.

My friends are precious to me. At any stop on the Simeon Rice timeline, you will find one constant: a group of friends who are enhancing the quality of my life in some way. You'll also find that my relationships with them are more like the relationships you find between family members. Guys like Bennie and Lamon and Sean and Kevin and Ty and John are like a security blanket for me.

If we were together in a foxhole and someone rolled a grenade in between us, I'm the type of guy who would jump on it—if I was quick enough to beat the other dudes. That's the depth of commitment we have toward one another.

Often I think that the closeness of these relationships is the reason so many romances have failed for me in my life. I am so devoted to my friendships that women get insecure. They say, "Why aren't *we* like that?" Also, I would start comparing the trust and devotion I have for a woman to that which I had for my friends. It doesn't take much imagination to see how that plays out. Looking back, I can think of two or three dating relationships that would have become much more spectacular had my friendships not been as tight.

I can also say that this has kept me from forming close friendships in professional football. With the exception of Tommy Bennett, I have never developed a true friendship with a teammate or an opponent or a coach or a member of the media. The relationships in pro sports, at least in the modern era, are extremely complex on the one hand and yet extraordinarily shallow on the other. You have financial issues and issues of competition to deal with. Also, can you truly trust someone who ultimately must answer to team, family, coach, accountant, agent, et cetera, before he answers to you?

When I run into old-timers, they tell me how the friendships they started as players are still going strong, like soldiers who shared the same battle scars. Maybe it's me, but I doubt that today's players are going to take that kind of bond with them when they leave the game. We don't have the down time the old guys did. Football is more like a business. You're always looking at your itinerary, someone's always pulling this way or that, and it's rare you get a couple of hours to shoot the breeze with the guys anymore. Don't get me wrong. I'm friendly with a lot of players. I just never formed any really tight friendships in the league.

I think it's because I'm meeting them "fully formed." I never had a chance to grow with that person, I've never had to walk his same path. When we get to that point where a close friendship might develop, either something external has affected it, or we get to a deeper level and find we just don't relate. The fellowship of the football field is great, but for me it doesn't provide the common ground I'm ultimately searching for.

Look, everyone wanted Jordan and Pippen to be friends, and everyone wanted Shaq and Kobe to be friends, and everyone wanted me and Warren Sapp to be friends, but the fact that we wear the same uniform, hoisted the same trophy, and achieved the same level of brilliance didn't bring any of us any closer to each other once we changed into our street clothes. Maybe when we hang up our jerseys, we'll find our common ground in the old football stories, and the friendships will form then. Maybe this deranged life we live now will become the impetus for creating close bonds in the future. I won't rule it out. Hell, that's what you live life for, to find out. But man, I just don't see it now.

My friends today are basically the guys I grew up with, along with a couple I met at the University of Illinois. I can't tell you how important it is for someone in my position to have established strong ties before reaching the NFL, because after you go high-profile, the people you meet are different. They come from different worlds and different things motivate them. When you have a shared past with someone you have all that context to fall back on, and the comfort level is extraordinary. It's nothing for us to be talking, and then refer back to part of another conversation we had when we were thirteen.

With that kind of inner circle, I know I can have the worst day and pick up the phone and they'll make me forget all the troubling things in my life, and soon I'll be laughing. What I get from them is priceless, and they get the same back from me. We give everything to each other. It's a beautiful thing, especially when you see the relationships most players have with their friends. NFL players are surrounded by what I call "Do-boys." They do things, they attend to the details, they're glorified go-fers. My boys are like the kids in that movie *The Sandlot*. The friendships have evolved over time, and exist regardless of the circumstances. We can talk for hours and bounce a lot of nothings off each other—the essence of what a friendship should be.

I am so tight with my friends that when I formed my apparel company, T3K, I didn't hesitate to ask them for their help. We all know each other's strengths and weaknesses, we all have a track record in business, and we all understand what it means to be part of a corporation. Although technically T3K is my business, it is structured as a partnership in the sense that their input is as valued as mine, and if they execute their portions of the business plan, we all reap the rewards. Together, we all work like a well-oiled machine.

The tricky thing, of course, is when the machine needs a slight adjustment. You have to take off your friend hat and put on your boss hat. I'm no Suge Knight, I'm not a slave driver, but as a boss I do set objectives and expect people to follow a plan to meet those objectives. If someone is coming up short on his responsibilities, I'll take him aside, let him know we're about to talk man-to-man and not friend-to-friend, and have an intelligent business conversation.

The reality is that this hardly ever has to take place. It's not a friend-filled company—only Kevin, Lamon, Cleshon, and Ty are actual employees. Besides, if we're talking about a day-to-day issue, SJR Enterprises—the parent company of my various business ventures—has a traditional management structure that deals with these things in the appropriate way, at the appropriate level. It's a far cry from the Juggernaut days.

Time and distance can affect a friendship, but I wouldn't say that I've ever really had to "work" at a friendship. I've nurtured them and allowed them to grow, and my friends have done the same. But yo, I'm realistic. I recognize that things change. When Bennie got married and had a child, he became less of a fixture in my life. This has changed a relationship that I have had since third grade, and forced us to find new ways to make it work. We talked two or three times a day for years, but he's not in a position to do that anymore.

My relationship with my cousin John has dwindled somewhat, too. We're still tight, but we don't communicate with each other as regularly as we did a few years ago. Life is complex, and it makes me sad sometimes when friendships loosen. I almost felt a little abandoned at first, but after a while I adjusted and these friendships just entered a new phase. As long as the love is still there—and as long as we know each others' secrets, subtleties, insecurities, and idiosyncrasies—we'll always have that bond.

Sooner or later, I'll get married, too. There is no doubt in my mind that the woman I marry will have to be a real friend before I make that kind of commitment. I guess I no longer expect to enjoy the identical rapport I have with my lifelong friends, but it'll have to be damn near the same. I know that's an impossibly high standard to hold someone to, but I'm willing to wait.

One of the hurdles that this special woman will have to clear is holding up her end of a conversation. And she should know that the conversations I enjoy most are the philosophical ones. In college, we used to stay up all night talking about life, and we'd barely experienced it at that point. But our minds were working, and we were trying to expand our way of thinking. As I've grown older and experienced more, those conversations have gained more depth and meaning. And because I'm having those conversations with mostly the same people, they've acquired a subtext and a history all their own.

I like to turn things over in my head and view them from different angles. I'm fascinated by how other people from different walks of life see the same issue. I'm always asking questions, always prodding people. I have the ability to store what people say and then pull it out weeks or months or even years later, when we get back on the same subject. When I was a kid, I always questioned everything. Organized religion was a big part of my family's culture, so of course I didn't always get satisfactory answers to my questions. I had to take a lot on faith. This could be a comfort at times, and incredibly frustrating at other times. Over the years, I may have drifted away from religion per se, but I have evolved into a very spiritual individual.

The irony is that my core beliefs are strangely similar to what I was taught as a child. I believe, for instance, that we were not put on this earth to live forever, so you make the most of the time you're here. There is so much death and so much pain and so much sadness in life that you have to treat the happy times like a bonus. I know I do. And in between, you mourn the tragedies and give thanks that you're not one of them. That's what enables me to smile when I'm down. That's what's real about religion.

I've learned a lot about what's not real in my thirty-plus years. And I've learned a lot about illusions. I've learned that people do some crazy things to chase them, and I've learned that the reality they mask can be very brutal. Yet I've also learned that some illusions are worth believing in, if only to help you find answers where there are none, and help you make it through the day. If you only deal with realities, life can seem like an endless string of car crashes.

The illusion of Simeon Rice, like most illusions, is based on scattered facts, fleeting impressions, and the assumptions everyone tends to make about athletes and celebrities. On the field, I'm viewed as a "skills" player. That has always been uttered as a backhanded compliment, and I've always taken it that way. But as a student of football history, I know a time will come when the illusion will come closer to the reality, which is that I helped change what football teams look for when they draft defensive ends.

In the locker room, the illusion is that I'm moody, aloof, disrespectful to coaches, and that I screw with the press. These also happen to be the cartoon-character traits of a "bad guy" in the NFL, which should tell you something about their accuracy. The reality is that I begin every season believing that we can win the Super Bowl, and until the season is over I keep my head in the game, play hard on every down, and try to be as honest and forthright as possible.

Off the field, the illusion is that I do my own thing whether it's good for the team or not. The reality, of course, is that virtually every decision—from the time I wake up every morning until the time I go to bed—is made with one underlying consideration: Will this keep me from playing football at the peak of my abilities? I know I've stated this several times, but if there's one thing a football fan should take from this book, this is it. I can't speak for other players in terms of the depth of their commitment to the game, but I can't imagine anyone works harder to stay in optimum condition—both physically and mentally—than I do.

Now tell me, in what way is that type of philosophy harmful to the goals of a football team? I'm not saying I'm a paragon of virtue, I'm not saying I'm the second coming of Mother Teresa, I'm not saying I don't make mistakes in my life. But if every player approached his life off the field with a level of commitment to the game similar to mine, I think you'd see the difference on the football field.

As for the illusion that wealth and success and fame make for a problem-free existence, well, that's just naive. Again, I don't like to speak for others, but I can say without hesitation that people in my position have to deal with bad shit all the time. Life can get very complicated and chaotic for so-called celebrities, and the solutions are often much more complex because of their position. It's almost like running a corporation—you can't just think of yourself, there are ramifications to everything you do or you don't do, and sometimes doing the right thing is not as simple as it initially seems.

Do I regret my station in life? Not at all. In fact, looking back, I have relatively few regrets. There are things I could have done better, things I could have understood more clearly. To me, though, that's what life's about. You learn from your mistakes. Since you can't live your life over, you move forward and try not to repeat the same mistakes. This just seems like common sense to me.

Enough about illusions. What's the reality of Simeon Rice?

If you look at my career, I think at this stage I'm right up there with the greats who have played this game. The defensive end position has evolved since the days of leather helmets, just as the sport itself has evolved. What Gino Marchetti did back in the day, when he turned a simple position into a multidimensional one with his combination of speed and power, made him the elite end of his era. What Deacon Jones did, essentially inventing the "sack" and forcing the league to devise new blocking schemes, made him the elite end of *his* era. You had freewheeling guys like L. C. Greenwood, relentless pursuers like Jack Youngblood, and intimidators like Howie Long all adding new dimensions to the position. You had Reggie White and Bruce Smith, who took what those guys did and repackaged it in a whole new way.

Now you have hybrid players like Jevon Kearse and myself, who have added athleticism normally associated with linebackers or even defensive backs to everything our predecessors have done. I thought it was interesting when the Eagles went out and signed Jevon. Andy Reid and Jim Johnson, their defensive coordinator—both of whom detest me, by the way—basically went after guys who matched the prototype I created. I get a kick when I watch the draft now and see these lean, mean defensive ends going in the first round. When *I* was drafted, I was supposedly too undersized to play the run and the pass. I proved an athlete who would normally slot in as a tight end in football or a power forward in basketball could excel at a position that was once considered off-limits to people like me.

The way the rest of football is changing, I believe you'll look back on my career and say, *Wow, he was the first of his breed, and he was the best.* When you give your heart and mind and soul to football, that's what you want in return when you hang up the jersey. Some people see it this way already, and I'm not ashamed to say that it makes me feel good to get that recognition. I'm a very approachable guy, so people are always coming up and talking to me. When they say I'm their favorite player, or a special player, or they love the way I play, that's cool. A lot of people approached me after Fox Sports did a piece on me, which was very complimentary. It pointed out some of the unique things I bring to my position, and I was glad to see it.

Of course, Howie Long came on right after that and said I wasn't really a defensive lineman, I was just a "skills" player. There it is again, the insult disguised as a compliment. Either he was saying that my game was different than his, and therefore I wasn't the classic defensive end, or he was taking the intellectual component out of the equation and saying that I was just some mindless force of nature. That's like saying Donovan McNabb and Michael Vick are great quarterbacks because they are "athletes." Yes, we are all elite athletes, and we all bring a new kind of athleticism to our positions, but ultimately it's what goes on above the neck that distinguishes the great players from the merely good ones. To suggest anything less cheapens what we do.

Howie was a great defensive end and a good commentator, and he is entitled to his viewpoint, whatever it is. But I'm entitled to mine, which is that if a player is doing great things, recognize those achievements without qualifying them, without looking for reasons why they don't fit the mold. If records are made to be broken, then molds are, too. I will never understand why people have a problem with that concept. By discarding the things that make me different, you are ignoring what makes me Simeon Rice—including the ability to think on my feet, the ability to run a business, and the ability to contribute to society instead of just taking from it.

In terms of being a media darling—or, rather, *not* being a media darling—obviously, I've come to grips with that. My experience at the Pro Bowl in 2004 only underscored for me which side of the good-guy/bad-guy line the league has decided I fit best. At least I know that, after you cut through all the hype, all the commercials, and all the marketing, when the game is on the field I'm going to rise to the top every time. And you know, I wasn't kidding when I said there's always a chance that my image will miraculously improve. According to the best minds in sportswriting, I finally learned how to tackle running backs in 2003 and I am now a "complete" player. That's what everyone was saying prior to the 2004 season, so you know it's true.

My life has taken on complexity and texture over the years, but at its core there is always football. Almost everything I own and everything I have achieved has come either directly or indirectly from the sport. Through football I have learned how to establish priorities, set boundaries, redefine expectations for myself and others, and, at a relatively young age, gain some perspective on where I fit into the big picture of life.

Although I have found a million reasons to appreciate football, what I love most about the game is that it has never lost its original appeal. It offers a level of fairness you don't find in real life. It rewards hard work and places a premium on creativity. And it delivers something for which humanity seems to have an insatiable appetite: Heroes. I love this about football. It is so charming and so innocent, and says so much about what we all want out of life. Not even the fact that I have often been cast as a villain has reduced my affection for the sport.